HOPING IN THE *LORD*

[T]hose who hope in the LORD will
renew their strength. They will soar
on wings like eagles; they will run
and not grow weary, they will walk
and not be faint.
—Isaiah 40:31

Timothy R. Harner, Esq.

Pleasant Word

Packaged by Pleasant Word, PO Box 428, Enumclaw, WA 98022. The views expressed or implied in this work do not necessarily reflect those of Pleasant Word. The author(s) is ultimately responsible for the design, content and editorial accuracy of this work.

Unless otherwise noted, all Scriptures are taken from the Holy Bible, New International Version, Copyright © 1973, 1978, 1984 by the International Bible Society. Used by permission of Zondervan Publishing House. The "NIV" and "New International Version" trademarks are registered in the United States Patent and Trademark Office by International Bible Society.

Scripture references marked KJV are taken from the King James Version of the Bible.

Scripture references marked NASB are taken from the New American Standard Bible, © 1960, 1963, 1968, 1971, 1972, 1973, 1975, 1977 by The Lockman Foundation. Used by permission.

ISBN 1-4141-0226-7
Library of Congress Catalog Card Number: 2004094777

[T]hose who hope in the LORD
will renew their strength.
They will soar on wings like eagles;
they will run and not grow weary,
they will walk and not be faint.

Isaiah 40:31

Table of Contents

PART ONE

God Gives Us Jesus

To Give Us Hope: Mary Learns That She Will Give Birth to Jesus

Over four hundred years have passed since the days when Ezra and Nehemiah worked together to heal the Promised Land. This is roughly the amount of time that separates us from when the Pilgrims arrived in America on the Mayflower.

Now God was intervening again in history to give his people new hope—new strength to heal the Promised Land. Only this time, instead of trusting in the leadership skills of a high official of the Persian government such as Nehemiah, God trusted in the pure heart and steadfast spirit of a young teenage girl named Mary. And this time, instead of sending a teacher and a priest such as Ezra, God came personally as Jesus to teach us and to be our priest.

We know that Mary lived in Nazareth, a town in the northern part of Israel near the Sea of Galilee. We also know that Mary was "a virgin pledged to be married to a man named Joseph, a descendant of David" (Luke 1:27).

Mary's mind must have been full of thoughts and hopes normal for a girl of her age and culture who was engaged to be married. As a virgin, she must have been looking ahead with some nervousness to the sexual intimacies of the wedding night. And she also must have longed to have children.

As far as we know, she had not the slightest inkling that she was destined to play a major role in the history of God's people and in the history of the world.

That stunning revelation burst into her life when none other than the angel Gabriel arrived in Nazareth to break the news to her. "The angel went to her and said, 'Greetings, you who are highly favored! The Lord is with you.'" (Luke 1:28). Not surprisingly, "Mary was greatly troubled at his words and wondered what kind of greeting this might be" (Luke 1:29).

To reassure her, the angel said, "Do not be afraid, Mary, you have found favor with God" (Luke 1:30). Since the angel found it necessary to tell Mary not to be afraid, I assume that Mary was very much afraid at this sudden, unexpected arrival of an angel.

Thus far, the angel had not explained to Mary in what sense she was "highly favored." For all she knew, the angel was about to drop off a pot of gold as a wedding gift!

So Mary must have become even more "greatly troubled at his words and wondered what kind of greeting this might be" as the angel proceeded to describe God's plans for her life and her child. The angel said, "You will be with child and give birth to a son, and you are to give him the name Jesus. He will be great and will be called the Son of the Most High. The Lord God will give him the throne of his father David, and he will reign over the house of Jacob forever; his kingdom will never end" (Luke 1:31–33).

The most natural assumption would have been that the angel was talking about a son who would be born to Mary after her marriage with Joseph was consummated. This would have seemed especially likely because the angel said that God would give her son "the throne of his father David" and Mary knew that Joseph was "a descendant of David" (Luke 1:32,27).

But the enormous implications of the angel's news that her son would be called "the Son of the Most High" and that "his kingdom will never end" must have made Mary wonder how her son would be conceived. She asked the angel, "How will this be . . . since I am a virgin?" (Luke 1:32–34).

The angel answered with words that confirmed that Mary's son would not be conceived in the normal way. He would not be the product of a sexual union between Mary and a man. Instead, the angel told her, "The Holy Spirit will come upon you, and the power of the Most High will overshadow you. So the holy one to be born will be called the Son of God . . . . . For nothing is impossible with God" (Luke 1:35–37).

Now we come to a miracle even greater than the virgin birth—Mary did not falter. Despite the fact that she was greatly troubled, afraid and full of wonder, she obeyed God immediately and perfectly. Mary's acceptance of God's will for her life sprang from her pure heart and her steadfast spirit (Psalm 51:10). "I am the Lord's servant," Mary answered. "May it be to me as you have said" (Luke 1:38).

Our awe at Mary's perfect obedience to the will of God—at her pure heart and her steadfast spirit—is increased when we remember how even the greatest of God's leaders balked under similar circumstances. The most famous example is Moses. When God spoke to him out of the burning bush, Moses thought up excuse after excuse to avoid going back to Egypt to confront the Pharaoh and free God's people from slavery (Exodus 3:1–4:17).

Furthermore, Mary had every reason *not* to want to get pregnant at this moment in her life. She must have feared what Joseph's reaction would be when he learned that she was pregnant with someone else's baby. She must have dreaded how her relatives and neighbors would scorn her for the rest of her life because she got pregnant before she got married. Nevertheless, Mary accepted this shame and humiliation because she was "the Lord's servant" (Luke 1:38).

No wonder Jesus learned so well how to obey God. Mary showed Jesus how humans obey God with purity of heart and a steadfast spirit—how humans establish the pure worship of the LORD in spirit and in truth. No wonder Jesus called Mary a "dear woman" (John 2:4).

I'm sure Mary taught Jesus that—since he was the Lord's servant—he must always say, "May it be to me as you have said." And just as Mary obeyed God regardless of how much shame and humiliation it cost her by being a pregnant bride, Jesus learned to obey God regardless of how much shame and humiliation it cost him.

No wonder Jesus always identified himself and his mission with passages in Isaiah that describe a righteous servant of the LORD. Jesus was nurtured by just such a righteous servant of the LORD: his mother, Mary.

And no wonder that in the Garden of Gethsemane, on the night before he suffered the shame and humiliation of his death on a cross, Jesus found the courage to pray, "Father, if you are willing, take this cup from me; yet not my will, but yours be done" (Luke 22:42). Like Mary, so many years before, Jesus followed God's will for his life perfectly, no matter what it cost him. Like his mother, Jesus suffered shame and humiliation with a pure heart and a steadfast spirit. And because we admire Mary and follow her son Jesus, we must go and do likewise. We must be *pure* in heart as we worship the LORD with a *steadfast* spirit.

Joseph Marries Mary

In a few short sentences, the Bible introduces us to Joseph, the man who became the father of Jesus on earth. For example, we learn that Joseph "was a righteous man" (Matthew 1:19). While we are not told all the ways in which he was righteous, presumably he generally kept the Ten Commandments and the rest of the Mosaic law as any good Jew of his time would. Most relevant to Mary was that he would not marry a woman who committed adultery.

Based on the initial information available to Joseph, he must have concluded that Mary was an adulteress—a faithless, wayward woman unfit to be his wife. Her pregnancy occurred during the period when she "was pledged to be married to Joseph" (Matthew 1:18). According to the customs and laws of that time, Joseph and Mary were legally and morally bound in marriage. This was true even though they had not yet reached the moment when the marriage ceremony consummated their marriage publicly and when sexual intimacy consummated their marriage privately.[1]

If Mary had been willing to lie, she could have told Joseph that someone raped her. But she made no such claim. Mary worshiped the LORD in *truth*. Perhaps she did not even tell Joseph the details about how she became pregnant. Or, perhaps she gave him an explanation that sounded preposterous, such as: "I'm pregnant because the Holy

Spirit came upon me and the power of the Most High overshadowed me."

Either way, Joseph must have believed that Mary betrayed him by having sexual intimacies with some other man. He may also have believed that she was a liar or mentally unstable. But in any event, he naturally came to the conclusion that he must not marry her.

It is a proof of Joseph's kind, gentle spirit—and of how much he loved Mary—that he decided to end their betrothal as quietly and as painlessly as possible. Since Joseph "did not want to expose [Mary] to public disgrace, he had in mind to divorce her quietly" (Matthew 1:19).

It is clear that Joseph was motivated by fear. He feared marrying a woman who he could not trust to remain faithful to him. He feared what people would think and say if he married Mary. Gossips would assume that he had slept with Mary before the wedding night and that the child was really his. He feared they would say that he was not a righteous man. He feared the constant whispering and cruelty of a small town[2] where people would always treat Mary and him with disdain because they were "sinners."

It took an angel of the Lord to overcome Joseph's fears. The angel appeared to Joseph in a dream and said, "Joseph son of David, do not be afraid to take Mary home as your wife, because what is conceived in her is from the Holy Spirit" (Matthew 1:20).

The angel assured Joseph that he should not worry about becoming the father of Mary's child—God had a wonderful plan for this child. The angel said, "[Mary] will give birth to a son, and you are to give him the name Jesus, because he will save his people from their sins" (Matthew 1:21).

It is doubtful that Joseph knew how Jesus would go about saving his people from their sins. Such lack of knowledge about the future makes Joseph like us.

We do not know God's plan for our lives and for the lives of those we love. We must live by faith, knowing only that our lives are a gift from the Holy Spirit and that God knows our names and has great plans for us.

Furthermore, the full significance of God's plans for us and for those we love will not usually be evident to us—at least not immediately. For example, I doubt that Joseph fully grasped the wonderful truth that we celebrate each Christmas: "All this took place to fulfill what the Lord had said through the prophet: 'The virgin will be with child and will give birth to a son, and they will call him Immanuel'—which means, 'God with us.'" (Matthew 1:22–23).

Nevertheless, despite such limitations in his understanding of God's plan, Joseph displayed in his life that same perfect obedience to God's plan for his life that we saw in the life of Mary and that we will see in the life of Jesus. "When Joseph woke up, he did what the angel of the Lord had commanded him and took Mary home as his wife" (Matthew 1:24).

Like Joseph, we must do whatever God commands us to do to the best of our ability. Despite our limited knowledge and understanding of God's ultimate plans and purposes. Despite the difficulty of knowing why God does what he does.

For example, why *did* God choose Joseph to become the father of Jesus on earth?

One reason was genealogical. Ancient prophecies promised that the Messiah would be descended from King David. And both Mary and Joseph were descendants of Israel's greatest king.[3]

But the most important reason must have been because God knew that Joseph would be a good father—a good example of our Father in Heaven.

What made Joseph a good father?

Joseph did what was best for his family, even when it wasn't easy. Even when it took self-discipline.

For example, Joseph accepted the responsibility of becoming a father, even though he was not the biological father of Mary's child. Joseph accepted the responsibility of becoming Mary's husband, even though it meant self-discipline—controlling his sexual passions for the benefit of his family—because Joseph "had no union with [Mary] until she gave birth to a son" (Matthew 1:25).

What made Joseph a good father?

He put what was best for his family ahead of what was best for his career. Even when it inconvenienced him. Even when it cost him money.

Joseph was a carpenter in Nazareth. Presumably he would have made the most money if he'd kept living in Nazareth. Nevertheless, Joseph lived in Bethlehem after Jesus was born—probably because he thought it best that this future king of Israel be raised near the ancient capital, Jerusalem. And when King Herod tried to kill the baby Jesus, Joseph fled to Egypt to keep Jesus safe.

What made Joseph a good father?

Joseph accepted God's plans for his child. Even when God's plans were not Joseph's plans. Even when God's plans would take his child away from him.

Joseph's plans for Jesus would presumably have led Jesus to become a carpenter living a quiet, respectable life. Nevertheless, Joseph was willing to encourage Jesus to fulfill a far greater purpose than supporting his aging parents in Nazareth. Joseph was willing to encourage Jesus to "save his people from their sins."

Joseph's acceptance of God's plan for Jesus was symbolized when he named Mary's child. As the angel commanded, Joseph "gave him the name Jesus." The name "Jesus" is the Greek form of the name "Joshua," which means "the LORD saves."[4]

What made Joseph a good father?

Joseph taught his child right from wrong. Even when Joseph was busy. Even when Joseph was tired.

We can perceive the wisdom of Joseph, a carpenter, in some of Jesus' most famous teachings.

As Joseph taught Jesus how to build houses, he taught Jesus the importance of building houses—and lives—on the right foundation so that we can survive the storms of life (Matthew 7:24–27).

As Joseph removed specks of sawdust from Jesus' eye, he taught Jesus not to be like the hypocrites who are blinded by the plank in their own eye as they try to remove a speck from another person's eye (Matthew 7:3–5).

I suspect that Jesus' passionate condemnation of hypocrites came from Joseph. Because I fear that there were many times when Joseph had to shield Jesus from the insults of such hypocritical, judgmental people. Self-righteous gossips must have sneered at Mary and Joseph because Mary became pregnant before she was married.

When Jesus taught us right from wrong, he showed nothing but contempt for such hypocrites. He said:

"Woe to you, teachers of the law and Pharisees, you hypo-crites! . . . You blind guides! You strain out a gnat but swallow a camel.

"Woe to you, teachers of the law and Pharisees, you hypo-crites! . . . [You] are full of greed and self-indulgence . . . .

"Woe to you, teachers of the law and Pharisees, you hypocrites! . . . [O]n the outside you appear to people as righteous but on the inside you are full of hypocrisy and wickedness . . . .

"You snakes! You brood of vipers! How will you escape being con-demned to hell?" (Matthew 23:23–33).

No wonder that Jesus refused to heed hypocrites who complained that he was a friend of "sinners." As a child, he must have known many hypocrites who thought they were "too good" for Joseph and Mary. So, when he grew up, Jesus defied such hypocrites by befriending sinners (Matthew 9:9–13).

No wonder that Jesus showed compassion to "fallen" women. He must have seen tears in Mary's eyes when the "better women" in town snubbed her and gossiped about her because years earlier she had be-come pregnant before she was married. So Jesus befriended the Samari-tan woman at the well who had had five husbands and who was living with a man who was not her husband (John 4:1–42). And so Jesus saved the woman taken in adultery from the hypocrites who wanted to stone her (John 8:1–11).

What made Joseph a good father? He taught Jesus to do the right thing regardless of what hypocrites say. He taught Jesus to worship the LORD with a *pure* heart—not a hypocritical heart. He taught Jesus to worship the Lord in a spirit of *truth*—not in a spirit of hypocrisy.

And what's the best *proof* that Joseph was a good father? The way his child, Jesus, lived.

Jesus was "a righteous man"—the same description the Bible gives for Joseph.

Jesus was obedient to God's plan for his life, even when it was hard. Even when it took self-discipline. Even when it meant dying on a cross.

Jesus did what was best for others—blessing all peoples by saving them from their sins. Even when it was hard. Even when it cost him not just his money, but his life.

Jesus taught us right from wrong. Even when he was busy. Even when he was tired. Even when he was tortured. Even when he was dying.

How do we know that Joseph was a good father? Because Jesus thought so.

Indeed, Jesus admired his father on earth so much that, when Jesus grew up, he paid Joseph a tremendous compliment. Jesus taught us to call God by the same name that Jesus called Joseph—the name "Father."[5]

Jesus Is Born

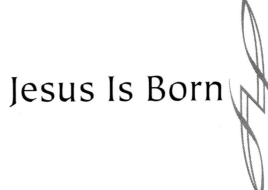

People like to say that only two things are certain in life: death and taxes. And so it was in Jesus' time.

The first Roman Emperor—Caesar Augustus—wanted to tax the people. In order to collect the tax, he ordered a census of the entire Roman world (Luke 2:1).

To register as a descendant of Israel's greatest king, King David, Joseph traveled to King David's hometown, Bethlehem. (Luke 2:3–4).

Mary came with him. The baby was due soon. We aren't told why Mary came along with Joseph in her delicate condition (Luke 2:5).

I can think of two reasons. Joseph didn't want to feed the gossips back home by having them witness the baby's birth less than nine months after the wedding. And Mary and Joseph knew that the Messiah was supposed to be born in Bethlehem.

Mary and Joseph couldn't do anything about defeating the power of taxes, but they were doing their best to defeat the power of death.

I like to say that the only answer to "death" is "life." By this I mean "life" in its broadest sense—anything of beauty or kindness or love or creativity. And the greatest act of "life" we can experience is having a baby.

Babies always bring new hope. And that was certainly true of the baby, Jesus.

He brought us eternal life in the broadest sense—everything of beauty and kindness and love and creativity. And he even defeated death itself!

Jesus hasn't ended taxes yet, but give him time. The difficult things—like rising from the dead—he does right away. The impossible things—like getting rid of taxes—take a lot longer!

Another thing about babies is that they don't come at the time *you* want. Babies come at the time *they* want—when they're good and ready. And then, there's no stopping them, even if you wish they'd wait a while longer!

This was true of the births of both of my children. And it was true of the birth of Jesus.

Both of my children were born more than a week after their due dates. Needless to say, my wife, Suzanne, was immensely discouraged because the babies weren't born by their due dates. For months she was pinning all her hopes on being done with the agonies of pregnancy by the due date. That date came and went. And she was still waddling around more than 9 months pregnant! She felt like a prisoner whose term was up, but the jailer wouldn't come with the key to let her out.

With our first child, Sarah, this agony of waiting reached its ultimate intensity. We actually went to the hospital, expecting to give birth that night. We got there about 11 o'clock. But the labor pains petered out! The next morning we had to go back home without a baby—*and* with an exhausted, distraught mother-to-be. The doctors called it "false labor." But as Suzanne always remembers, "That false labor *hurt* as much as the real thing."

On the other hand, once the baby decides to come, there's no stopping it! This was most vividly illustrated in the case of Andy.

We weren't expecting Suzanne to go into labor that evening when we came back home tired from my parents' house. Before going to bed, Suzanne prepared herself a gigantic strawberry shortcake smothered in whipped cream. She sat down on the couch beside me ready to dig in. She took one scrumptious bite. She turned a shade of green. She looked at me and said, "Here, you eat this. I'm not feeling well. I think maybe I'm in labor."

Sure enough. Suzanne spent all that night in labor as the pains grew stronger and more frequent. In the morning we went to the hospital.

After we got to the hospital, it seemed as if the labor pains were dwindling just like they had that first time we went to the hospital with Sarah. This time, however, Andy was so overdue (and we were so determined not to go through the same protracted agony as with Sarah—a total of 35 hours of "false" and "true" labor) that we decided to "induce" labor.

This involved running an I.V. line to Suzanne with a substance that intensified her labor. All that day, May 30th, the pain grew worse as the baby took his own sweet time about showing up.

At 4:30 P.M., the doctors assured me that the baby wouldn't come for at least an hour. I called the grandparents to tell them not to hurry to the hospital. There was plenty of time. I went to the hospital cafeteria to grab supper.

But about 20 minutes later—just as I was finishing my supper and about to dig into a delectable piece of pumpkin pie—an announcement started coming over the intercom. Even before they gave the announcement, I "knew" it was for me. And sure enough, I was told to report immediately to the delivery room.

I dashed through the hospital. Even so, I barely got to the delivery room in time to see Andy born!

Just like Sarah and Andy, the baby Jesus came at the time God wanted—not the time other people wanted him—and not the time that other people expected him.

People had been predicting the Messiah's birth and waiting for the Messiah's birth for centuries!

For example, in the first two chapters of the gospel of Matthew, there are repeated references to prophecies about Jesus' birth.[1]

By the time Jesus was born, these prophecies stretched back more than five hundred years to the time of Isaiah—roughly the amount of time that separates us from the Protestant Reformation and the discovery of America by Columbus!

So people had to wait a lot longer than they wanted—or expected—for Jesus to be born.

During those centuries, there were many times that they experienced "false labor." It seemed that the Messiah *must* come soon. But he didn't.

The agony, pain and frustration of the delay grew as the centuries passed. But humans could not "induce" the birth of the Messiah. The timing of his birth was in the hands of God.

On the other hand, once the right time came for Jesus to be born, there was no delaying his birth. Even though the timing was very inconvenient for Mary and Joseph.

The political situation was not good. The Romans ruled Israel.

The exact form of Roman rule varied. At the moment, their puppet was King Herod, ruling from Jerusalem. He was a cruel, paranoid man who resorted to murder without batting an eye.[2]

But if babies were only born when the political situation is good, when would anyone be born? It is always "the best of times and the worst of times."

When Mary and Joseph looked to the political times, they probably thought it was "the worst of times." But taking the longer view, it was "the best of times" for Jesus to come.

The Roman Empire was at its height. Its marvelous roads opened up the known world for the first Christian missionaries. The widespread use of the Latin and Greek languages made it easier to spread the good news about Jesus.

Furthermore, the timing was right in the grand scheme of human technological and sociological development.

Jesus came recently enough that we have reliable records about him. And the good news about him could spread widely around the whole world within a "mere" two thousand years.

On the other hand, the good news about Jesus spread worldwide just in time to help Humanity overcome worldwide perils such as nuclear weapons, ecological crises, racism and bigotry.

All of which justifies the optimism of the Apostle Paul. He knew that what seems to be "the worst of times" can really be "the best of times." As Paul wrote to the church at Rome: "[W]e know that in all things God works for the good of those who love him, who have been called according to his purpose" (Romans 8:28).

Unfortunately, Mary and Joseph did not have this inspiring verse of the Bible to encourage them as they faced their difficult personal circumstances when Jesus was born. Paul wouldn't write his letter to the church in Rome until about 60 years later (roughly the amount of time that separates us from World War II).[3]

And Mary and Joseph must have been perplexed by the difficulties in which they found themselves.

They knew that they loved God. And they knew that they had been called according to his purpose. Yet everything seemed to go wrong that could go wrong.[4]

It was "the worst of times" to be traveling. The roads were crowded by people responding to the Roman decree.

But the worst thing was that Mary was pregnant. Even her steadfast spirit must have been taxed by the discomforts and indignities of the trip to Bethlehem.

The final disaster came when Mary and Joseph got to Bethlehem. I'm sure that their spirits rose, thinking that *at last* they could rest. But no!

Mary began to feel labor pains. The baby was coming!

And then, in that pregnant line that has caught the world's imagination and sympathy ever since, Mary and Joseph learned "there was no room for them in the inn" (Luke 2:7).

I can't fully imagine the anguish and anger that Mary and Joseph must have felt at that moment. But I can grasp the emotion of that moment somewhat by times that we've driven hard all day towards Walt Disney World. At last, we stop for the night, hungry and exhausted. Only to learn that we've got to drive even further because all the motels are full at that exit on the Interstate.

Mary and Joseph couldn't solve their problem by driving to the next exit on an Interstate. But at least someone was willing to let them stay in a stable that night.

I'm not sure how good or bad it was to give birth in a stable. I've heard it said that it was actually a blessing in disguise. A stable was quiet and private. The inn would have been very noisy—essentially a chaotic courtyard where Mary would have had little privacy.[5]

On the other hand, I've heard it said that the kind of stable Jesus was born in differed dramatically from the quaint, clean stables of our nativity scenes. It was probably a dark cave filled more with the smell of manure than with the light of angels.

Perhaps the truth lies somewhere between the optimistic and the pessimistic view of what that particular stable was like.

What is certain is that the image of Jesus being born in a stable has captured the imagination of millions of people throughout the ages. The thought of the King of Kings being born humbly in a stable— surrounded by adoring animals—has touched us all.

And I think that the experience taught Mary and Joseph some of that compassion for those in need that so marked their son, Jesus. Mary and Joseph knew what it was like to be in desperate need. They knew what it was like to be exhausted and to be told that there was no room for them in the inn. And they knew how wonderful it was when someone did their best to help them—to be a "good neighbor" like the Good Samaritan—by letting them use a stable for the night.

Again and again, Jesus showed similar compassion for those in need. He filled the Promised Land with blessings for all peoples.

I hear Jesus telling the story of the Good Samaritan as he taught us that everyone is our neighbor who we should help (Luke 10:25–37).[6] I see Jesus having compassion on the hungry multitudes as he prepared to feed them (Matthew 14:13–21 and 15:29–38). I hear Jesus telling his disciples that he's not too busy to see little children (Matthew 19:13–15). I hear Jesus teaching us that if we've helped anyone who is hungry, thirsty, a stranger, without clothes, sick or in prison, it's just as if we've helped him (Matthew 25:31–46).

Furthermore, Jesus always wanted us to go the extra mile when helping others. Don't give people the stable that is dark and full of manure. Give people the stable that is clean and bright—full of fresh hay and friendly animals!

As Jesus said, give people in need "a cup of cold water" (Matthew 10:42). The key word here is "*cold*." In our modern society, we take it for granted that we can drink cold water (or some other cold drink) any time we want. But in Jesus' time (before refrigeration and running water), it took a great deal of extra effort to make sure the drink was cold.[7]

Mary and Joseph experienced one of the other great truths that Jesus taught us: if we seek first the kingdom of God and his righteousness, then all of our other needs will be met (Matthew 6:33).

Mary and Joseph gave up everything—including their good reputations with the gossips back home—to seek God's kingdom, the Promised Land. And God took care of them.

To the cynic, it looked as if God didn't take very *good* care of them—all they got was a stable full of manure, straw and animals. But to believers, God gave them the most wonderful gift of all time—God gave them the baby Jesus.

So always follow God as faithfully as Mary and Joseph did—even in those moments of anguish and despair when there is no room for you in the inn. Because—if you are faithful and keep seeking the Promised Land—you can be sure that "the worst of times" will become "the best of times." You will come to a time in your life when you find a cozy stable where you meet the baby Jesus. And you will fill the Promised Land with blessings for all peoples.

The Shepherds
Find Jesus

The first people who learned that God always has "room in the inn" for them were shepherds. They were "living out in the fields nearby, keeping watch over their flocks at night" (Luke 2:8).

In the culture of their time, shepherds were looked down upon. Not only were they smelly and dirty. They were not trusted.

But God always reaches out to those who are despised and rejected. Because in the Promised Land, *all* peoples will be blessed. So when the time came to announce the birth of his son, God sent angels to some shepherds nearby.

The news was broken first by just one angel. The message stressed that Jesus' birth was good news for *all* people. It was a message of hope for *all* Humanity.

Before getting to the heart of the message, the angel first had to reassure the shepherds that they were not in trouble or danger. When an "angel of the Lord appeared to [the shepherds], and the glory of the Lord shone around them, . . . they were terrified" (Luke 2:9). So the angel's first words to them were "Do not be afraid" (Luke 2:10).

I doubt that this one sentence was enough to overcome the fright of the startled shepherds. Nevertheless, the angel plowed ahead with his message: "I bring you good news of great joy that will be for all the people. Today in the town of David a Savior has been born to you; he is Christ the Lord" (Luke 2:10–11).

It's hard to imagine a message of greater hope. This was indeed "good news of great joy."

It was good news for more than just a few shepherds on a hillside. It was good news of great joy to "all the people."

It was more than a promise about something that would come in the distant future. It was good news about something that had happened *today*.

At last, after waiting for centuries, the long promised and long awaited Messiah had been born. Since he was a descendant of King David, he had been born in Bethlehem—the "town of David." He was to be "a Savior."

The angel didn't specify what the baby would save the shepherds and all the people from. But such details didn't matter at the moment. It was enough to know that this newborn infant bore the title of "Christ" (which is Greek for "Messiah")[1] and that this baby was "the Lord."

As the shepherds began to absorb this good news, the birthday party really got going. There had been just one angel. Now, "[s]uddenly a great company of the heavenly host appeared with the angel, praising God and saying,

'Glory to God in the highest,
    and on earth peace to men on whom
        his favor rests.'"

(Luke 2:13–14)

When God throws a party, he does it right. Imagine the scene as "a great company of the heavenly host" praised God.

The image that appears in your mind will vary with how you like to praise God.

For some people, it will be a very staid, formal, stiff affair. The angels will be wearing the celestial equivalent of tuxedos.

Other people will picture the celestial equivalent of a rock concert. The angels will be rocking and rolling through the skies with their hands waving in the air—big smiles on their faces and boisterous "Amens" on their lips.

Whatever the celebration looked and sounded like, the message of hope was loud and clear. The angels gave glory to God. The angels proclaimed peace to Humanity.

This good news was not for just a few people. This good news of great joy was for all the people.

No wonder that the spirit of that celebration still touches our hearts each Christmas even though two thousand years have passed.

The angels' message certainly touched the hearts of those shepherds. They had been caught in a dead-end job watching sheep. They had been terrified of the angel. Now they hurried off to see if the message of hope they'd received from the Lord was true.

They raced to Bethlehem. The angel had told them that they'd find a sign that the good news was true: "You will find a baby wrapped in cloths and lying in a manger" (Luke 2:12). And sure enough, the shepherds "found Mary and Joseph, and the baby, who was lying in the manger" (Luke 2:16).

After their encounter with the baby Jesus, the shepherds could not restrain themselves. They returned to their same old jobs—watching their flocks at night. But they'd caught a whole new spirit—the Christmas spirit.

And so—even though the angels were gone—the shepherds kept the celebration going. They "returned, glorifying and praising God for all the things they had heard and seen, which were just as they had been told" (Luke 2:20).

The shepherds were not the only ones whose hearts were touched that night. Mary's heart was also touched by the message of hope from the angels and the shepherds. We are told that "Mary treasured up all these things and pondered them in her heart" (Luke 2:19).

Like any new mother, Mary had much to treasure and ponder. But it is fascinating to realize that Mary would not have known about the angels celebrating the birth of her son if the shepherds had not been faithful in looking for the baby Jesus.

I'm sure Mary had been afraid and discouraged as the pain of childbirth enveloped her and she could not even find room at the inn.

I'm sure that—just like my wife after giving birth to each of our children—Mary's spirits soared when she held Jesus in her arms that first time and looked into his puffy, new-born face.

And I'm sure that Mary's sense of wonder and joy must have known no bounds when she learned from the shepherds that the son she'd just given birth to was as special as she believed.

As Mary pondered the humble circumstances of Jesus' birth and the lowly status of the shepherds who sought him, perhaps her thoughts returned to those truths she pondered when she was first pregnant with Jesus—when she endured the shame and stigma of being pregnant before her wedding night. They were words she repeated to her cousin Elizabeth when she went to visit her. We know Mary's words as the Magnificant:

> [God] has performed mighty deeds with
> his arm;
> he has scattered those who are proud
> in their inmost thoughts.
> He has brought down rulers from their
> thrones
> but has lifted up the humble.
> He has filled the hungry with good
> things
> but has sent the rich away empty.
>
> (Luke 1:51–53)

As Mary treasured the news of the angels and shepherds, cuddled her baby, and gazed into Jesus' eyes, her thoughts must have turned to how blessed she was. Like any new mother treasuring the miracle of life and hope she holds in her arms, Mary must have thought:

> My soul glorifies the Lord
> and my spirit rejoices in God my
> Savior,
> for he has been mindful
> of the humble state of his servant.
> From now on all generations will call
> me blessed,
> for the Mighty One has done great
> things for me—
> holy is his name.

His mercy extends to those who fear
    him,
  from generation to generation.

                              (Luke 1:46–50)

This was good news of great joy that Mary treasured all her life.

And it is good news of great joy for us, too. Good news that should always give us great joy, as we ponder and treasure the Christmas magic of new life and new hope in the face of the baby Jesus.

The Magi Follow
the Star

In our minds, the story of the three wise men is always tied inseparably to the story of the shepherds. On our Christmas cards and in our Nativity scenes we always show the three wise men at the stable with the shepherds worshiping the baby Jesus.

However, a careful reading of the story of the three wise men shows that they did not come to see the baby Jesus at a stable. Instead, they visited Jesus in a house (Matthew 2:11).

A number of months may have passed since Jesus' birth. At least King Herod thought so. That was why King Herod killed every boy in Bethlehem and its vicinity who was two years old and under.

Wicked (and paranoid) King Herod had "found out from [the wise men] the exact time the star had appeared" (Matthew 2:8). Based on what the wise men told him, Herod evidently felt it necessary to kill every boy up to two years old in order to make sure that he killed any boy with a claim to his throne (Matthew 2:7,16).

The Bible does not tell us how many wise men there were. It only tells us there were three gifts: gold, incense and myrrh (Matthew 2:11). So we have no way of knowing exactly how many wise men came to see Jesus.

Since our Christmas cards and traditions have so distorted the story of the wise men, let's review what the Bible tells us about them.

The story occurs "[a]fter Jesus was born in Bethlehem" (Matthew 2:1). Nothing is said about exactly how long after Jesus' birth the story takes place, except that it was while King Herod still lived.

This is not the King Herod who we hear about in the story of Jesus' crucifixion. ("Herod" was the family name for five rulers of Palestine under the Roman emperors.[1])

The King Herod who met the wise men (known as "Herod the Great") died a few years after Jesus was born. He spent a great deal of effort and money rebuilding the temple in Jerusalem to make it more magnificent. But he was a cruel and paranoid tyrant who was well known for killing anyone who he suspected might overthrow him.[2]

We are told that the wise men (called "Magi" in the New International Version of the Bible) came to Jerusalem "from the east" (Matthew 2:1). But we do not know where "from the east" they came. If we did, it would be easier to guess how long it took them to get to Jerusalem after they saw the star marking Jesus' birth.

The Magi may have come from as far away as modern day Iran or Iraq. And they were steeped in the religious lore of those lands.

The closest parallel to a "religion" of today would be astrology. That was why the Magi were paying such close attention to the sky that they noticed the star marking Jesus' birth.

The Magi were like many people today who are seeking Jesus. They start out with a very imperfect idea about who he is. And they must travel a long way to find him.

Each person starts from a different point in their lifelong journey to find Jesus and get closer to him. The nature of that starting point varies from person to person—just as ideas vary about what the "star" was that attracted the attention of the Magi.

Some people tie the star to a naturally occurring event such as Halley's Comet. We know that Halley's Comet appeared in the skies at roughly the time Jesus was born. (Keep in mind that there is some uncertainty among scholars about exactly what year Jesus was born.)

One reason for believing that Halley's Comet (or some other comet) was the "star" is that a comet generally is visible twice during its journey around the sun.

A comet first becomes visible when it approaches the sun. Then the comet becomes lost in the glare of the sun as it passes around the opposite side of the sun from the Earth. The comet becomes visible again when it begins to leave the sun on its way back out to the cold, distant reaches of the Solar System.

Since the Magi saw the "star" twice, (first when Jesus was born and second when they arrived in Bethlehem (Matthew 2:1–2,9–10)), it may be that the "star" they were seeing was a comet—perhaps even Halley's Comet itself.

In the same way, some people first awaken to God's call by observing the majesty of nature.

For example, just before writing the first draft of this chapter on March 12, 1997, I stepped outside to see Comet Hale-Bopp. I had checked my *Sky & Telescope* magazine the night before so I would know where to look. I thought it would be hard to spot the comet because I've had trouble before finding comets in the sky. However, I saw it immediately in the northeastern sky.

It was bright—like the brightest star in the sky. And the comet's distinct head and tail made it look like the classic portraits of how a comet should look.

That was not all that awed me. At 5:30 A.M., the very first glow of dawn was beginning to brighten the sky. The clear sky around the comet was just beginning to turn a transparent blue. And lower toward the horizon were gigantic billowing clouds that were beginning to glow pink.

It was an awesome sight. Majestic, yet fearful. For who can totally overcome their fear of these strange, sudden visitors from the heavens—no matter how much science tells us that they are merely hunks of rock and ice.

Knowing that I would soon come back indoors and start writing about the Star of Bethlehem, I couldn't help but wonder if it was a similar stunning view of a comet that started the Magi searching for Jesus until they found him.

There are many other experiences of nature that lead us to ponder the meaning of life and to wonder who created such beauty and majesty.

You can feel it as mighty waves pound the rocky cliffs of Maine. You can feel it as warm ocean surf gurgles over your toes on the beach on Maui as the sun rises and as whales spout just off shore.[3]

Perhaps you feel it best when you are a parent. I could feel it when I put my hand on my wife's tummy and felt our babies move for the first time. I could feel it when I held their bloody, bluish bodies in those magic moments just after they were born. I could feel it when I saw their first smiles. I could feel it when I heard their first words.

Such experiences of life and nature are so wonderful that we must search and search until we find the Purpose of it all and until we worship the Creator of it all.

God honors whatever spurs us to begin the search for him—whatever our personal "Star of Bethlehem" may be.

Perhaps the Magi did not see a comet.

Perhaps the Star of Bethlehem was a nova—a star that briefly shines much brighter than normal in the sky.

Or perhaps the Star of Bethlehem was a special, miraculous star created by God for the purpose of honoring the birth of his son. My wife and I bought balloons and hung them outside the house to let everyone know that our baby was born. Why wouldn't God want to do something special such as create a star to let everyone know that his son had been born?

Therefore, whether our starting point is a routine, cyclical event in nature such as the predictable return of Halley's Comet, or whether it is an unusual (yet explainable) event in nature such as a new comet or a nova, or whether it is the beauty and majesty of life itself, or whether it is a special miracle of God, we should respond to the artistic yearnings of our souls and seek the God who sent such wonder our way.

The other major explanation for the Star of Bethlehem is that it was an astrological event. I think that this explanation is the most likely to be true. Since the Magi were astrologers, they would be trained to interpret events in the sky according to the ground rules of astrology.

I've read various ideas about what astrological event might have led the Magi to believe that someone had been born to be the king to the Jews. Most likely, the Magi saw a conjunction of planets in some constellation of the sky. A "conjunction" of planets occurs when several planets appear in approximately the same part of the sky at the same time. Astrologers draw meanings from which planets are in conjunction and which constellation the conjunction appears in.

Such a conjunction might linger for several months, giving the Magi time to make their journey to Jerusalem. Furthermore, depending on where the planets are in relationship to the Earth's orbit at the time the conjunction begins, the planets sometimes appear to move apart and then come back together again later. Such a conjunction of the planets could have prompted the initial search of the Magi for Jesus and then have "reappeared" as the Magi neared Bethlehem, confirming that they had found the king of the Jews.

At first blush, this idea that the Star of Bethlehem was an astrological event is disturbing. Astrology is not scientific. It's merely a superstition. It's a way to exploit and manipulate gullible people. So how can we accept the idea that someone following astrology could have been so right about Jesus' birth?

But, as I reflected on this, I realized that God can—and does—use many religions, superstitions and ideologies as a starting point to help people begin searching for Jesus.

Jesus is the Light of the world. So his Light is reflected in many other religions and philosophies that have much that is good in them.

As Paul told the Athenians when he arrived as a missionary, the Ancient Greeks had been worshiping God all along. Paul was merely there to explain to them with accuracy something that they had not fully comprehended before (Acts 17:22–30; Romans 2:13–15).

Furthermore, even attending church is only a starting point to help people begin searching for Jesus. Many people who claim to be Christians sit in church pews for *years* without fully understanding and responding to what they are hearing. They need something unusual—a Star of Bethlehem in their lives—to get them out of their pews and into the search for the living Jesus.

One of my favorite illustrations of how God uses many different ways to get people to come to him involves the cat named "Bootsey." This black cat with white markings started living with my future wife, Suzanne, before she started dating me. Bootsey never forgave Suzanne for marrying me because I took his place in her bed. He lived 18 years—until Sarah was 11 and Andy was 7. So Bootsey became a member of our family who we will always miss.

This story about Bootsey describes an adventure that befell him while we were building our first house—one year before Sarah was born.

The construction of our house had reached the point where the basic wood structure was in place. We could walk on wood floors. And the builder had begun adding other features to the house.

Most important to this story, the runs for the heating and air conditioning had been installed. But there were no covers over the entrances to these cat-sized "tunnels."

We brought Bootsey over to the new house for the first time so that he could begin to get used to it.

We took him upstairs to where our bedroom would be and set him loose. Whoosh! He raced for the opening that led to the heat run along the floor.

Before we could stop him, he was gone!

This particular heat run went about five feet along the floor under the bathroom. Fortunately, it didn't connect with anything else with a space big enough for Bootsey to squeeze through. Nor did it have a cat-sized hole that would send Bootsey plunging two stories to his death.

So at least we knew where Bootsey was. But there was no way we could reach into the heat run far enough to pull him out.

Suzanne was nearly hysterical. She called and called to Bootsey. But he was too scared to come to her.

Fortunately for Bootsey, Suzanne knew him very well. And she loved him too much to ever give up trying to save him by getting him to come to her.

So Suzanne ran next door and got some tuna fish. She held it near the opening.

The smell reached Bootsey. In the hope of getting his favorite food, Bootsey crawled toward her.

Finally, Bootsey got so close that Suzanne could reach down and pull him to safety. She hugged him and hugged him. And then she gave him the tuna fish.

God uses the "Stars of Bethlehem" in our lives the same way that Suzanne used that can of tuna fish with Bootsey.

We are separated from God. In our fear we run away from him. Seeking safety, we choose a dangerous place to hide.

We are all alone in the dark.

We are paralyzed by our fears.

God calls to us again and again. But we ignore his voice.

Fortunately, God knows us very well. And he is even more determined to save us than Suzanne was to save her beloved cat.

So God finds a "can of tuna fish" to lure us out of the lonely darkness towards him. For the Magi, the "can of tuna fish" was the "Star of Bethlehem."

The journey that we begin after we catch this scent of a better life and after we see this star of hope may not be easy or short. Like the Magi, people often go to the wrong places as they search for Jesus. But at least they're searching for him diligently!

And the exact nature of the "can of tuna fish" and the "Star of Bethlehem" varies from person to person. But it is always something that gives us hope that we can find a better life—*if* we can overcome our fears and crawl in the direction that God wants us to go.

It is always a light of hope shining in the darkness of our lonely, fearful lives. Just as the Magi saw the Star of Bethlehem shining in the darkness.

We should not be surprised that God brings people to him the same way that Suzanne brought Bootsey to her.

Bootsey's journey started because he wanted to eat the tuna fish, not because he trusted the sound of her voice calling him. And Bootsey's journey ended when Suzanne took him in her arms and hugged him.

In the same way, God often must use something other than his voice to motivate people to start searching for him. God then waits patiently until the person reaches that moment in his or her life when it is best for God to reveal himself.

Then—in God's good time and in God's good way—God reaches down, lifts them to safety, and hugs them in the Promised Land.

And God gives them their "can of tuna fish" because God always gives us all that is best in life when we "seek first his kingdom and his righteousness" (Matthew 6:33).

The Bible plays a key role in this process of fully revealing God to people. For example, it is fascinating that the thing that finally set the Magi on the right course to finding Jesus was the Bible. Even when the Bible was interpreted by people who did not care enough about its message to investigate whether its message was true, the Bible told the Magi where to find Jesus (Matthew 2:4–6).

But I am getting ahead of myself. Before seeing what led the Magi to the place where Jesus actually lived, let's look at how they went to the wrong place looking for Jesus. Because it is a great encouragement to me that, even if we start looking for Jesus in the *wrong* place, God eventually leads us to the *right* place, as long as we sincerely, diligently search for Jesus with all our hearts. (See the Appendix titled "*Force Majeure*: Does God Forgive Non-Christians?")

Since the Magi were looking for the newborn king of the Jews, they went to the natural place to look for a newborn king—the king's palace in the capital, Jerusalem.

Unfortunately—as so often in life—the obvious answer is the wrong answer.

We look for God with the rich and famous. But in reality, he's with smelly shepherds in a stable.

We look for God to transform our lives with miracles to serve our selfish desires. But we can't find God until he transforms our hearts by making us realize that God's power is made perfect in our weakness (Luke 9:46–48; 2 Corinthians 12:9; and James 3:13–4:7).

When the Magi got to Jerusalem, they caused quite a stir by asking, "Where is the one who has been born king of the Jews? We saw his star in the east and have come to worship him" (Matthew 2:2).

It was as if an ambassador from a distant country arrived in Washington, D.C. saying, "Where's the person who's going to be the next President?" The current occupant of the White House would be very interested to learn who the next President would be—especially if there were no term limit and if the current President planned to stay in office until the day he or she died.

So "[w]hen King Herod heard this he was disturbed, and all Jerusalem with him" (Matthew 2:3).

I doubt that King Herod believed that the actual Messiah had been born. But he knew the power of rumor and superstition to undermine his power. He was determined to put a stop to any ideas anyone might harbor that there was any king of the Jews except him.

It is sobering to realize that, when it came to learning about Jesus, wicked King Herod was smarter and shrewder than the Magi.

King Herod was smarter than the Magi because he knew where the answer could be found—the Bible. He "called together all the people's chief priests and teachers of the law [and] he asked them where the Christ was to be born" (Matthew 2:4).

These religious leaders and scholars knew the correct answer. They quickly found the relevant Bible verses and told King Herod that the Christ was to be born in Bethlehem (Matthew 2:5–6).

King Herod was also shrewder than the Magi. He knew that they would not help him find this newborn threat to his throne, if he told them that he planned to kill the child. Therefore, he lied.

King Herod told them, "Go and make a careful search for the child. As soon as you find him, report to me, so that I too may go and worship him" (Matthew 2:8).

How typical of wicked people that they pursue their wicked schemes by pretending that they want to worship God!

It is scary to realize that the people who knew best how to find Jesus—the religious leaders and scholars—showed no interest in searching for him.

They were content to know all about God intellectually—as long as their knowledge didn't change their daily routine.

They enjoyed the pomp and circumstance of being called to the palace by the king. They enjoyed flaunting their intellectual knowledge about the Bible. But their hearts had no interest in finding God—no interest in finding the Promised Land where they could bless other peoples.

How like them we often are! We love to sit in a pew and enjoy the music. We love to talk in a Bible study group to show how smart we are. But we are so slow to live the kind of life that the Bible says we should live—we are so slow to bless others by establishing the pure worship of the LORD in spirit and in truth.

We don't change our daily routine to go find Jesus. We don't want to inconvenience ourselves. We don't want to change our comfortable lives.

It's not that we don't believe God exists. We do.

It's not that we disagree with what God wants us to do. It's just that we're too comfortable in our pews to go looking for more things to do.

We're so busy learning about Jesus that we don't have time to live like Jesus lived.

So it is immensely comforting to know that God helps all those who are willing to leave their comfort zone to go search for Jesus.

The Magi followed the wrong religion. The Magi looked for Jesus in the wrong place. The Magi trusted the wrong people.

Nevertheless, the Magi found Jesus.

The Magi succeeded because they sincerely wanted to meet Jesus and worship him. They cared enough about finding Jesus that they were willing to uproot their entire lives to go find him—no matter how long and how difficult their journey might be.

The Magi succeeded because God helped them. God made sure the Magi got correct advice from the Bible, even though the people telling them what the Bible said were not good people. And God sent "the star they had seen in the east . . . ahead of them until it stopped over the place where [Jesus] was" (Matthew 2:9).

As I said before, we don't know for sure what the "star" was. And in our lives, the "star" that first inspires us to seek for God will vary from person to person.

But one thing remains the same regardless of the century and regardless of the person. God will always send "stars" to guide us to him.

Your guiding "star" may disappear for a while—especially if you've been searching for God in the wrong places and hanging around with the wrong people.

Nevertheless—in God's good time and in God's good way—God will send you your guiding "star" again until you find Jesus.

You can count on it!

If you search for Jesus long enough and hard enough, you'll come to that moment when it leads you to the place where Jesus is—the Promised Land.

Like the Magi, when you find Jesus you'll be overjoyed. You'll bow down and worship Jesus. You'll give Jesus the best gifts you have. And you'll "return[] to [your] country by another route" (Matthew 2:10–12).

You won't be misled by the King Herods in your life anymore. You'll go home a changed person. A better person. A person who has met Jesus face-to-face. A person who has found the Promised Land.

Hoping in the Lord

It seems as if God often uses trips to teach people about himself—whether Mary and Joseph are looking for an inn, shepherds are looking for a baby, or the Magi are following a star.

So here are a few thoughts stimulated by our family's trip to Hawaii while I was writing these thoughts about the birth of Jesus.

During the long flights to and from Hawaii, I pondered a recent sermon at our church.[1] In his sermon, the pastor drew two analogies to the Christian life from how jets fly.

First, once a jet starts flying, they don't turn the engine off. If they did, the plane would plunge to the ground and crash. Similarly, the Christian life doesn't consist of making a good start and then trying to coast. We have to keep our Christian commitment up full blast. Otherwise, we'll crash in flames.

Second, when a jet lands, the pilot must keep the engines on full power. Otherwise, wind shear will start rocking the plane and can cause it to crash. Similarly, in our Christian life, we must keep going full power right to the end.

Another thought came to me several times during the trip because my children kept trying to build things with sand, write words in the sand, or leave their footprints in the sand. They'd always get frustrated and upset when they'd see a wave come pounding in and destroy what they'd tried to build.

I thought back to my writings about "Establishing the Work of Your Hands" based on the life of Moses. And I realized again how fleeting anything we try to accomplish in this life is, except the things we build with God's help. Unless God establishes the work of our hands, our efforts are as futile and as fleeting as those buildings in the sand—quickly washed away in waves of time.

Another thought came to me walking along the beach on Maui with Sarah to watch the sun rise. If we tried walking or running parallel to the incoming waves, then when a big wave hit us we'd stumble—and sometimes we'd even fall. So we learned that when a big wave came, we had to stop, face it, and keep both feet on the ground. Then we could stand firm.

I realized that facing big problems in life is like facing big waves on the beach. If we ignore the problems and just keep walking or running along, they'll trip us up. But if we face our problems head-on with both feet on the ground, we can survive them and move on down the beach after they subside.

Finally, a scary, disturbing thought came to me as we waited in Atlanta for our final flight home from Atlanta to Rochester. We were exhausted by this point in our trip. We'd left Maui at 3 P.M. the day before (8 P.M. eastern standard time). We'd sat several hours at the Honolulu airport while our flight was delayed an hour. We'd flown all night long for seven and a half hours without hardly any sleep. We'd waited several hours in Atlanta for this final leg of our journey home. Then, when my wife went to get our boarding passes for the flight to Rochester, the man in charge of the gate said we weren't in the computer and there was no room on the heavily over-booked flight.

That story ended happily. After about fifteen angry, anguished minutes, they gave us seat assignments and we flew home, actually arriving about half an hour early.

But a terrifying thought crossed my mind when we were waiting to see if there was room on the flight—how much worse it will be for those people who find out after they've died that they don't have the necessary "ticket" to get to heaven.

They've gone along for the journey. They've taken a lot of flights. They've enjoyed the sun and surf in Hawaii. They've eaten well.

But then, at the last moment, when it's too late to do anything about it, they'll find out that they're not getting into heaven. They'll be told that they don't have the right "ticket"—a living faith in Jesus Christ.

Jesus spoke about the horror of that moment. He warned us (much like our pastor warned us before we set off for Hawaii):

"Not everyone who says to me, 'Lord, Lord,' will enter the kingdom of heaven, but only he who does the will of my Father who is in heaven. Many will say to me on that day, 'Lord, Lord, did we not prophesy in your name, and in your name drive out demons and perform many miracles?' Then I will tell them plainly, 'I never knew you. Away from me, you evildoers!'"

(Matthew 7:21–23)

Make sure you heed this warning. Do the will of our Father who is in heaven by blessing all peoples. Keep your heart pure and your spirit steadfast. Establish the works of your hands by loving the Lord your God with all your heart and with all your soul and with all your mind and by loving your neighbor as yourself. Face all your problems head-on with your feet firmly grounded because you have a living faith in Jesus Christ. And have the discipline to keep the jet engines of your faith going full thrust right to the end.

During such a faithful journey through life, we always find Jesus—we always reach the Promised Land. We are always like Mary and Joseph who reached their Promised Land when they found God's gift to them, Jesus. We are always like the shepherds who reached their Promised Land when they found their savior, Jesus. And we are always like the Magi who reached their Promised Land when they found their king, Jesus.

During such a faithful journey through life worshiping the LORD in spirit and in truth, we always find the hope that Jesus gives us. Therefore, with the pure heart and the steadfast spirit that are the fruit of the Holy Spirit, we always find the strength to reach the Promised Land.

[Because] those who hope in the LORD
    will renew their strength.
They will soar on wings like eagles;

they will run and not grow weary,
they will walk and not be faint.

(Isaiah 40:31)

PART TWO

God Calls Jesus to Set Us Free from Sin

Mary and Joseph Lose Jesus in Jerusalem

Now we come to one of my favorite stories in the Bible. In many ways it's a very simple story—the story of a child lost in the big city and of his parents' frantic search for him. But because it's a story about Mary, Joseph and Jesus, it is also a very profound story. It has much to tell us about parents, their children, and Jesus.

Even though the story is a familiar one, let's recap it briefly.

Jesus was now twelve years old. He'd been living in Nazareth with his parents, Mary and Joseph. Nazareth was a town of some importance. It had about 20,000 people and lay at an important crossroads. But still, Nazareth was nothing compared to the "big city" of Jerusalem.

Although we know nothing specific about how wealthy and important Jesus' family was, we assume that they were a humble "middle class" family. Joseph was a carpenter (Matthew 13:55). Presumably, Jesus became a carpenter, too.

Jesus and his father must have gazed in awe at the magnificent buildings of Jerusalem, compared to the modest structures they helped build in Nazareth. The most magnificent building of all was the Temple. Jesus and his father must have marveled at the woodworking of the Temple and its furnishings.

We know that Jesus and his parents visited Jerusalem regularly as he grew up. We are told that "[e]very year his parents went to Jerusalem for the Feast of the Passover" (Luke 2:41).

This Feast celebrated a key event in Israel's history—the escape of the Jews from slavery in Egypt. As devout Jews, Mary and Joseph were expected to attend such major festivals in Jerusalem annually if at all possible.

I'm sure that Mary and Joseph made every effort to come to Jerusalem each year.

They knew that Jesus was a very special child—a future king who would save his people from their sins (Luke 1:32–33; Matthew 1:21). They must have wanted to expose him to Jerusalem and its Temple as much as possible.

In addition, I'm sure they had a good time—the closest thing they had to a vacation. Their annual pilgrimage to Jerusalem must have been similar in many ways to our family's annual "pilgrimage" to Walt Disney World with our children.

Our annual trip to Walt Disney World was an educational experience for our children. Some years we also stopped briefly in Washington while driving south because we wanted them to see our nation's capital—just as Mary and Joseph wanted Jesus to see his nation's capital, Jerusalem.

Our annual trip to Walt Disney World was a time to remember our grandest dreams and to recapture our hopes for a wonderful future.

In the Magic Kingdom, there is the boat ride where colorful, animated children from every nation sing over and over again that "It's A Small World After All." In the Temple, Jesus heard people singing over and over again that God's love endures forever (Psalm 136).

At Epcot, there is a laser light show to celebrate what is best about the diverse peoples of our small world. The music and magnificence of the Temple had a similar effect on Mary, Joseph and Jesus as the Disney Magic of modern technology has on us today. Imagine hearing the music in the Temple! In Jesus' time there were no stereos or headsets. There were no movies or television to detract from the awe of the pageantry at the Temple.

At Epcot, there is also an American "temple" where "robots" who look like Benjamin Franklin and Mark Twain talk about the triumphs and tragedies of the American people. In the Temple, the greatest teachers of Judaism talked about the triumphs and tragedies of God's people.

Two other things must have been as true of Jerusalem in Jesus' time as of Walt Disney World today—the crowds and the frantic pace. The crush of people in Jerusalem must have been equivalent to the crush of people in Walt Disney World when it's crowded. And the frantic pace of travel must have been similar to the haste with which we packed our car and drove all night towards Walt Disney World.

The crowds and the frantic pace help explain the confusion that caused Mary and Joseph to lose Jesus in Jerusalem. We are told that "[a]fter the Feast was over, while his parents were returning home, the boy Jesus stayed behind in Jerusalem, but they were unaware of it" (Luke 2:43). So "[t]hinking he was in their company, they traveled on for a day" (Luke 2:44).

How could this be? How could parents lose track of their child for a whole day and not even know he was missing?

Actually, the mistake was fairly easy to make when we consider the way that Mary and Joseph were traveling. They weren't hopping into the family car to drive back home. Presumably, they were traveling in a large group of friends and relatives from Nazareth. Furthermore, the women and men traveled in separate groups.

Since Jesus was twelve years old, Mary probably thought that Jesus was traveling with the men. But Jesus was still young enough that Joseph probably thought that he was traveling with the women and children. It was not until evening—when the men and women were gathering together for the night—that Mary and Joseph learned that Jesus hadn't been with either of them that day.

Mary and Joseph must have been nervous and embarrassed. Where was Jesus? "[T]hey began looking for him among their relatives and friends" (Luke 2:44).

At some point, they must have become frantic. My wife and I never lost either of our children for more than a few minutes—but those few minutes are among the most anguishing anyone can live through.

Joseph and Mary must have been distraught when they confirmed that Jesus was missing. There were no telephones to call Jerusalem and ask the police to find Jesus. So "[w]hen they did not find him, they went back to Jerusalem to look for him" (Luke 2:45).

Their search for Jesus did not end quickly. They must not have been able to guess where Jesus would go if he were alone in Jerusalem.

Perhaps they checked the homes of friends and relatives. Perhaps they checked the palace and the marketplace. But—like the Magi—it took them awhile to look in the right place for Jesus.

By this time they must have been completely baffled how to find Jesus. At last, "[a]fter three days they found him in the temple courts, sitting among the teachers, listening to them and asking them questions. Everyone who heard him was amazed at his understanding and his answers" (Luke 2:46–47).

Mary and Joseph had certainly not expected this! "When his parents saw him, they were astonished. His mother said to him, 'Son, why have you treated us like this? Your father and I have been anxiously searching for you.'" (Luke 2:48).

I wish we could hear Mary's tone of voice and see her face as she said this to Jesus. I imagine she said it with a combination of relief and fury—the same way that my wife and I spoke to our children when we found them after they'd been missing for merely a few minutes.

Jesus answered Mary with that frustrating naivety that is typical for a child of twelve. I know that because it's typical of how my 12-year old children answered me under similar circumstances whenever I was astonished that they were doing something that didn't make sense to my adult mind.

Jesus couldn't understand what his parents were all upset about. "'Why were you searching for me?' he asked. 'Didn't you know I had to be in my Father's house?'" (Luke 2:49).

Mary and Joseph "did not understand what he was saying to them" (Luke 2:50). I can sympathize with them because I had the same problem understanding such childish responses to my own questions and complaints.

The key difference between Jesus and other children was that Jesus did not become disrespectful or disobedient towards his parents. Even though they "didn't get it," he didn't yell and scream at them. He didn't tell them they were stupid. Instead, Jesus "went down to Nazareth with them and was obedient to them" (Luke 2:51).

Of course, Jesus was fortunate to have such good parents. It was easier to obey Mary and Joseph than to obey most parents. Most parents would berate their child for disrupting the parents' travel plans. Most parents would ridicule their child for being so stupid.

But Mary—after her initial exasperation and fear vented themselves—did not ridicule or condemn Jesus for his astonishing behavior. Instead—like any good mother—Mary "treasured all these things in her heart" (Luke 2:51).

Fortunately, Mary had many wonderful memories to cherish about her son. In ways more numerous than the Bible records, "Jesus grew in wisdom and stature, and in favor with God and men" (Luke 2:52).

For parents, this story holds a number of lessons about how to help their children grow "in wisdom and stature, and in favor with God and men."

For one thing, parents need to learn that it's OK to make mistakes as parents. Everyone makes mistakes. Even Mary and Joseph. Let's review the mistakes they made.

First, Mary and Joseph lost track of Jesus *physically*.

There are plenty of excuses for why they left Jesus behind in Jerusalem. They were busy. There were lots of people running around. There was some confusion whether a 12-year old boy would travel with the men or with the women.

But despite all these excuses, the truth was that Mary and Joseph made a mistake. They didn't spend enough time talking with their child and their spouse to make sure that everybody knew what was going on.

Mary and Joseph's second mistake was that they lost track of Jesus *spiritually* and *emotionally*.

This is a natural consequence of being too busy and distracted to keep track of a child physically. Because if we can't even keep track of a child's physical location, how are we going to keep track of the many ways they change emotionally and spiritually as they grow?

To me (as to Jesus) it was odd that Mary and Joseph had such trouble figuring out where Jesus would be in Jerusalem. In hindsight, it's obvious that Jesus had an intense interest in spiritual matters, especially teaching. So where else would he go in Jerusalem than to the center of spiritual matters and teaching—the Temple!

Mary and Joseph somehow had missed out on this critical aspect of Jesus' development.

Skeptical critics of the Bible's accuracy are so struck by Mary and Joseph's inability to realize that Jesus would be in the Temple and by their astonishment at his amazing abilities that these skeptics regard it as "proof" that the stories about Jesus' birth are not historical. Why, these skeptics ask, would Mary and Joseph be astonished that Jesus was in the Temple amazing everyone with his understanding and his answers if they'd been visited by angels, the shepherds and the Magi?

Perhaps these skeptics have never been parents. If they had had their own children, they should realize that parents almost always are unable to fathom what is going on inside their children—especially as they make the transition from child to adult. Mary and Joseph were no different—even though God chose them as the best parents he could find to raise Jesus.

Furthermore, the angels, shepherds and Magi told Mary and Joseph very little about the specifics of Jesus' ministry. The angel told Mary that Jesus would "be great;" that he would "be called the Son of the Most High;" that he would be given "the throne of his father David;" that he would "reign over the house of Jacob forever;" and that "his kingdom will never end" (Luke 1:32–33). There was nothing in the angel's statements that specifically mentioned that Jesus would be a great teacher or that he would love the Temple—that he would establish the pure worship of the LORD in spirit and in truth.

Nor do the other statements about Jesus recorded in the nativity stories describe Jesus as a teacher or describe his love for the Temple. The statements about Jesus didn't get into the specifics about how he would "save his people from their sins" (Matthew 1:21)—how he would bless all peoples in the Promised Land.

The most natural thought that probably occurred to Mary and Joseph was that, since God was going to "give him the throne of his father David" (Luke 1:32), Jesus would be a great warrior like David. After all, the most memorable story about the boy David was the story about how he defeated Goliath. So perhaps Mary and Joseph looked for the boy Jesus among those who were learning to make *war.*

Next Mary and Joseph might have looked for Jesus among those who were learning to make *laws,* because Jesus was supposed to "reign over the house of Jacob forever" (Luke 1:33).

Then, remembering that David was a gifted musician, perhaps Mary and Joseph looked for Jesus among those who were learning to make *music*.

It would have taken careful reflection to remember how much David loved to worship in the house of the LORD. To remember how much David yearned to build a Temple for the LORD. To remember how much David wanted to "dwell in the house of the LORD forever" (Psalm 23:6). To remember how much David wanted a pure heart and a steadfast spirit so that he could worship the LORD in spirit and in truth.

Therefore, a major reason why Mary and Joseph failed to understand their child's hopes and dreams was probably because—just as other parents—they were blinded by their preconceptions about who their child is, how their child should live, and what their child should do when he or she grows up.

Another major reason why Mary and Joseph failed to understand their child's hopes and dreams was probably because—just as parents today—they were too busy to pay close attention to the signs that came their way.

Mary and Joseph must have missed Jesus' fascination with the teachers in the Temple. If they'd been observing his reactions in the Temple, they'd probably have known it would be the first place he'd go—just as I could guess where in Walt Disney World my children would go.

Furthermore, Mary and Joseph must not have listened carefully enough to what Jesus said about what interested him. We do not know whether Jesus loved music. But Jesus loved the truth too much—and tolerated hypocrites too little—to enjoy politics. And from everything we know about Jesus as an adult, it's hard to believe that Jesus ever wanted to pursue a military career.

In contrast, from all we know about Jesus as an adult, can anyone doubt that from his earliest childhood he must have studied the Bible, prayed without ceasing, told people about God, and talked about how we should live?

Hindsight is always 20–20. So I've tried to do better than Mary and Joseph at listening to my children and helping them become the people *they* want to become instead of the people *I* want them to become. Nevertheless, it's easy for me to make the same mistakes as Mary and Joseph made.

I don't pay enough attention to who my children are. I'm too busy. And anyway, I think I've already got it all figured out so there's no need to listen and observe carefully to understand who my children really are and how God really wants them to live. Finally, I fail many times as a parent in a way that Mary and Joseph failed here—they blamed their child for their own mistakes!

When Mary and Joseph found Jesus in the Temple, they were "astonished" at the way Jesus was "sitting among the teachers, listening to them and asking them questions." They must also have been "astonished" at how "[e]veryone who heard him was amazed at his understanding and his answers" (Luke 2:46–48).

But did Mary and Joseph tell Jesus how proud they were of him? Did they realize that they were the ones who "got lost"—that they should have told Jesus more carefully about their plans for traveling home? No! Of course not! Like any parent (or at least like me), they blamed the child!

In that moment when Mary and Joseph should have been proudest of Jesus, Mary was human enough to vent her stress, anguish and relief by complaining: "Son, why have you treated us like this? Your father and I have been anxiously searching for you" (Luke 2:48).

Even when Jesus explained why he was right and they were wrong, Mary and Joseph still couldn't figure out their child. "'Why were you searching for me?' he asked. 'Didn't you know I had to be in my Father's house?'" But Mary and Joseph still "did not understand what he was saying to them" (Luke 2:49–50).

It's scary to think how hard it is to be a good parent. Even Mary and Joseph made mistakes! Even Mary and Joseph failed to understand their child! Even Mary and Joseph sometimes got mad at their child for the wrong reason!

How can I hope to get things right as a parent?

But then I take heart. Even though Mary and Joseph made *mistakes* as parents, they still *succeeded* as parents. So if I do the things they did right as parents, I can be confident that the mistakes I make as a parent will be washed away by all the good things I do as a parent.

Two things made Mary and Joseph outstanding parents. First, they cared more about their child, Jesus, than about anything else in the world—including their own self-interest. Second, they made sure that their child learned to know God and God's ways.

We've already seen how Mary and Joseph sacrificed everything for Jesus when he was born. Mary sacrificed her good name and was willing to destroy her marriage to Joseph by showing up pregnant before the wedding with a child that was not his. Joseph sacrificed his respectability by marrying a woman in circumstances that suggested he'd had sex with her before the wedding.

Mary and Joseph fled to Egypt with the baby Jesus when they feared King Herod would kill him (Matthew 2:13–20). They traveled to Jerusalem every year at great expense and inconvenience—at least partly so that Jesus would learn about the wide world and the ways of God's people. When they lost track of Jesus, they hurried back to Jerusalem to find him. They searched anxiously for him until they found him.

And even though they sometimes misunderstood Jesus and got mad at him when they were really the ones at fault, when they calmed down and reflected on things, they weren't angry at Jesus anymore. Instead, Mary—as any good mother or father—"treasured all these things in her heart" (Luke 2:51).

We need to show our children that we love them and treasure them just as Mary and Joseph showed Jesus how much they loved and treasured him.

Second, Mary and Joseph made sure that Jesus was raised to know God and God's ways. We know this partly because on trips such as this pilgrimage to Jerusalem they provided Jesus with opportunities to become better educated—just as we took our children on vacations to broaden their understanding of the world and to show them things that may inspire them for the rest of their lives. A space shuttle launching. A whale breaching. The power of Freedom at the Lincoln Memorial. The power of God at Niagara Falls.

But mostly we know that Mary and Joseph raised Jesus to know God and God's ways because of what we know about the kind of person Jesus grew up to be. Jesus was always quoting the Bible and applying it correctly to the circumstances of life. And even more important, Jesus applied God's ways to his own life so that he was always doing the right thing: Jesus was always loving the Lord his God with all his heart and with all his soul and with all his mind and he was always loving his neighbor as himself.

I'm sure that Mary and Joseph lived the kind of lives that taught Jesus how to live this way on a practical, day-to-day basis. Indeed, this is the ultimate challenge for every parent—to teach our children so well by our words and our deeds that our children grow "in wisdom and stature, and in favor with God and men."

One such lesson that our children must learn is that they must never let discouragement or criticism stop them from pursuing their dreams and achieving their visions. They must not get discouraged because adults such as their parents or their teachers don't understand them. Sometimes adults will even criticize them for doing the very things we ought to be praising them for. For example, Jesus' mother was exasperated (at first) because he was so interested in learning about God's ways that he lost track of "unimportant things" such as when the family was supposed to go home.[1]

Another lesson to learn from this story is that it's OK for children to make childish mistakes—such as forgetting their homework. It's normal for children to forget such things—to be so caught up in being a child that they forget the dull details of life. After all, Jesus was so "out of things" that he forgot to join the family for the trip home. And he was so "irresponsible" that he didn't even realize his mistake for three days until his parents showed up! Despite these childish mistakes, Jesus grew up to be just fine—so children today can grow up to be just fine even if they make mistakes, too.

This story about Jesus in the Temple also teaches us much about who Jesus was and how he grew up. Indeed, perhaps no other story shows us so simply and profoundly that Jesus was both fully Human and fully God.

How can there be a better story to show that Jesus was so fully Human?

Jesus didn't spring from thin air. He was born in a manger and grew up. Jesus knew what it was like to be absent-minded—to be so caught up in the innocent intensity of a child that he forgot to wonder why he hadn't seen his parents for three days. Jesus knew the wonder of discovering things for the first time—such as admiring the magnificence of the Temple and enjoying a stimulating intellectual discussion with the most learned religious thinkers of his time. Jesus knew what it was like to be criticized by his mother—even when his mother was wrong and he was right. Jesus knew how hard it was to leave what he really wanted to do so he could go back to Nazareth with his parents and be "obedient to them" (Luke 2:51).

Jesus experienced all the growing pains of a child as he "grew in wisdom and stature, and in favor with God and men" (Luke 2:52). Yet—with hindsight—it became apparent that Jesus was the Son of God, fully God as well as fully Human.

Jesus had such a deep understanding of the thoughts and ways of God that even at the age of twelve "[e]veryone who heard him was amazed at his understanding and his answers" (Luke 2:47). Jesus had a perfect attitude. Of what other child could it be said he "was obedient to [his parents]?" (Luke 2:51). But most of all, who else ever had such a perfect conviction that God was his father? No wonder his parents "did not understand what he was saying to them" when Jesus told them "I had to be in my Father's house" (Luke 2:49–50).

In the culture in which Jesus grew up, it was particularly odd that Jesus would think of God as his father. As followers of Jesus we are familiar with the idea that God is our "Heavenly Father." Indeed, we start most of our prayers with some such reference to God as our "Father in Heaven."

But it was rare to think of God as a "father" in the Old Testament—and if he was talked about as a father, he was usually a stern, distant disciplinarian. There usually was no sense of that gentle, kind intimacy that led Jesus to call God the equivalent of "Daddy" instead of the more formal word "Father."[2]

Indeed, by calling God his "Daddy," Jesus gave us an example of how he "grew in wisdom" by being fully Human as well as fully God. As the Son of God, Jesus had a perfect relationship—a perfect communion—with God, stretching beyond the existence of time and of this universe. As a human child, he experienced for a few years the simple joys of a small child's relationship—a joyous communion—with his mommy and daddy. And, as an adult, Jesus drew upon both experiences to deepen our understanding of what it means have a perfect relationship—a perfect, joyous communion—with God. Jesus taught us to call God our "Daddy."

Jesus Is Baptized

We have to skip ahead on the DVD.

About twenty years have passed since the boy Jesus amazed and astonished everyone who heard him in the Temple. We have no record in the Bible about what happened to Jesus in those "silent years."

Now Jesus "was about thirty years old." He was about to begin his ministry (Luke 3:23). At this time, Jesus made a choice that was as astonishing as the wisdom he displayed as a boy in the Temple. Instead of heading to Jerusalem to begin his ministry, he first sought out John the Baptist at the Jordan River.

John was Jesus' relative. John was a few months older than Jesus. As you may recall, John's mother, Elizabeth, was six months pregnant, when the angel, Gabriel, told Mary that she would become pregnant with Jesus.

Indeed, Gabriel referred to the fact that Elizabeth had become pregnant despite being "in her old age" (after being barren all her life), as proof that God could enable Mary to conceive Jesus even though Mary was still a virgin. As Gabriel told Mary, such miracles could happen: "For nothing is impossible with God" (Luke 1:36–37).

We infer that John and Jesus knew each other as they were growing up. Since Mary visited Elizabeth when they were pregnant (Luke 1:39–56), presumably Mary also visited Elizabeth after their babies were born.

Furthermore, John knew Jesus well enough that John was amazed when Jesus asked John to baptize him.

John's hesitation to baptize Jesus is all the more amazing because John was already a figure of fame and importance at the time that Jesus came to the Jordan River to have John baptize him. There were "crowds coming out to be baptized by him" (Luke 3:7).

John's belief that Jesus did not need to be baptized is also amazing because it proves that Jesus lived a righteous life for the first thirty years of his life. John had high standards of conduct—standards similar to those that Jesus insisted on in the Sermon on the Mount.

For example, when the crowds asked John what they should do, "John answered, 'The man with two tunics should share with him who has none, and the one who has food should do the same.'" (Luke 3:11).

If John compared my life to such high standards of conduct, he would declare me a terrible sinner. First, John would warn me "to flee from the coming wrath" (Matthew 3:7). Then, assuming I was willing to change my ways, John would whisk me right into the Jordan to baptize me, urging me to "[p]roduce fruit in keeping with repentance" (Matthew 3:8).

But when "Jesus came from Galilee to the Jordan to be baptized by John," John tried to change Jesus' mind. John told Jesus, "I need to be baptized by you, and do you come to me?" (Matthew 3:13).

In order to change John's mind, Jesus did not say, "I'm a sinner. I need to repent." Any of us would have to say that. But not Jesus! He had been living the way God wants us to live.

So instead of claiming to be a sinner in need of repentance "Jesus replied, 'Let it be so now; it is proper for us to do this to fulfill all righteousness.' Then John consented" (Matthew 3:15).

As happens so often with Jesus, his answers raise more questions than they answer. Why did Jesus make the long trip from Galilee to the Jordan so that John could baptize him? Why was this "proper" for John and Jesus "to do . . . to fulfill all righteousness?" (Matthew 3:15).

I've heard many sermons and Sunday School lessons try to answer these questions, but I still am not convinced that I fully understand why Jesus decided to be baptized.

In part, I think my inability to understand is because understanding Jesus' words is an art rather than a science. Just as a beautiful painting or a poem can be admired again and again and still yield fresh insights, Jesus' words are always yielding fresh insights about Jesus, my life, and our world—no matter how many times I hear them and study them.

And in part, I think my inability to understand Jesus' words better is because of my "hardness of heart." Jesus' insights and perspectives are radically different from my natural insights and perspectives about what ought to be done. Therefore, I keep trying to rationalize away the clear meaning of his teachings.

For example, I would find it very hard to let John baptize me publicly, even if I knew I had acted like the "brood of vipers" (Matthew 3:7) that John denounced. But it would never occur to me (except that Jesus himself did it) that I should humiliate myself by getting baptized like a sinner even if (like Jesus) I knew perfectly well that I was not a sinner.

If it weren't for the wisdom and insight I gain from studying what Jesus did and taught, I would think that the best way for Jesus to begin his ministry would be by some splashy proclamation about how great he was. That's the way political campaigns always get launched. And it's a rare pastor seeking a church who starts out by downplaying his own talents and righteousness.

So if I'd been advising Jesus, I'd have suggested that when he got to the Jordan, he should have had John the Baptist introduce him to the crowd and give him a ringing endorsement. Then Jesus should have started upstaging John by giving better speeches than John and doing lots of miracles.

Or, perhaps I would have advised Jesus to go first to Jerusalem and repeat his performance as a child prodigy. Dazzle them with his teaching! Do a bunch of miracles! Start things off with a bang!

Jesus' decision to begin his public career by humbling himself by getting baptized seems so foolish!

But, of course, as Paul wrote to the church at Corinth: "God made foolish the wisdom of the world" by sending righteous Jesus to die on the cross to save sinners because "the wisdom of this world is foolishness in God's sight" (1 Corinthians 1:20;3:19). So let me suggest several reasons why Jesus was wise to be baptized by John—why Jesus let John baptize him "to fulfill all righteousness" (Matthew 3:15).

As he was about to begin his ministry, Jesus wanted to affirm what *kind* of Messiah he would be. Jesus would not be the conquering military hero who the masses dreamed of—the kind of Messiah who brings "peace" by "winning" wars. Jesus would be the kind of Messiah who brings peace by winning hearts—the kind of Messiah who teaches people to be good neighbors and best friends.

And to be good neighbors and best friends, we must learn the Way of humility and submission. Instead of imposing our will on others, we must submit our will to God and commit our lives to serving others.

So Jesus submitted to being baptized. But why was baptism chosen as a symbol of Jesus' submission—especially a baptism of repentance for sins that Jesus had never committed?

If I had been Jesus, I would have been afraid of what other people would think of me. Surely they would think that I was a sinner. Why else would I be hanging around with all these sinners, asking to be baptized?

But Jesus could never stand such hypocrisy. He could never stand anyone who thought they were "too good" to associate with "sinners."

Jesus was determined to bridge the gap between "sinners" and God. So he began building that bridge by allowing himself to be baptized with the sinners.

A related thought was picked up by Luke when he wrote his gospel. Luke wrote, "[w]hen all the people were being baptized, Jesus was baptized too" (Luke 3:21). Since Jesus came to touch all people with God's love, he had to be with "all the people" as they came to be baptized for their sins.

No longer was the *boy* Jesus content to sit in his Father's house—the Temple in Jerusalem—learning what to do. Now the *man* Jesus was ready to be among "all the people," doing whatever needed to be done to bring them hope—even though they were sinners.

At this critical moment in Jesus' life, God affirmed Jesus' choice of which kind of Messiah he should be. God's affirmation came just after Jesus was baptized, as Jesus was praying.

The Bible doesn't say what Jesus was praying for. Nevertheless, we can be pretty sure that he was praying for what would be best for "all the people"—all the sinners—who were being baptized and who were chang-ing their ways. And we can be pretty sure that Jesus was praying for wisdom so that he could best minister to their needs—could best bless all the peoples in the Promised Land.

As a sign of his pleasure, God answered Jesus' prayer in a dramatic fashion: "heaven was opened and the Holy Spirit descended on him in bodily form like a dove. And a voice came from heaven: 'You are my Son, whom I love; with you I am well pleased.'" (Luke 3:21–22).

It's unlikely that we will receive such a dramatic manifestation of God's pleasure with us. But we can be sure that God will be pleased with us if we go to be with sinners to help them, even though it means humbling ourselves. In one way or another, we will sense that heaven has opened, that the Holy Spirit has come upon us, that we are part of God's family, that God loves us, and that God is well pleased with us.

Jesus Is Tempted

Now came a moment of hard testing for Jesus.

It is noteworthy that this time of tempting did not come because Jesus had sinned or become distant from the will of God for his life. On the contrary, this severe tempting by the devil took place immediately after Jesus' baptism—one of the spiritual high points of Jesus' life when God told him that he was his Son, that God loved him, and that God was "well pleased" with him (Matthew 3:17).

Nor did Jesus come to the place and moment of temptation because of some mistake he'd made or because he was doing something other than what God wanted him to do. We are told that "Jesus was led by the Spirit into the desert to be tempted by the devil" (Matthew 4:1). There is not the slightest doubt that Jesus was in close communion with God as he entered this time of testing because we are told that Jesus was "full of the Holy Spirit" at this time (Luke 4:1).

The fact that Jesus was subjected to strong temptations even when he was full of the Holy Spirit doing what God most wanted him to do is immensely encouraging. Too often we get discouraged when we are tempted to do something wrong. We feel that if we were "full of the Holy Spirit" the way we ought to be such wicked ideas would not enter our minds. This is part of the deception that keeps us from hoping in the LORD. And when we lose hope, we are much more likely to give in to the despair that leads to sin and defeat in our lives.

The truth is exactly the opposite. The fact that we are being strongly tempted is a good sign that we are full of the Holy Spirit. If we are already walking on the path to evil, there's no need to feel tempted by evil. Furthermore, the Deceiver does not want us to awaken to our peril by thinking about where we are going with our life. The Enemy of Our Souls would rather keep us busy and preoccupied so that we don't pay attention to the road signs and the maps that would tell us that our lives are going the wrong way.

In reality, we are tempted most when we are closest to God—just as Jesus was tempted immediately after his baptism and after God's affirmation that he was well pleased with Jesus. Furthermore, instead of temptation being a sign that we are too wicked in our thoughts to serve God well, the temptations are a sign that God wants us to begin a bolder, more fruitful life than we have ever experienced before.

Jesus was about to begin his public ministry. In three short years, his teachings and example would inspire and change the world forever. Yet, despite his great potential—indeed, *because* of his great potential (because the devil wanted to deflect Jesus from his true mission)—Jesus was subjected to great temptations.

So we should not be discouraged when our thoughts turn toward evil. It is probably a sign that we have been doing many things right and that God plans for our lives to become even more fruitful. We must not get discouraged at such difficult times of testing. Instead, we must hope in the LORD, waiting for him to carry us through the temptations that so easily and forcefully beset us.

Indeed, temptations grow naturally out of the circumstances in which we find ourselves—just as the temptations that Jesus faced arose naturally out of the situation facing him.

The first temptation[1] arose from Jesus' physical circumstances. Jesus was "in the desert, where for forty days he was tempted by the devil. He ate nothing during those days, and at the end of them he was hungry" (Luke 4:1–2).

Wanting to take advantage of Jesus' physical hunger to get him to put his personal comfort above the disciplines of God, the devil said to him, "If you are the Son of God, tell this stone to become bread." But Jesus refused. He answered by quoting the Bible: "It is written: 'Man does not live on bread alone.'" (Luke 4:3–4).

The next two temptations related to Jesus' career objectives. Since Jesus was about to begin his public ministry, he was undoubtedly thinking a great deal about how to gain many followers and how to prove to everyone that he was the Son of God. The devil was quick to give Jesus some wrong advice.

The devil "showed him in an instant all the kingdoms of the world" and told him: "I will give you all their authority and splendor, for it has been given to me, and I can give it to anyone I want to. So if you worship me, it will all be yours." But Jesus refused to worship the devil. He answered by quoting the Bible again: "It is written: 'Worship the Lord your God and serve him only.'" (Luke 4:5–8).

The devil also had ideas about a quick and easy way that Jesus could prove that he was the Son of God. "The devil led him to Jerusalem and had him stand on the highest point of the temple. 'If you are the Son of God,' he said, 'throw yourself down from here.'" Then—to show that he could quote the Bible too—the devil said, "For it is written:

'He will command his angels
        concerning you
    to guard you carefully;
they will lift you up in their hands,
    so that you will not strike your foot
        against a stone.'"

Jesus refused. He answered by quoting the Bible for the third time: "It says: 'Do not put the Lord your God to the test.'" (Luke 4:9–12).

Frustrated, "[w]hen the devil had finished all this tempting, he left [Jesus] until an opportune time" (Luke 4:13).

There's good news and bad news for us here. The good news is that if we resist temptation long enough, it will finally end. The bad news is that the temptations never completely stop. They'll return at "an opportune time" when we are most vulnerable.

Temptations will return at a time when we hunger for material things as Jesus did when he hungered for bread. Temptations will return at a time when we desperately want to feel successful and powerful as Jesus did when he went forth to find followers. And temptations will return at a time when we desperately want everyone to see how righteous and in tune with God we are, as Jesus did when he went forth to show people that he was the Son of God.

The specifics of the temptations vary between us and Jesus, obviously. But the basic insecurities of our existence are the same: a hunger for material things, a hunger for power, and a hunger for glory.

Jesus overcame all such insecurities. He defeated all temptations.

For in Jesus we do not have a friend "who is unable to sympathize with our weaknesses, but we have [a friend] who has been tempted in every way, just as we are—yet was without sin" (Hebrews 4:15). Therefore, to defeat temptations, we should be guided by how Jesus surmounted the temptations he felt.

Although many valuable lessons can be drawn from Jesus' experiences resisting temptation, the four lessons that I am going to discuss are: (1) the importance of self-discipline; (2) the importance of knowing the Bible well so its words can guide us; (3) the importance of telling others about those weak areas where we are often tempted so that our friends can strengthen our resolve to resist the temptations; and (4) the importance of hoping in the LORD (instead of hoping in our own power, hoping in the power of anyone or anything other than the Lord, or hoping that we can manipulate the LORD for our selfish purposes).

First, we must have great self-discipline.

Remember that Jesus called us to be his "*disciples*" (Matthew 28:19). We cannot be "disciples" without "*discipline.*"

Following Jesus is like running a marathon. People who run marathons run miles every day. They practice carefully and diligently. And then one day—the day of the race—they are ready.

Our lives must be like that when it comes to following Jesus.

It's not a matter of just practicing while we sit in the pew on Sunday. That would be like preparing for a marathon by reading about it and doing a few warm-up exercises.

We have to practice living the Way Jesus did *every day* in *every way* and in *every thing*. Then some day—such as when Jesus faced great temptations in the desert—we'll be ready to face great temptations and difficulties whenever and however they may strike.

Jesus had developed such self-discipline.

The most obvious proof of Jesus' self-discipline was his ability to fast for forty days. Despite my most vehement vows, I cannot stay away from food for more than a few hours.

In fact, I so lack discipline that I find it almost impossible to resist "junk food" for an entire day even though I have unlimited amounts of "good food" available to eat. So I am simply in awe of anyone who can fast for an entire day—much less someone such as Jesus who could fast for an entire "forty days."

But the most important disciplines that Jesus learned—and that we must learn—were not disciplines in eating. They were disciplines of learning about God and doing what God wanted.

In the story of the boy Jesus in the Temple, we've already seen how Jesus thirsted to learn God's teachings and God's ways, even as a child. And in the story of how Jesus let John baptize him, we've already seen how Jesus was committed to doing whatever was best "to fulfill all righteousness."

Through such disciplines, Jesus was already completely self-confident about who he was and what he should be doing. Therefore, he was much less likely to fall victim to the insecurities that cause us to fall so easily for temptations that deceptively and falsely promise that they will remove our insecurities.

Second, it is essential to know the Bible well.

This means memorizing verses. This means reading the Bible over and over again so that its words come naturally to mind. This also means studying hard to learn the context of the words so that we understand fully what they meant when they were first written. And, most important of all, this means learning how to think and analyze with a well-educated mind so that we apply the general principles of the Bible properly to the specific facts and circumstances in which we find ourselves.

To illustrate the importance of such an accurate, wise application of the Bible to resist temptations, let's look in detail at each of the three temptations that Jesus faced and how he used the Bible to refute the deceptive lies of the devil.

In the first temptation, Jesus was hungry and "[t]he tempter came to him and said, 'If you are the Son of God, tell these stones to become bread.'" (Matthew 4:3).

The first thing I notice about this passage is that "[t]he tempter came to him." We don't need to go looking for trouble. Trouble comes looking for us!

The next thing I notice is how cleverly the temptation attacks Jesus on several levels simultaneously. In temptations—as in so many other aspects of life—the whole is greater than the sum of its parts.

I can see at least three ways in which this temptation taunted and tempted Jesus: (1) it tempted him to rely on his own power to supply his physical needs instead of trusting God to take care of him; (2) it questioned whether Jesus "really" was the Son of God; and (3) it taunted him with the insult that, even if he "really" was the Son of God, he must be a big disappointment to his Father.

Most of us never get past the first level of temptation. We find it impossible to trust God to take care of us instead of relying on our own powers and talents to supply our physical needs.

So when we get hungry, we get tired of waiting and hoping that God will help us. We can't turn stones into bread. But we can work so hard that it destroys our family. Or we can worry so much that we take the joy from life and never accomplish anything. Or we can bend our ethical and legal standards because "everybody else is doing it"—we "have to do it" to put food on our table and a Mercedes in our garage.

And, although we do not experience the precise temptation that Jesus felt, (questioning whether we are "really" one of the persons of the Trinity), we do experience questioning whether we are "really" Christians. Does God "really" love us? Are we "really" following him? Does God even "really" exist?

And related to such questioning, are the doubting taunts that, even if we "really" are Christians, we are not very good ones. God must be very disappointed and ashamed of us. Look at all the ways we fail to please him.

To counteract such questioning and taunting, we too often rely on our own strengths and talents—whatever they may be—to convince ourselves and others that we "really" are Christians and that we "really" are spectacularly great Christians at that! Vainly fighting such questioning and doubting by hoping in our strength instead of hoping in the Lord leads us straight into the hypocrisy and self-righteousness that Jesus condemned again and again in the Pharisees.

Jesus found the perfect passage in the Bible to refute the lies and insecurities that lead us into such sins. Because of all his hard, disciplined study of the Scriptures, Jesus remembered some advice from Moses' farewell speech to the Israelites just before Moses' death. So Jesus answered the tempter by saying, "It is written: 'Man does not live on bread alone, but on every word that comes from the mouth of God.'" (Matthew 4:4).

People must not live by relying on physical things—or in a broader sense by relying on anything that *people* can do. People must live by relying on the things of God.

We cannot sustain ourselves. Only God can sustain us.

I'm sure that the reason Jesus thought of this advice from Moses was not just because the words fit, but because the facts and circumstances that prompted the advice were so similar to the facts and circumstances that Jesus faced at that moment. The full passage from Moses' farewell speech that Jesus quoted reads as follows:

> "Be careful to follow every command I am giving you today, so that you may live and increase and may enter and possess the land that the LORD promised on oath to your forefathers. Remember how the LORD your God led you all the way in the desert these forty years, to humble you and to test you in order to know what was in your heart, whether or not you would keep his commands. He humbled you, causing you to hunger and then feeding you with manna, which neither you nor your fathers had known, to teach you that man does not live on bread alone but on every word that comes from the mouth of the LORD. Your clothes did not wear out and your feet did not swell during these forty years. Know then in your heart that as a man disciplines his son, so the LORD your God disciplines you" (Deuteronomy 8:1–5).

The parallels between this experience of Moses in the desert and the experience of Jesus in the desert are startling.

Moses wanted to lead the Israelites to the physical Promised Land. Jesus wanted to lead God's people to the spiritual "Promised Land" of the Kingdom of God that figured so prominently in the teachings of the prophets and John the Baptist.

Moses and the Israelites spent "forty years" in the desert. Jesus spent "forty days" in the desert.

During their time in the desert, God humbled and tested Moses and the Israelites in order to know what was in their hearts—whether they would keep God's commands. During Jesus' time in the desert, he was also tested in order to show what was in his heart.

In each case, the person being tested was sustained by God to show that "man does not live on bread alone but on every word that comes from the mouth of the LORD."

And then we come full circle. Moses' farewell advice commends discipline—the very virtue that I listed as one of the keys to successfully resisting temptation. Moses summed up the point of being tested in the desert by saying: "Know then in your heart that as a man disciplines his son, so the Lord your God disciplines you."

So the fact that Jesus was hungry did not mean that Jesus was not "really" the Son of God. His hunger was not a sign that he was somehow a disappointment to God. Moses knew (and Jesus remembered) that such difficult circumstances are precisely the way that God shows he loves us as a father loves his son. He loves us enough to discipline us![2]

If we remember these insights of Moses and Jesus, we can find the hope in the LORD that we need to sustain us in the midst of those questions and taunts that naturally arise when we find ourselves in difficult circumstances.

A third key to resisting temptations is to be willing to admit to others that we are tempted. Although Jesus was alone in the desert so he could not talk to anyone at that moment, we know that he must have told someone later—probably his disciples so that they could learn how to defeat temptations. Because if Jesus hadn't told this story to someone, it could never have gotten into our Bibles.

Just as an alcoholic can only begin the road to recovery when he or she is able to admit that they are an alcoholic, we have to be willing to admit we're being tempted before we can defeat the temptation. And just as an alcoholic needs the support of many people to sustain him or her as he or she struggles against the temptation to drink alcohol, we benefit immeasurably by having people to turn to who will pray with us and encourage us as we struggle with whatever temptations occur most often in our lives.

If we learn discipline, know the Bible well, and have friends to help us, we maximize our chances of resisting the temptation to rely on our own strength to "turn stones into bread" when we are physically or spiritually "hungry." Instead, we will learn to hope in the LORD instead of hoping in our own power.

We also maximize our chances of resisting the two other temptations thrown at Jesus in this moment of great vulnerability: the temptation of hoping in the power of anyone or anything other than the LORD to help us and the temptation of hoping that we can manipulate the Lord for our selfish purposes.

In order to tempt Jesus to hope in the devil instead of in the LORD, "[t]he devil led him up to a high place and showed him in an instant all the kingdoms of the world. And he said to him, 'I will give you all their authority and splendor, for it has been given to me, and I can give it to anyone I want to. So if you worship me, it will all be yours.'" (Luke 4:5–7).

There are several interesting features to this temptation.

First, was the devil telling the truth when he said he could give all the authority and splendor of the kingdoms of the world to Jesus?[3] We can't know for sure. But it is certainly dangerous to trust the devil. As Jesus said at another time and place: "[T]here is no truth in [the devil]. When he lies, he speaks his native language, for he is a liar and the father of lies" (John 8:44).

Second, is the related problem of whether you can trust the devil when he promises he will do something.[4] I always say that the most important question to ask before entering into a contract with anyone is whether you can trust them. Certainly, anyone would be very naive to think that Satan would keep his side of any bargain.

Third, it is the nature of temptation to make us do something *wrong today* in the hope that we'll get something *good in the future*.[5] Good ends are always tempting us to use evil means.

And finally, being a lawyer, I can't help but notice a subtlety in what the devil asked Jesus to do. The devil asked Jesus to worship him. But the devil did not insist that Jesus worship *only* the devil. In contrast, when Jesus quoted the Scripture that refuted the devil, he said, "It is written: 'Worship the Lord your God and serve him only.'" (Luke 4:8).

79

God insists on being the *only* one we worship. But the devil knows that if he can get us to worship the devil just a *little* bit, the devil will succeed.

This is the lie that so often snares us. We think that it's OK to worship the devil at work as long as we worship God the rest of the time. In a similar fashion, most of the Ancient Israelites were perfectly happy to worship the LORD as one of their gods. The problem was that they also wanted to worship additional gods such as Baal or whatever other god the dominant superpower of the day (such as Egypt or Assyria) liked.[6]

And, that's why I say that, in its broadest sense, the essence of this temptation is to get us to hope in anyone or anything other than the LORD in some aspect of our life.

Perhaps it's becoming overly dependent on a parent or spouse. Perhaps it's vainly seeking security in our career. Perhaps it's vainly seeking security by having lots of money.

Whatever it is, it will ultimately fail us. As Jesus knew, the only "security" in life—the only splendor or authority that can satisfy you instead of destroying you—comes when you "Worship the Lord your God and serve him only" (Luke 4:8).

The context of the passage of Scripture that Jesus quoted helps us to understand better what Jesus meant by worshiping and serving the LORD. Jesus was quoting Deuteronomy 6:13 which is translated as follows in the New International Version of the Bible: "Fear the LORD your God, serve him only . . . ." This statement follows one of the most important messages Moses ever gave God's people:

> Hear, O Israel: The Lord our God, the LORD is one. Love the LORD your God with all your heart and with all your soul and with all your strength.
>
> (Deuteronomy 6:4–5)

This was the passage that Jesus would later call "the first and greatest commandment" (Matthew 22:37–38).

Moses next gave the advice that Mary and Joseph must have followed so well in raising Jesus:

These commandments that I give you today are to be upon your hearts. Impress them on your children. Talk about them when you sit at home and when you walk along the road, when you lie down and when you get up.

(Deuteronomy 6:6–7)

This is how Mary and Joseph impressed God's commands on their hearts and on the heart of Jesus—by constantly talking about the Scriptures and by constantly following the Scriptures in every aspect of life. This was why Jesus could quote the Bible so accurately and so appropriately when he needed wisdom and strength to resist temptation.

The Scripture that Jesus quoted to refute the third temptation of the devil also came from this same speech by Moses: "Do not test the Lord your God as you did at Massah" (Deuteronomy 6:16). For this temptation, "[t]he devil led [Jesus] to Jerusalem and had him stand on the highest point of the temple" (Luke 4:9). Then the devil tempted him. "If you are the Son of God," he said, "throw yourself down from here" (Luke 4:9).

It is fascinating to me that the devil tempted Jesus by taking him to the very place where you would assume a person would be the safest from temptation—the holy city of Jerusalem and its holiest spot, the Temple. This shows that we should be on our guard against temptation under every circumstance—even when sitting in a pew at church or when busily engaged in religious activities.

It is also sobering to realize that the devil can quote Scripture to deceive us. Frustrated that Jesus had quoted Scripture twice to defeat temptation, the devil decided that two could play at that game! After tempting Jesus to throw himself down from the highest point of the temple as a stunt to "prove" that he was "really" the Son of God, the devil said, "For it is written:

'He will command his angels
concerning you
to guard you carefully;
they will lift you up in their hands,
so that you will not strike your foot
against a stone.'"

(Luke 4:10–11)

81

This poetic passage of Scripture comes from Psalm 91. As with any poetry, the words express an artistic truth rather than a mechanical recipe. In other words, these words are not proven false just because I stub my toe now and then.

Even more important, the devil took the passage out of context. If you read the entire psalm, it talks about God's protection for those who are following him. The psalm assures someone "who dwells in the shelter of the Most High" that they "will rest in the shadow of the Almighty" (Psalm 91:1). It applies "[i]f you make the Most High your dwelling" (Psalm 91:9). In this psalm, the LORD says he will rescue and protect someone "[b]ecause he loves me" and "he acknowledges my name" (Psalm 91:14). So in order to hope in the LORD, we must be sheltering in the Most High and resting in the shadow of the Almighty because we love the LORD and acknowledge his name.

The devil was tempting Jesus to claim the *benefits* of hoping in the Lord without bearing any of the *burdens* of hoping in the LORD.

Jumping off the Temple would have been nothing but a stunt. It would not have shown faith, but foolishness. It would not have glorified the Lord. It would have glorified Jesus. It would not have shown *trust* in God. It would have shown *contempt* for God—a belief that God could be manipulated. Therefore, such a stunt would have been the exact opposite of what the psalm commanded: sheltering and resting in the Lord because we love him and acknowledge him.

Jesus saw through the devil's deception. And so Jesus answered, "It says: 'Do not put the Lord your God to the test.'" (Luke 4:12). And—unlike the devil—Jesus chose a passage of Scripture that exactly fit the circumstances in which Jesus found himself.

The Scripture that Jesus quoted came from Deuteronomy 6:16. This verse came just a few sentences after the verse that Jesus quoted when he refused to worship the devil: "Worship the Lord your God and serve him only" (Luke 4:8, quoting Deuteronomy 6:13). And, indeed, the thoughts of the two temptations and the two verses are intertwined.

If you worship God and serve him only, you will seek what honors God and makes God look good. But if you worship yourself, you will seek what honors you and makes you look good. You'll succumb to the temptation to do something ostentatious like jumping off the top of the Temple so that God sends angels to catch you. That way everybody will be impressed by how important you are and by how you can get God and angels to come at your command.

You'll be manipulating God instead of worshiping and serving God.

Moses succumbed to such a temptation. In fact, Jesus' quote from Scripture referred to the very circumstances that tempted Moses to sin in this way. The full sentence from Moses' farewell speech reads as follows: "Do not test the LORD your God as you did at Massah" (Deuteronomy 6:16).

What happened at Massah? What was Moses remembering? What was Jesus thinking about?

The reference is to Moses getting water from a rock when the Israelites were thirsty as they traveled through the wilderness—much as Jesus was thirsty after 40 days of fasting in the wilderness. The Israelites grumbled against Moses and God because of the difficult circumstances in which they found themselves.

This happened twice. The first time came soon after they left Egypt at "Massah"—a word that means "testing."[7] The second time came many years later at a place called "Meribah"—a word that means "quarreling."[8]

At the first time of testing, Moses succeeded as a leader of God's people. But at the second time of testing, Moses failed as a leader of God's people.

Oh, Moses brought water out of the rock the second time. But the trouble was that Moses brought water from the rock in a manner contrary to the way God told him to do it. Moses *struck* the rock instead of *speaking* to the rock. Furthermore, just before he struck the rock, Moses (with Aaron at his side) angrily said: "Listen, you rebels, must we bring you water out of this rock?" (Numbers 20:7–11).

In short, Moses handled the whole matter in a way that brought honor to himself instead of honor to God. So God was angry with Moses and Aaron and told them, "Because you did not trust in me enough to honor me as holy in the sight of the Israelites, you will not bring this community into the land I give them" (Numbers 20:12). In other words, Moses and Aaron were not allowed to enter "the Promised Land."

By defeating a similar temptation, Jesus proved that he was worthy to lead God's people into "the Promised Land." Unlike Moses—who struck the rock in a fashion that made it a stunt to prove how great he was—Jesus refused to jump from the top of the Temple in a stunt to prove how great he was.

Having failed to tempt Jesus into sinning, the devil left. But he did not leave forever. The devil only "left him until an opportune time" (Luke 4:13).

Our battle against temptation is never ending. Temptations will always arise again at the most difficult times of our lives—when we are most vulnerable to sinning.

But, fortunately, God always sends us help.

Some of the help comes before the temptation even begins—the way Jesus was given countless opportunities to learn the Scriptures that guided him through the temptations. Furthermore, after Jesus was baptized, God affirmed that Jesus was his Son and that he was pleased with him. This reassurance from God came at the perfect time—just before the devil tried so hard to convince Jesus that he was not God's Son and that he was acting foolishly.

And some of the help comes after the temptation is ended—the way "angels came and attended" Jesus after the devil left him (Matthew 4:11). In our case, such help from God's messengers is likely to come from Christian friends and family members who reach out to us during and after a time of testing to support us and reaffirm God's hand in our lives.

Now that I've completed discussing each temptation separately, there are several observations that I have about the temptations in general.

First, Jesus' use of Scripture is one of the most important examples we have about the authority, accuracy and application of Scripture. As you know, scholars and denominations seem to debate and divide unceasingly about such issues. Here we have an example from Jesus himself about how to use the Bible. So I always like to return to it to guide me when the arguments of scholars become too confusing and discouraging.

With regard to the issue of the authority of Scripture, Jesus treated Scripture as authoritative when making decisions about the most fundamental issues of living.

When faced with temptation, he didn't rely on various social sciences to give him the answers. He didn't consult an economics text when asked to turn stones to bread. He didn't consult a psychiatric text when asked to worship someone or something other than the Lord God. And he didn't consult a sociologist when asked to win friends and influence people by jumping off the highest point of the Temple. Instead, Jesus quoted Scripture.

And when faced with temptation, Jesus didn't rely on the authority of any other person or group of persons to determine what was right. When challenged about how to live his life, he didn't quote the advice of his parents, teachers or peer group. When asked to prove that he was the Son of God, he didn't rely on the views of a government official, a religious leader, or a ruling body. Instead, Jesus quoted Scripture.

With regard to the accuracy of Scripture, Jesus had no qualms about its accuracy. Jesus quoted Scripture word for word. He didn't paraphrase it. Nor did he question or wonder whether its text might contain errors. Furthermore, Jesus implicitly accepted the historical accuracy of each Scripture because the historical context of each quote had so much in common with the circumstances in which he found himself.

And with regard to the application of Scripture to the specific circumstances of his own life, Jesus had no theological, philosophical or scientific doubts that Scripture could be applied to his life and conduct. Jesus did not doubt that God existed, that God cared about him personally, and that God had a specific, knowable plan and purpose for Jesus' life. Jesus did not doubt that humans can know the ultimate reality of the universe and the ultimate truths about themselves. He knew that God's ability to create us and communicate with us transcends all limits, including those limits that philosophers quarrel about. And Jesus did not doubt that he could discern objective, universal truths, despite any limits that philosophers, lawyers, psychiatrists, sociologists, anthropologists and biologists might assert.

In every way, Jesus' use of Scripture supports the ringing affirmation of Scripture's authority, accuracy and applicability contained in the Apostle Paul's second letter to Timothy: "All Scripture is God-breathed and is useful for teaching, rebuking, correcting and training in righteousness, so that the [person] of God may be thoroughly equipped for every good work" (2 Timothy 3:16–17).[9]

A second general observation about these three temptations is that they relate to three areas where Christian leaders have stumbled again and again through the millennia. Therefore, they may be seen as being temptations that apply generally to Christian leaders. Indeed, in an even broader sense, they are temptations that apply to any leader of any kind of group.

Again and again, leaders use their talents and power for their personal gratification. When you have power, there are many kinds of "stones" that can be turned into many kinds of "bread." Many leaders succumb to the temptation to use their positions to gain money for themselves. In every age and in every way, people take bribes, kickbacks and other financial benefits gained by misusing the powers with which they are entrusted.

Judas Iscariot is an example of someone who misused power for personal gain. He betrayed Jesus for thirty silver coins.

Other leaders succumb to the temptation to use their positions to gain sex for themselves. If the tabloids aren't full of gossip about someone taking bribes, they're full of the latest gossip about who is sleeping with someone they aren't supposed to.

King David is an example of a leader of God's people who fell to this temptation to misuse his powers to obtain sexual gratification. When he sent for Bathsheba to spend a night enjoying her charms, he started a dreadful chain of events that led to him ordering the murder of her husband and led to the death of his son, Absalom, in a rebellion that almost cost David his throne.

Leaders are also notorious for compromising their principles—often betraying the very causes they stood for. Sometimes leaders are falsely condemned in this regard when they are actually making courageous compromises for the longterm good of the people they lead. Such people are statesmen—the kind of leaders who are "crucified" one way or another by their own people in their own day, but who are "resurrected" in glory and honor by those who were once their enemies in times to come.

Perhaps no leader better exemplifies this mixture of nobility and baseness in the same leader than Richard Nixon. In the matter of Watergate, he succumbed to the temptation to "worship the devil" in order to retain the "authority and splendor" of the kingdoms of the world. But in the matter of overcoming a generation of Cold War hatred and suspicion with "Red China," Nixon was a statesman of immense importance to ending the Cold War without a nuclear holocaust.

It only takes a moment of worshiping what is wrong to undermine a lifetime of worshiping and serving what is right. That is why Jesus insisted on worshiping and serving *only* the Lord his God.

In the Bible, a leader who fell into this temptation was King Solomon. He started life so well. He built the temple in Jerusalem for the LORD. But, as he grew older, he compromised his principles. In order to maintain the alliances that helped him retain his authority and splendor, he married many foreign wives. And, in the end, they led him astray into worshiping their foreign gods. Solomon kept worshiping the Lord his God, but he ignored the word "only" to his peril. And the result of forgetting the "only" led to the division of Israel into two kingdoms after his death and, ultimately, to the destruction of both kingdoms.

And what leader can resist the temptation to show off? What politician can pass up a photo opportunity such as jumping off the highest point on the Temple and having angels swoop down to rescue him? Not even Moses could resist this temptation. That was why he failed God as a leader and was not permitted to enter the Promised Land.

King Hezekiah also fell for this temptation. He was so proud about defeating the Assyrian siege of Jerusalem and being healed miraculously during the siege, that he couldn't resist showing off to the Babylonian envoys who came to visit after his victory. As a result, he foolishly showed the Babylonians all his wealth and resources. When Isaiah heard about King Hezekiah showing off for the Babylonians, he correctly prophesied that the Babylonians would come some day and carry all Hezekiah's wealth and descendants to Babylon.

I sensed the universal nature of these three temptations once while sitting in Sunday School class.[10] We were studying the Gospel of John. And that Sunday we were studying the passage where Jesus is comforting his disciples at the Last Supper the night before he will be crucified.

During part of the lesson, we discussed Jesus' statement to the disciples: "I tell you the truth, anyone who has faith in me will do what I have been doing. He will do even greater things than these, because I am going to the Father" (John 14:12).

To stimulate discussion, the teacher asked people, "When you think that you can do greater things than Jesus did, what are the 'greater things' that you want to do?" Immediately, the answer flashed across my mind: "I want to turn stones into bread, have all the authority and splendor of the world, and jump off the Temple and have angels catch me." It took only an instant before my thinking cleared and I thought, "No, that's not right! That is not what makes you great! Those are precisely the temptations that Jesus had to defeat to become truly great!" That episode showed me again how deeply ingrained our sinful nature is. Instinctively, I seek the wrong kind of greatness. It is only with a supreme effort of will, and years of discipline and training, that I am able to see through the deception of such "false greatness" as seeking personal gratification, the fleeting authority and splendor of the world, and stunts that make me look good.

The danger of such temptations never ends. As with Jesus, they only leave us until another opportune moment comes for the temptations to flash through our minds and hearts again.

For example, the most memorable moment when I experienced one of these temptations came years ago. It came in 1981 during my last night in New York City as a law clerk.

When I was a law clerk for Judge Meskill on the U.S. Court of Appeals for the Second Circuit, I lived in Farmington, Connecticut near the Judge's chambers in New Britain, Connecticut. But roughly one week out of each month I stayed in New York City while the Judge heard cases argued in the Federal Court House in Foley Square.

Most of that week was spent working very hard at the courthouse or in my hotel room. There was barely time to squeeze in a greasy supper at a no frills "diner" next to the hotel.[11]

But on the last night in New York, the work was mostly done so there was time to enjoy a stroll around mid-Manhattan in the evening. On that last night, I remember pausing for a moment at a corner, gazing up at the sign for one of the headquarters for one of the broadcast networks. I think it was ABC. Some intoxicatingly beautiful women had just passed me by. And as I gazed at the sign for the network, I was amazed for a moment to think of all the power wielded by the small group of people who worked in that building.

I started thinking, "Are you a fool for leaving all this? Why do you want to go back home to Rochester to work in a law firm there? Why do you want to go home this weekend to be with Suzanne? Look at all the beautiful women here—all eager to hop into bed with you at the drop of a hat! Look at all the power here—at places like that TV network! This is where you belong! You've worked so hard. This is where you've earned the *right* to be! Don't be a fool and throw it all away!"

For an instant, there flashed through my mind an image of all "the splendor and authority" of the world. And I thought, "Think how much more good you could do working here where the power is! Why throw it all away by running away to a tiny dump like Rochester? Think how much prettier and sexier the women here will be compared to living in Rochester with Suzanne!" (Obviously, this was a deception of the devil because there was—and is—no woman prettier or sexier than my wife.)

I could feel the yearning for that power and those beautiful women just like I feel the yearning for a handful of M&M chocolate covered peanuts when I'm hungry. First, I look at them. Then I smell them. And the next thing you know, they're in my mouth.

But in the next instant, other thoughts flashed through my mind. I thought, "No, this is wrong! This is not the way to 'power.' No truly great people ever sought power this way. They sought power in the little, backwards places like Rochester with nice, normal people like Suzanne. Think of Jesus refusing all the power and glory of the kingdoms of the world. Think of Moses. He was trained in all the wisdom of the Egyptians just like I was trained at Harvard Law School. But he spurned all the riches and glories of Egypt to flee into the desert and, later, to lead a bunch of slaves into the desert. Think of Abraham who had to leave all the riches and glory of the empire where he grew up to go wander around Canaan in a tent. That is always the way that God trains his leaders. That is the only way to true greatness and true power and true glory."

And so, with a wrenching effort of willpower I stopped gazing at the network's sign and shouted in my head, "NO! I *will* not choose that path. I *will* return home. And probably I'll marry Suzanne."

All that night and the next day, I felt somewhat shaken by the power of the "vision" I'd had of all the power and glory I was throwing away. Was I really doing the right thing?

Perhaps my consternation was written on my face as I took the subway the next day to leave New York City. I had my suitcase with me. I was going back home. From there my parents were driving Suzanne (my future wife) and me to Watertown for the weekend to visit Linda and Alden (my sister and brother-in-law).

Obviously, the possibility of marriage was in the air. Why else was Suzanne being subjected to so much interaction with my family?

I don't remember for sure how I traveled home. Probably I took a train out of Grand Central Station. Anyway, I remember riding on the subway with my huge blue suitcase when a hideously fat and ugly man struck up a conversation with me. He was dressed all in green—kind of in a "leisure suit." And he was wearing a bright ribbon to show his support and concern for the children of Atlanta who were falling prey to a serial killer of children who the police simply could not seem to find.

I don't remember what we talked about. Maybe I told him I was going home to be with my family and girl friend for the weekend. I don't know.

It was clear that the poor man was morbidly obese. His face was puffy and swollen from fat and water retention. All in all it was hard to imagine a more ugly, repulsive looking person. And he was dressed in such an outlandish color that it made him look even fatter!

But clearly a nice person dwelt beneath the fat and the hideous clothes.

We reached my stop. As I rose, dragging my heavy suitcase, and spinning to my left to go out the sliding subway door, his parting words were, "God will go with you!"

As I stepped through the door onto the subway platform, I felt a chill of lightning flash through me. And these words flashed through my mind, "Do not despair! You will succeed!"

These words had become a constant encouragement to me at that time in my life. They were an amalgam of the refrain and theme of a fantasy series I had been reading—*The Chronicles of Thomas Covenant the Unbeliever.* In the books, Thomas Covenant, a leper, travels to a fantasy world where he struggles to overcome evil and despair. So whenever I needed a lift, I'd say to myself the message that sustained Thomas Covenant—"Do not despair! You will succeed!"

In that moment, I knew God had given me the assurance I needed that I had chosen wisely. And how fitting that it came from someone who looked so repulsive on the outside, but who was so wonderful on the inside. Those are the kind of people who God always loves to use to do his work.

And so, as I prepared to write this passage, I was struck by the fact that after Jesus successfully resisted temptations, "angels came and attended him" (Matthew 4:11). I realized that fat man in the hideous green suit had been an "angel" who strengthened me after my time of temptation—a good "neighbor," a Good Samaritan, to a stranger in need.

There was another "angel" who attended me that magic weekend to assure me that I made the right choice by shunning the power and glory of New York City in order to return home to live and work in Rochester. As we sat in the back seat of the car on that long ride to Watertown, Suzanne and I talked and cuddled. I remember one moment in particular, gazing at the picturesque farms, meadows and forests that were rolling by. I felt angelic Suzanne's warmth and softness. I thought of that blessing and benediction from the fat green man. I knew as certainly as I'd ever known anything that I'd made the right choices. I knew that someday Suzanne and I would have wonderful children—hopefully both a boy and a girl—and we'd live happily ever after.

And that's how I found my Promised Land.

PART THREE

---

*Jesus Shows
He Is the Messiah*

Jesus Turns Water Into Wine

The scene now shifts from the wilderness to a wedding—from Jesus hungry and tempted to Jesus enjoying himself with his friends and relatives.[1]

We are not told who was getting married. But we know that the wedding was in Cana in Galilee. Mary, "Jesus' mother was there, and Jesus and his disciples had also been invited to the wedding" (John 2:1–2).

A problem arose at the wedding—"the wine was gone." So Jesus' mother went to him and said, "They have no more wine." (John 2:3).[2] The obvious implication was that Jesus should somehow—presumably miraculously—provide some wine.

What follows is a precious vignette between a mother and her son. At first, Jesus seemed to discourage his mother from getting him involved. He replied, "Dear woman, why do you involve me? . . . My time has not yet come" (John 2:4).[3] But no mother takes "No" as an answer from her son! Mary refused to be put off by Jesus. Instead, she "said to the servants, 'Do whatever he tells you.'" (John 2:5). What's a son to do! Rather than disappoint his mother, Jesus decided to do what she wanted.

Jesus had the servants fill six stone water jars with water. These jars were huge. They were used by Jews for ceremonial washings and each held from twenty to thirty gallons (John 2:6).

At Jesus' command, the servants drew the "water" from the jars and gave it to the master of the banquet. Only now it was no longer water. It was wine! Furthermore, when the master of the banquet tasted this wine he said, "[Y]ou have saved the best till now" (John 2:8–10).

"[Jesus] thus revealed his glory, and his disciples put their faith in him" (John 2:11).

Here indeed was glory.

Not the fake, fleeting glory of those who yield to the temptation to do anything (even "worship the devil") in their quest for all the "authority and splendor" of the kingdoms of the world (Luke 4:5–7).

This is the glory that only comes by doing what your mother asks. This is the glory that only comes by helping your friends and family have a good time—by rejoicing with those who rejoice. This is the glory that only comes from changing the "water" of a humdrum life into the "wine" of an abundant life. This is the glory that only comes from hoping in the LORD!

There is one other twist to the story that I like. The master of the banquet didn't know where the best wine came from. Neither he nor most of the guests knew about the miracle. But "the servants who had drawn the water knew" (John 2:9).4 If you want to see God work miracles, you have to be a servant.

Jesus Tells Nicodemus He Must Be Born Again

Unfortunately, we cannot always serve God in places that are as pleasurable as a wedding. Sometimes we must serve God in places where we are hated and despised. Sometimes we must *confront* people rather than *comfort* people. After the wedding in Cana, Jesus faced such a difficult experience.

Jesus went to Jerusalem for the Passover Feast. This should have been a happy time for worshiping God. But instead, when Jesus went to the temple, he was outraged by what he saw! "In the temple courts he found men selling cattle, sheep and doves, and others sitting at tables exchanging money" (John 2:13–14).

Jesus must have seen such commercial activity at the temple many times before. We know that he visited Jerusalem and its temple periodically as he grew up. For example, Jesus amazed the teachers at the temple when he was twelve years old (Luke 2:41–51).

We don't know why Jesus became so upset with the merchants during this particular visit.

As long as these merchants treated people fairly, they served useful purposes. They sold people animals for sacrifices at the temple. They also exchanged people's money from throughout the Roman Empire for money that could be used at the temple. People came from great distances to worship at the temple. Therefore, it was difficult or impossible for them to bring their sacrifices from home. These visitors benefited from being able to buy their sacrifices at a convenient location. For example, we can assume that Mary and Joseph themselves used such merchants to purchase the birds they sacrificed at the temple when they brought Jesus there as an infant to be consecrated to the Lord (Luke 2:21–24).

Something about the way the merchants were conducting their businesses must have upset Jesus.

Probably part of what offended him was the location of the merchants. They were located inside the temple itself! A place for the merchants could have been found outside the temple courts. Instead, they were located where they detracted from the dignity of the temple. The noise and commotion must have distracted and interfered with people who were trying to meditate, pray and worship. The presence of merchants in the temple showed that the religious leaders had the wrong priorities—they cared more about taking money from people than about helping people meditate, pray and worship. There is no monetary profit in helping people worship the LORD in spirit and in truth.

Furthermore, I suspect that what angered Jesus the most was that the merchants treated people unfairly. They were extorting money from people. The merchants had a monopoly on selling animals for sacrifices near the temple. As a practical matter, visitors had to pay whatever the businesses charged for the animals or to exchange money.

Jesus would have been especially infuriated if he'd seen a poor person unable to worship God because the merchants overcharged him or her. Jesus could never have tolerated extorting money from people because they wanted to worship at the temple.[1] The temple was a Promised Land where all peoples should be blessed.

Perhaps Jesus thought about his poor parents struggling to pay for the sacrifice to consecrate him as an infant. (We assume that they were poor because they bought two birds instead of two sheep for the sacrifice (Luke 2:24)).

Jesus always identified with the oppressed and mistreated. So I can imagine the fury that filled his eyes as he saw such extortion and thievery taking place in the temple itself!

Even so, Jesus did not take *hasty* action.

I remember hearing a preacher emphasize the importance of the detail that Jesus "made a whip out of cords" in order to drive the merchants out of the temple. It takes time to make such a whip. Therefore, Jesus took forceful, planned action. He didn't lose his temper and do something foolish that he latter regretted. Instead, when he was ready, Jesus acted.

Jesus "drove all from the temple area, both sheep and cattle; he scattered the coins of the money changers and overturned their tables" (John 2:15). When he reached those who sold doves to people (such as the young Mary and Joseph) who didn't have much money, Jesus said, "Get these out of here! How dare you turn my Father's house into a market!" (John 2:16).

Naturally, Jesus' bold action to "cleanse" the temple made him an object of intense scrutiny. I'm sure the merchants reacted angrily and used all their economic and political clout to get Jesus into trouble. Meanwhile, ordinary people applauded this "consumer activist" who was trying to save them money. Anyone who wanted to use the temple for meditation, prayer and worship must have been glad the merchants were tossed out.

Furthermore, Jesus performed a number of "miraculous signs" (John 2:23). Although we aren't told what miraculous signs Jesus performed, Jesus was probably healing people. Jesus performed other types of miracles (such as turning water into wine). However, most of Jesus' miracles healed people from various physical and mental afflictions.

On the surface, the reaction of many people was exactly what Jesus should have hoped for. "[W]hile he was in Jerusalem at the Passover Feast, many people saw the miraculous signs he was doing and believed in his name" (John 2:23).

However, Jesus realized that such people were fickle followers. They'd be with him while he was performing miracles that benefitted them, but they'd desert him when he called for discipline and sacrifice. So "Jesus would not entrust himself to them" (John 2:24).

In the midst of such turmoil and controversy, the Jewish ruling council[2] must have debated at length what to do. And one of their members—named Nicodemus—decided to visit Jesus.

We don't know whether Nicodemus came on his own or whether he came as an emissary from a group of people on the ruling council. However, since he came to see Jesus at night (John 3:1–2), Nicodemus probably wanted to keep his visit a secret from most of the people on the council and from the public.

One thing we *do* know about Nicodemus is that he "was a man of the Pharisees" (John 3:1). As you probably know, the Pharisees were Jews who observed their laws and traditions very strictly. They were immensely zealous about keeping their long list of "Do's" and "Don'ts." But, unfortunately, they were long on sacrifice and short on justice, love and mercy.

Many Pharisees put the *appearance* of doing the right thing above the *reality* of doing the loving thing. And to protect their "purity," they avoided contact with those who most needed the touch of God's love. So most Pharisees became bitter enemies of Jesus. They hatched schemes and plots to make Jesus look bad. And, eventually, they succeeded in having Jesus crucified.

Unfortunately, I find it very easy to become a Pharisee. So can anyone who has gone to church for a long time—a Church-Goer. Just like the Pharisees, we Church-Goers often think that we know everything there is to know about what people should and shouldn't do. Just like Pharisees, we Church-Goers often love to be friends only with Church-Goers like us. Just like Pharisees, we Church-Goers often fear what people will say if we make friends with "sinners." And just like Pharisees, we Church-Goers often get so caught up looking at the trees of "Do's" and "Don'ts" that we lose sight of the forests of justice, love and mercy.

Worse yet, I'm a lawyer. Being a Pharisee—a Churchgoer—comes naturally to lawyers. We often spend our careers showing that we are smarter, wiser and better than anyone else. And we often spend far more time following rules and procedures than following the ways of justice, love and mercy.

Therefore, as a Church-Goer and a lawyer, it is critical that I take to heart the message that Jesus had for that other Pharisee, Nicodemus.

Nicodemus was a skilled politician. That's how he got on the Jewish ruling council. He started the meeting like any skilled politician would. He flattered Jesus. Nicodemus said, "Rabbi, we know you are a teacher who has come from God. For no one could perform the miraculous signs you are doing if God were not with him" (John 3:2).

This is one of those conversations where I wish we had a video so we could see body language and hear the tone of voice in which the words were spoken.

For example, perhaps Nicodemus said these words in a sincere manner. But I doubt it. For one thing, if he fully believed these words, he would not have come to Jesus secretly at night. Furthermore, Jesus would have praised him for his discernment instead of rebuking him for his lack of God's spirit and his ignorance of God's ways.

Instead, I think Nicodemus said these words much like we Church-Goers say so many words when we come to church on Sunday. We're so used to saying "the right thing" that we no longer attach much meaning to what we're saying. Like Nicodemus, we say that we believe that Jesus came from God and that Jesus performed miraculous signs that God was with him. But we don't act as if we believe these stunning truths.

There were also two subtle problems with what Nicodemus said. These problems typically plague all Pharisees like me.

First of all, he obviously believed that Jesus should be flattered and impressed that "*we* know you are a teacher." Whoever "we" was, Nicodemus was acting as if "we" were important and as if "we" knew what was right and wrong, wise and foolish. Nicodemus implicitly assumed that "we" were the ultimate authorities on religious teachings.

Nicodemus' second attitude problem was that he focused on "miraculous signs" in order to determine whether God was with Jesus. While it's true that Jesus did various miraculous signs to show that he was the Messiah, Jesus argued again and again with people who wanted *miracles* to satisfy their *cravings* instead of *truths* to improve their *lives*. As a trained teacher of the law, Nicodemus should have focused on the *truth* of what Jesus *taught* and on the *spirit* in which Jesus *ministered* as being the "miraculous signs" proving that Jesus was the Messiah.

Jesus perceived all these failings in Nicodemus. So in reply to Nicodemus' flattery and misconceptions, "Jesus declared, 'I tell you the truth, no one can see the kingdom of God unless he is born again.'" (John 3:3).

It is scary to realize how Pharisees like me evade the thrust of this declaration by Jesus to this very day. When Church-Goers say "You must be born again" we invariably say it to someone who we believe is a "sinner." We almost never apply it the way Jesus did—to Pharisees and Church-Goers like us. Yet it was Nicodemus—the good "Church-Goer"—who most needed to start over spiritually by being born again.

The words Jesus chose could have either a literal, physical meaning about a physical birth of a baby or a symbolic, spiritual meaning about being "born from above."[3] In the context in which Jesus used them, it was obvious that he meant a spiritual birth. Certainly anyone as learned as Nicodemus must have understood this.

But just like we Church-Goers today, Nicodemus decided to evade the application of Jesus' teachings by getting distracted in a dispute over words. It was far easier to quibble over words than to transform his life by learning how to be "born from above."

Think how often we do the same thing in church or Sunday School today. We're vastly more comfortable discussing the meanings and definitions of words than facing up to the need to change our actions and attitudes.

So—just like the skilled teacher, lawyer and politician that he was—Nicodemus made a remark that sounded perceptive and learned. He asked, "'How can a man be born when he is old?' . . . . 'Surely he cannot enter a second time into his mother's womb to be born!'" (John 3:4). But Nicodemus' remark was actually a distraction from facing the real issue—changing the way he was living.

Jesus was too good a teacher and pastor to let Nicodemus draw him into an irrelevant discussion of foolish quibbling over words. Jesus' reply made it clear that he was talking about a spiritual birth (John 3:5–6). And Jesus burst Nicodemus' pretensions. Jesus rebuked this pompous scholar, saying: "You should not be surprised at my saying, 'You must be born again.' . . . . You are Israel's teacher . . . and do you not understand these things?" (John 3:7,10).

Then Jesus gave Nicodemus another illustration of what he meant: "The wind blows wherever it pleases. You hear its sound, but you cannot tell where it comes from or where it is going. So it is with everyone born of the Spirit." (John 3:8)—with everyone who worships the Lord in spirit and in truth.

This is a message that every Pharisee needs to hear from Jesus—whether it's Nicodemus 2000 years ago or we Church-Goers sitting in the pews next Sunday. We can't limit how and when God works in our lives and in the lives of other people. The wind of God's Spirit will blow on *whoever* God chooses. The Promised Land will bless *all* peoples.

Despite our arrogance, we Church-Goers haven't learned everything we should and shouldn't do. We can't just stay with "good" Church-Goers like us. The wind of God's spirit blows on all people—even on those who we look down on because they are different from us and on those who we fear because they disagree with us.

We must not fear what people will say if we make friends with such "sinners." We must not get so caught up in looking good that we become bad. We must not get so caught up in looking at the trees of "Do's" and "Don'ts" that we lose sight of the forests of justice, love and mercy. Hard as it is to believe, we Church-Goers aren't smarter and wiser and better than all those other people.

We Church-Goers need to be born again. We Church-Goers need to experience the wind of God's Spirit stirring our hearts and changing our lives. And we Church-Goers must insist on justice, love and mercy.

We must be like Jesus in the temple. We must "cleanse" the temple of our hearts and our lives. We must remove any distractions that hinder meditation, prayer and worship. We must stop treating people unfairly.

Just as Jesus brought the winds of change to the temple, God must bring the winds of change to the hearts and lives of we Church-Goers. We Church-Goers must worship the LORD in spirit and in truth. We Church-Goers must bless all peoples. We Church-Goers must be born again.

Jesus Talks with a Samaritan Woman

In Jesus' Promised Land, everyone will be born again—everyone will worship the LORD in spirit and in truth. Because Jesus didn't just tell the successful Jewish scholar, Nicodemus, that the Spirit of God is like the wind, blowing whenever and wherever God pleases so that anyone may be blessed. Jesus also blessed a Samaritan woman by enabling her to start a new life. Jesus taught this hated, despised, rejected sinner that despite her sins and failures in the past she could be born again spiritually—could be blessed in the Promised Land by worshiping the Lord in spirit and in truth.

Just as in our lives, this opportunity to spread God's love came in the ordinary course of Jesus' day. He had to travel through Samaria with his disciples. Jesus was tired. He rested near Jacob's well outside a town while his disciples went into the town to buy food (John 4:4–6,8).

I always find it comforting to know that Jesus got tired. It means there's nothing wrong with me getting tired either. It's all right to take a break from life's journey to sit and rest beside a well.

But even when we are tired, the opportunity to touch another person with God's love must not be passed up.

If Jesus had been a typical Jewish traveler, he almost certainly would have ignored the Samaritan woman who came to the well to draw water. She was from a foreign country that "good" followers of God hated and despised because they had corrupted the "one true religion" by refusing to worship God in Jerusalem.

Furthermore, given the low status of women in that culture, a typical male would not "waste" his time talking to her, especially when he was tired. But Jesus was never too tired to help other people. And Jesus never hated, despised or rejected anyone because of their past sins, present failures, or low social standing. So he started a conversation with the Samaritan woman.

Jesus began with an obvious request under the circumstances. He asked, "Will you give me a drink?" (John 4:7).

The Samaritan woman was surprised that this Jewish man would have anything to do with her "[f]or Jews do not associate with Samaritans" (John 4:9). She replied, "You are a Jew and I am a Samaritan woman. How can you ask me for a drink?" (John 4:9).

Instead of defending his actions, Jesus took the offensive, challenging the woman to broaden her perspectives. "Jesus answered her, 'If you knew the gift of God and who it is that asks you for a drink, you would have asked him and he would have given you living water.'" (John 4:10).

The woman must have thought she had a real weirdo on her hands now. Or perhaps she thought Jesus was making fun of her, treating her like a "dumb woman." She responded by pointing out the obvious: "Sir, . . . you have nothing to draw with and the well is deep. Where can you get this living water?" (John 4:11).

She must have thought, "Just who does this Jew think he is, anyway!" She asked him (probably in an angry, taunting tone of voice): "Are you greater than our father Jacob, who gave us the well and drank from it himself, as did also his sons and his flocks and herds?" (John 4:12).

Jesus did not respond with anger. Instead, he explained himself further, again challenging the woman to broaden her perspectives, to be "born again" so she could be "born from above" spiritually. "Jesus answered, 'Everyone who drinks this water will be thirsty again, but whoever drinks the water I give him will never thirst. Indeed, the water I give him will become in him a spring of water welling up to eternal life.'" (John 4:13–14).

The woman was interested now. But like us, she failed to grasp how wonderful the gift was that Jesus was offering her. She thought it would merely relieve her from the drudgery of her everyday existence. So she told Jesus, "Sir, give me this water so that I won't get thirsty and have to keep coming here to draw water" (John 4:15).

Before the woman could receive Jesus' gift, Jesus had to confront her with some unpleasant truths about her life—some things that blocked the springs of water in her life that would give her eternal life. In this woman's case, she evidently lacked sexual faithfulness and integrity. To bring this issue to the fore, Jesus told her, "Go, call your husband and come back" (John 4:16).

Before we can change our lives, we have to be honest about our lives and how we have failed to measure up to God's standards for our lives. Jesus was testing the woman to see if she could be honest with him about her sexual misconduct. She could have lied and said her husband was too busy to come. But instead, she acknowledged part of the truth: "'I have no husband,' she replied" (John 4:17).

Jesus demands not just the truth about our lives. Jesus demands the *whole* truth and *nothing but* the truth. He said to her (in a voice that I imagine was full of compassion and mercy even as he confronted her with her shortcomings): "You are right when you say you have no husband. The fact is, you have had five husbands, and the man you now have is not your husband. What you have just said is quite true" (John 4:17–18).

The woman was stunned by Jesus' knowledge of her personal life. Perhaps Jesus had heard other women from the town gossiping about her as she made her way to the well. Or perhaps Jesus used supernatural powers to look into the woman's mind and heart. She certainly thought he did. For she said, "Sir, . . . I can see that you are a prophet" (John 4:19).

Now she was on precarious ground. God knew all about her. God's gift was available to change her life for the better. All she had to do was accept Jesus' offer of eternal life.

But she drew back. She sought a distraction to draw attention away from her personal life, her failures and her sins. She wanted to deflect Jesus away from her life and onto a theological controversy that had raged between the Samaritans and the Jews for almost a thousand years: where should God be worshiped? She said, "Our fathers worshiped on this mountain, but you Jews claim that the place where we must worship is in Jerusalem" (John 4:20).

Again and again, I've seen Christians, including me, use this same strategy to avoid facing the truth about ourselves and how we should change our lives. It is easier to argue about the correct translation of a Greek word in the New Testament than to ponder whether I help the poor enough. It is easier to define the term "neighbor" than to help someone I don't like. It is easier to tell my children how to act than to act that way myself as a good role model.

Jesus does not like such distractions. He always tries to get us back to the real issues—our thoughts, our motives and our conduct.

Rather than rehash centuries of theological controversies, Jesus kept the focus on whether the woman was worshiping God in spirit and in truth. And Jesus broadened the woman's perspectives so she could see the forest of God's love instead of the trees of people's arguments. Jesus explained that "a time is coming when you will worship the Father neither on this mountain nor in Jerusalem" (John 4:21).

This did not mean that—like so many contemporary philosophers believe—there is no right or wrong. Jesus politely, but firmly, told the woman that the Samaritans did *not* know what they worshiped and that the Jews *did* know what was right: "for salvation is from the Jews" (John 4:22).

But instead of making the truth a *club* to drive the woman *away* from God, Jesus made the truth a *light* to guide the woman *toward* God. Jesus told her that "a time is coming and has now come when the true worshipers will worship the Father in spirit and truth, for they are the kind of worshipers the Father seeks" (John 4:23).

Jesus had high standards. And he insisted that the woman change her life to meet God's high standards. Jesus told her, "God is spirit, and his worshipers must worship in spirit and in truth" (John 4:24).

Nevertheless, Jesus continued to offer to give the woman "water" so that she could enjoy eternal life. And I sense hope in the woman's eyes and voice as she told Jesus, "I know that Messiah . . . is coming. When he comes, he will explain everything to us" (John 4:25).

I think that even as she asked the question, the woman had a pretty good idea that she was talking to the Messiah. And sure enough, Jesus gave her the answer she longed to hear: "I who speak to you am he" (John 4:26).

"Just then his disciples returned and were surprised to find him talking with a woman. But no one asked, 'What do you want?' or 'Why are you talking with her?'" (John 4:27). The Samaritan woman went back to the town. She told people to come and meet Jesus (John 4:28–29).

Having given the Samaritan woman hope that she could change her life, Jesus now gave his disciples hope that they could change the lives of anyone they met. As the crowd of Samaritans drew near, thirsty for the "water" Jesus wanted to give them, Jesus drove the point home to his disciples. There was no need to wait to spread God's good news. There was no barrier of nation, creed, or sex that could limit the gift of eternal life. Jesus told his disciples: "Do you not say, 'Four months more and then the harvest'? I tell you, open your eyes and look at the fields! They are ripe for harvest." (John 4:35).

No matter how tired or thirsty or hungry we may be, there are always ripe fields that we can harvest—there are always Promised Lands full of people who need to be blessed. A single conversation can overcome centuries of hatred. A single conversation can turn someone's old life of failure into a new life of success—worshiping the LORD in spirit and in truth. A single conversation can give hated, despised, rejected failures a new life with "a spring of water welling up to eternal life" (John 4:14). A single conversation can give hated, despised, rejected sinners a new life of hoping in the LORD.

Jesus Preaches in His Hometown of Nazareth

If one thing is clear from Jesus' visit to his hometown of Nazareth, it's that we're far better off hoping in the LORD than hoping in our hometown.[1]

[T]his visit to Nazareth came in the early part of Jesus' ministry. The Gospel of Luke says that at this time in Jesus' life:

> Jesus returned to Galilee in the power of the Spirit, and news about him spread through the whole countryside. He taught in their synagogues, and everyone praised him.
>
> (Luke 4:14–15)

During this period of growing fame and popularity, Jesus decided to visit his hometown of Nazareth "where he had been brought up" (Luke 4:16).

I imagine that Jesus visited with some boyhood friends and many relatives. I also imagine that many people sought out their "old pal" Jesus—even if, in fact, they'd had little or nothing to do with him when he was growing up.

Nothing succeeds like success. So—now that "the news about him spread through the whole countryside" and "everyone praised him"—people would have been eager to see Jesus and take some credit for his fame.

Since most of this was phony friendship, I assume that Jesus was not impressed. In fact, given Jesus' usual directness in punching holes in people's pretensions and facades, I imagine he quickly turned a fair number of these "fair weather friends" into grumbling gossips and enemies. I suspect that some of them even dared to dust off old gossip about Mary becoming pregnant before she was married.

Jesus probably already foresaw that things would not go smoothly if he spoke in the synagogue. But Jesus was never one to shrink from controversy. He accepted the honor of preaching in the synagogue that Sabbath.

Jesus read from a prophesy in the scroll of Isaiah the prophet that fit perfectly with Jesus' vision of the kind of Messiah he would be:

"The Spirit of the Lord is on me,
    because he has anointed me
    to preach good news to the poor.
He has sent me to proclaim freedom
    for the prisoners
    and recovery of sight for the blind,
to release the oppressed,
    to proclaim the year of the Lord's
    favor."

(Luke 4:16–19)

The passage did not speak of a conquering military hero who would drive the Romans from Israel. The passage did not speak of a showy miracle-worker who would cater to everyone's selfish desires for power, fame, wealth and sex.

Instead, the passage spoke of a disciplined servant of God who fasts in the desert, rejecting the temptations to become a self-indulgent Messiah. The passage spoke of a good friend, turning water into wine at a wedding so that everyone's joy would become complete. The passage spoke of a patient teacher, freeing the Pharisee, Nicodemus, from narrow-minded preconceptions so that he could be born again from above. The passage spoke of a kind counselor, bridging ancient distrust, hatred and prejudices so that a Samaritan woman could learn to worship God in spirit and in truth. The passage spoke of a Promised Land where all peoples would be blessed.

Jesus stopped reading the passage in the middle of a couplet. The full poetic couplet read: "to proclaim the year of the LORD's favor and the day of vengeance of our God" (Isaiah 61:2). By leaving off the part about "the day of vengeance," Jesus emphasized his role in giving us hope by proclaiming "the year of the LORD's favor."

Whether because of this variation from the normal reading of the passage or because people had heard so much about Jesus that they were transfixed with anticipation, "[t]he eyes of everyone in the synagogue were fastened on him" as "he rolled up the scroll, gave it back to the attendant and sat down" (Luke 4:20).

Then Jesus began his sermon by making a bold claim. He said, "Today this scripture is fulfilled in your hearing" (Luke 4:21).

We aren't told what the next part of Jesus' sermon was about. Apparently, the initial reaction was favorable. Luke tells us: "All spoke well of him and were amazed at the gracious words that came from his lips" (Luke 4:22).

Then the tide of public opinion turned against him.[2] They started asking, "Isn't this Joseph's son?" (Luke 4:22). They couldn't accept Jesus for who he really was. They couldn't accept that Jesus and his family were better or more important than they were. A passage in the gospel of Matthew sets forth their reasoning and their anger, their contempt and their scoffing this way:

> "Where did this man get this wisdom and these miraculous powers?" they asked. "Isn't this the carpenter's son? Isn't his mother's name Mary, and aren't his brothers James, Joseph, Simon and Judas? Aren't all his sisters with us? Where then did this man get all these things?" And they took offense at him.
>
> (Matthew 13:54–57)[3]

Jesus rebuked these scoffers. They were demanding that he "prove himself" by performing miracles like he had in Capernaum. But when Satan tempted him in the desert, Jesus refused to prove he was the Messiah by performing dazzling miracles or by showing off by doing such stunts as jumping off the top of the temple and having angels catch him. Now Jesus resisted the similar temptation to prove himself to these local yokels in his hometown by performing miracles (Luke 4:23).

Instead, Jesus tried to change their perspectives about who he was and broaden their horizons about how God acts. With Nicodemus, Jesus helped him to see that he needed to be born again and let the wind of God's Spirit blow on whoever God chose. With the Samaritan woman, Jesus helped her to see that she needed to worship God in spirit and in truth regardless of what sins and prejudices were in her past. With the people in his hometown, he also tried to get them to see such truths—to get them to see that the Promised Land blesses *all* peoples.

Jesus said, "I tell you the truth . . . no prophet is accepted in his hometown" (Luke 4:24). To prove this observation, he reminded them about events in the lives of two of Israel's greatest prophets: Elijah and Elisha. When there was a severe famine, Elijah was not sent to a widow in Israel, but to a widow in the region of modern Lebanon. And when Elisha healed a leper, he did not heal a leper from Israel. Instead, he healed a foreigner, Naaman the Syrian, who commanded the army of Israel's enemy (Luke 4:25–27; 1 Kings 17:7–24; 2 Kings 5:1–27).

Jesus' illustrations did not convince his hometown detractors. Instead, "[a]ll the people in the synagogue were furious when they heard this" (Luke 4:28). Their scoffing turned to rage. "They got up, drove him out of the town, and took him to the brow of the hill on which the town was built, in order to throw him down the cliff" (Luke 4:29).

So when people reject your wise advice and good counsel, try not to take it to heart. Jesus had the same problem. There was nothing wrong with Jesus. He had "the power of the Spirit" in his life. He had a clear purpose and a noble mission for his life (Luke 4:14,18–19). Nevertheless, his hearers rejected him. They even tried to kill him!

Perhaps this was one of the incidents that Jesus had in mind when he told this proverb: "Do not give dogs what is sacred; do not throw your pearls to pigs. If you do, they may trample them under their feet, and then turn and tear you to pieces" (Matthew 7:6).

Fortunately, this mob did not succeed in killing him. Instead, "[Jesus] walked right through the crowd and went on his way" (Luke 4:30). Presumably, Jesus escaped through some combination of miraculous help from God and timely assistance from his friends and relatives.

Even more amazing than that Jesus escaped the mob, is that he did not give up his ministry.

After barely escaping death, Jesus "went on his way." If it had been me, "my way" would probably have been as far away from controversy and danger as possible. But not Jesus. He went to another town and "began to teach the people." And he did not preach timidly. The people "were amazed at his teaching, because his message had authority" (Luke 4:30–32).

Where did Jesus find the courage and determination to carry on his mission in the face of rejection by his own hometown? He found it from hoping in the LORD.

If he'd been hoping in his hometown, he'd have given up. But he was secure in the knowledge that God still had a purpose for his life even though so many old "friends" and "neighbors" scoffed at him and rejected this purpose. Jesus drew renewed strength from his certainty that:

> "The Spirit of the Lord is on me,
>   because he has anointed me
>   to preach good news to the poor.
> He has sent me to proclaim freedom
>   for the prisoners
>   and recovery of sight for the blind,
> to release the oppressed,
>   to proclaim the year of the Lord's
>   favor."
>
> (Luke 4:18–19)

Since we follow Jesus, *his* mission *then* is still *our* mission *today*. And that same mission—that same purpose for our lives—can renew our strength today just as it renewed Jesus' strength then. Unlike our hometown, it is a hope that will never fail us.

After Praying, Jesus Chooses the Twelve Apostles

Another reason that Jesus kept finding the courage and determination to press ahead with his mission and purpose was that he "often withdrew to lonely places and prayed" (Luke 5:16).

Part of this discipline of withdrawing from the hustle and bustle of life is merely good psychology.

I know that many of my best ideas come when I'm out jogging, when I flop on the couch to listen to music, when I wake up in the middle of the night, when I'm stopped at a red light, or when I'm shaving. We have to step back from frantic details to let our brains process all the available information. Then we can use our intuition and creativity to come up with a good answer. We must step back from the trees so that we can see the forest.

I know that every once in a while I had to stress this truth with Sarah. She'd be frantically trying to finish her homework late at night. But she just couldn't figure out the math problem or find the answer to the social studies question. Finally, I'd intervene and take the book away from her. I'd explain that I was sure she'd figure the problem out quickly and easily in the morning when she was rested. And I was always pleased when I saw the look of joy and increased wisdom on her face in the morning when my prediction came true.

For similar reasons, I try never to do any work on the weekends. I'm so much more efficient at work if I'm fresh and well rested.

And in my life at work and at home, I can certainly identify with Jesus having people crowd around him asking for help. Sometimes at work, the phone keeps ringing and ringing, the mail, e-mail and voice mail keep piling up, and the people keep popping into my office with one problem or another. Then, when I get home, I'm barely through the door when Andy wants to play baseball, Sarah wants to talk about her homework, and my wife's mad that I'm late and supper's overcooked.

No wonder I get cranky. But Jesus never got cranky. And one reason for his better mood was that he was much better than me at taking time to pray.

Because when Jesus withdrew to lonely places, he didn't listen to music or read a book. Jesus prayed.

And Jesus' prayers weren't short "comic book" kinds of prayers— brief and predictable. His prayers were the spiritual equivalent of writing *War and Peace.*

For example, we are told that Jesus prayed the whole night before he chose the Twelve Apostles.

The only time I find the strength and enthusiasm to stay up all night is when we drive to Walt Disney World! No wonder Jesus got better results from his prayers than I do.

But we must also be realistic. Even with all Jesus' insight, wisdom and prayers, everything didn't go smoothly in his life.

In the previous chapter, we saw that his sermon in his hometown got people so mad they tried to kill him. And one of the twelve people who Jesus chose to be an apostle was "Judas Iscariot, who became a traitor" (Luke 6:16).

Nevertheless, things will go much better in *our* lives if we follow Jesus in this aspect of *his* life. As the pressure of life's constant changes, frantic days, and deep disappointments threaten to overwhelm us, we must constantly renew our strength by withdrawing to lonely places and praying.

After the Sermon on the Mount, Jesus Touches a Leper

The Sermon on the Mount is one of those parts of the Bible that should be read at one sitting to get its full impact. If we chop it up a few verses at a time, we lose the overwhelming force of its commands.

Plus, it's essential to read the end of the Sermon in order to grasp its full significance for our lives. The tendency is to read a portion of the Sermon that seems impossible to do—such as loving our enemies or not lusting after beautiful women—and then trying to find a reason why we don't *really* have to live that way. But when we read the end of the Sermon, we learn that the whole point of the Sermon is that we must put Jesus' words into practice or else we are like a foolish man who built a house on sand—a "house" that crashed when the "storms of life" beat upon it.

Furthermore, I always like to read a few verses beyond the end of the Sermon because I think that the story of Jesus curing the leper is essential to feeling the full impact of the Sermon. The point of the story is that Jesus didn't just talk about doing good things. He put his words into action. He touched someone with a loathsome disease who probably oozed pus and smelled bad. The leper also probably looked hideous because leprosy disfigures and scars its victims.

Nevertheless, when Jesus came off the mountainside where he'd delivered the Sermon on the Mount, he immediately touched the leper,

119

curing him. Similarly, Jesus will touch and cure anyone who realizes that—compared to the standards of righteousness required by the Sermon on the Mount—he or she is a spiritual leper. Spiritually, we ooze pus, we smell, we look hideous, our lives are disfigured, and our hearts are hardened by scars. Nevertheless, Jesus loves us so much that he touches us and heals our spiritual leprosy.

Indeed, we have no hope of being released from the leprous power of Sin unless Jesus touches us and makes us clean. Yet we have hope because Jesus loves to touch spiritual lepers such as us so that we can be cured from the ill-effects of Sin.

Fortunately, Jesus loves to touch spiritual lepers like me who find it impossible to be meet the standard for righteous that the Sermon on the Mount requires. Here are some of the passages from the Sermon on the Mount that are most meaningful to me. That means that here are some of the passages that I find it hardest to obey.

It is impossible for me to be "poor in spirit" (Matthew 5:3). As Sarah constantly reminded me (especially after she became a teenager), I can be incredibly vain—a common problem among those who graduated from Harvard Law School.

I get mad when people say bad things about me. So how can I possibly "[r]ejoice and be glad" when I am persecuted? (Matthew 5:11–12).

I am very shy. So how can I possibly be "the salt of the earth" and "the light of the world?" (Matthew 5:13–16).

I get angry very easily (Matthew 5:21–22).

I find it essentially impossible not to lust after a pretty woman when I see her (Matthew 5:27–28).

If someone does something bad to me, I want to retaliate by treating them twice as badly as they treated me (Matthew 5:38–39,43–44).

As I read the Sermon on the Mount, the list goes on and on about all the ways that I sin and fall short of the glory of God—about all the ways that I find it impossible to "[b]e perfect . . . as [my] heavenly Father is perfect" (Matthew 5:48).

Furthermore, I spend immense energies storing up treasures on earth where moth and rust destroy. Since I know it's true that I cannot serve both God and Money, I have an awfully strong suspicion that—when push comes to shove—I am really devoted to Money and despise God (Matthew 6:19–21,24).

Like any "good" pagan and any "good" American, I constantly "run after" things such as clothing, food and drinks. And I constantly worry about things in the future that I can't do anything about (Matthew 6:25–34).

Since such worries often keep me from doing what I know I should do, I often fail to do unto others what I would like them to do unto me (Matthew 7:12).

All this makes me extremely nervous when I read that "wide is the gate and broad is the road that leads to destruction, and many enter through it" (Matthew 7:13). Because I have a bad feeling that I'm in that crowd who gets angry, lusts after women, retaliates against my enemies, accumulates material possessions, and worries about tomorrow instead of doing unto others what I would like them to do unto me.

And I am in a state of total despair and fear when I read that "small is the gate and narrow the road that leads to life, and only a few find it" (Matthew 7:14). Because after reading about the standards of conduct that Jesus requires in my life, I realize just how narrow that gate really is and just how few people really find it.

Then Jesus hammers the same point home with an illustration that he must have learned as a carpenter. If I put his words into practice, I'm like a wise man who built his house on the rock. So when the storms of life come upon me, my house will not fall. But if, as is all too often the case, I do not put Jesus' words into practice, I am like a foolish man who built his house on sand. So when the storms of life come upon me (as they come upon everyone from time to time), the house of my life will fall "with a great crash!" (Matthew 7:24–27).

Then, as I read about Jesus coming down from the mountainside to touch and heal a leper (Matthew 8:1–3), I feel even more despair. Because Jesus really *did* practice what he preached! And I'm so far from having the courage to touch the "lepers" of this world that there's no way that I qualify as a wise man who builds the house of his life on the rock.

But then, I realize that there really *is* hope for me. Now that I realize I am a spiritual leper, I can do the same thing that the leper did when

Jesus came down from the mountainside after preaching this Sermon. I can beg for mercy by coming, kneeling before Jesus and saying, "Lord, if you are willing, you can make me clean" (Matthew 8:2).

If I hope in the LORD this way, I can be sure that my hopes will be justified. For Jesus will treat me the same way he treated that other leper two thousand years ago.

With a smile on his face and gentleness in his voice, Jesus will reach out his hand, touch me, and say, "I am willing . . . Be clean!" And—like the leper—immediately I will be "cured" from whatever "leprosies" afflict me! (Matthew 8:3).

Since we are all spiritual lepers, I urge you to come to Jesus to be touched whenever you need to be cured from the power of Sin. Because, whenever we realize that we are spiritual lepers who need the touch of Jesus to be cured, we satisfy the first standard that Jesus required in the Sermon on the Mount for becoming citizens of his Kingdom—citizens of the Promised Land:

"Blessed are the poor in spirit,
for theirs is the kingdom of heaven."

(Matthew 5:3)

Despite His Family's Wishes, Jesus Continues His Work

The tempo and danger of Jesus' ministry were reaching a nearly un bearable pitch! The crowds were becoming so large that they interfered with Jesus' ministry. After Jesus healed a leper—perhaps the very leper who he touched when he came down from the mountainside after preaching the Sermon on the Mount—the news about Jesus spread so widely that "Jesus could no longer enter a town openly but stayed outside in lonely places. Yet the people still came to him from everywhere" (Mark 1:45).

When Jesus did try to minister in a town, the crush of people was so great that people could not get through the crowd to see Jesus. For example, in Capernaum the crowd was so great that four friends were unable to get their paralytic friend to Jesus. In desperation, they cut a hole in the roof of the house and lowered their friend to Jesus (Mark 2:1–12). The crowds were so large and dense that Jesus' own mother and brothers could not walk through the crowds to talk with Jesus! (Luke 8:19).

The danger had grown with the crowds.

We have already seen that a mob in Jesus' hometown of Nazareth tried to kill him (Luke 4:14–30). But now those who wanted to kill Jesus were becoming more organized, determined and powerful. After Jesus healed a man on the Sabbath, "the Pharisees[, the strictest religious party,] went out and began to plot with the Herodians[, a powerful political party,] how they might kill Jesus" (Mark 3:6).

To Jesus' family it seemed that things were getting out of hand. Undoubtedly, his mother, Mary, was becoming very worried about his safety. What mother does not worry about her "baby boy"!

I am not inclined to be harsh (or surprised) that Mary did not fully understand what Jesus would have to go through as the Messiah. Which one of us fully grasps God's purposes in the life of another? And even though Mary had had an angel explain to her that Jesus was a very special child, she had not (as far as we know from the accounts in Scripture) been told very much—if anything—about the specifics of his life and how he was to become the Messiah.[1]

The concerns of Jesus' family broke into the open when Jesus "entered a house, and again a crowd gathered, so that he and his disciples were not even able to eat" (Mark 3:20). This was the final straw as far as Mary was concerned. "When his family heard about this, they went to take charge of him, for they said, 'He is out of his mind.'" (Mark 3:21).

I don't take this remark as a belief that Jesus was literally "out of his mind." We've all said that we thought somebody was "out of their mind" or "nuts" when they were doing something we thought would get them into trouble—such as riding a gigantic roller coast or plunging down the Tower of Terror in Walt Disney World.

Like any good mother, Mary was going to help her son! First she'd get him away from the crowd! Then she'd talk some sense into him!

The situation when Mary and Jesus' brothers arrived must have confirmed their worst fears. Jesus was just finishing an argument with some "teachers of the law" who had come down from Jerusalem. These important, educated, powerful people had just denounced Jesus.

They said, "He has an evil spirit" (Mark 3:30). Indeed, they accused him of being possessed not just by an ordinary evil spirit, but by the leader of all evil spirits—Satan himself! Using the name "Beelzebub" for Satan, they said: "He is possessed by Beelzebub! By the prince of demons he is driving out demons" (Mark 3:22).

Jesus did not ignore this scathing attack. He ridiculed their wicked slander, saying: "How can Satan drive out Satan? If a kingdom is divided against itself, that kingdom cannot stand. If a house is divided against itself, that house cannot stand. And if Satan opposes himself and is divided, he cannot stand; his end has come" (Mark 3:23–26).[2]

It is fascinating that Jesus used this illustration of a house being divided at the precise moment when his personal house—his family—was divided. His mother and his brothers disagreed with him and wanted him to stop—or at least curtail—his activities. Indeed, perhaps it was that very division in his own family that brought such an illustration to his mind.

At any rate, Jesus could not let anyone stop or limit his ministry—not even his beloved, well-meaning mother. He must do God's will no matter how much it cost to him. He must do God's will no matter how much anguish and how many divisions it caused in his own family.

Jesus made this point tactfully, but firmly, when his mother and brothers arrived. Since they could not get through the crowd to see him, they stood outside and "sent someone in to call him." So the "crowd . . . sitting around him . . . told him, 'Your mother and brothers are outside looking for you.'" (Mark 3:31–32).

Jesus did not hurry away to see what they wanted. Indeed, I suspect that he knew very well what they wanted based on some prior arguments within his family about his activities and about the turmoil and dangers he was causing.

Instead, like any good teacher, Jesus asked a question. He asked, "Who are my mother and my brothers?" (Mark 3:33).

Perplexed looks probably crossed people's brows. They must have wondered what point Jesus was trying to make by this question.

Then, when Jesus had their full attention, he made his point. "[H]e looked at those seated in a circle around him and said, 'Here are my mother and my brothers! Whoever does God's will is my brother and sister and mother.'" (Mark 3:34–35). "My mother and brothers are those who hear God's word *and* put it into practice" (Luke 8:21 (emphasis added)).

This statement was a tactful reminder to his family that he must do God's will regardless of the costs and dangers to himself, and regardless of the wishes of his family.

It remains a good reminder to me as a parent. I must encourage my children to do God's will—even if I worry about the costs and dangers to them.

It is also a marvelous description of our relationship to Jesus. We are like his brother, sister and mother.

Jesus doesn't have favorites based on who our parents are, which nation we come from, which sex we are, how smart we are, or how much money we have. Jesus only cares about whether we are doing God's will.

And what does it mean to do God's will? What does it mean to hear God's word *and* put it into practice?

The whole idea of doing "God's will" is a scary one. To me, the concept of "God's will" conjures up images of immense burdens of doing and not doing things. But this is the way a Pharisee approaches the idea of "God's will."

Jesus had a much more "user friendly" idea of doing God's will—of hearing God's word *and* putting it into practice.

To be sure, there are things we must do and not do. And sometimes we'd rather not do them—just as Jesus prayed so fervently in the Garden of Gethsemane, asking to be spared the agonies and shame of crucifixion the next day (Matthew 26:36–46).

But, at its heart, Jesus taught us that doing God's will is like being in a family. Therefore, we should be like Jesus and say: "Whoever does God's will is my brother and sister and mother" (Mark 3:35). "My mother and brothers are those who hear God's word *and* put it into practice" (Luke 8:21 (emphasis added)).

What does it mean to treat everyone like a brother and sister and mother?

It means that we should put into practice the teachings of Jesus in the Sermon on the Mount. For it is in our families that we come closest to implementing those ideals of the Christian life. It is in our families that we have the best chance to "hear God's word *and* put it into practice" (Luke 8:21 (emphasis added)).

Therefore, in our families, we should always be peacemakers (Matthew 5:9). In our families, we should not be angry with each other or say nasty, derogatory things to each other (Matthew 5:22). In our families, we should quickly settle any disputes we may have with each other (Matthew 5:23–26). In our families, we should remain faithful to our spouses (Matthew 5:27–32). In our families, we should "[g]ive to the one who asks you, and . . . not turn away from the one who wants to borrow from you" (Matthew 5:42). And, in our families, if (God forbid!) we become enemies with any member of our family, we should "[l]ove [our] enemies and pray for those who persecute [us]" (Matthew 5:44).

Even within our immediate families, it is hard to live this way. But perhaps now you can see why it is so important that we do our very best to have families that implement the Sermon on the Mount. Because our families are the training ground and the model for how Jesus envisions touching and changing the entire world with God's justice, love and mercy.[3] Because our families are the training ground and the model for being "best friends" who follow Jesus' Golden Rule: "in everything, do to others what you would have them do to you" (Matthew 7:12).

Jesus Tells the Parable of the Sower

That same day Jesus went out of the house [where his family tried to get him to stop preaching] and sat by the lake. Such large crowds gathered around him that he got into a boat and sat in it, while all the people stood on the shore (Matthew 13:1–2 (emphasis added)).

Jesus did not stop his ministry despite worries caused by the slanders of the Pharisees, by the danger that the Pharisees would kill him, by the crushing workload, or by the well-intentioned, but misguided, advice of his family to quit while he still could.

Instead, *on that same day*, Jesus left the crowded house and went to the lake so that even more people could hear him. Indeed, the crowd grew so great that Jesus had to speak to them while sitting in a boat with the people standing on the shore.

Jesus must have been struck by the sharp contrast between the eagerness of his family to *stop* his preaching and the eagerness of the crowds to *hear* his preaching. If his life was going to fulfill God's purposes, Jesus must press on, despite all trouble, persecutions and worries. To teach this truth, he told the crowds this parable:

"A farmer went out to sow his seed. As he was scattering the seed, some fell along the path, and the birds came and ate it up. Some fell on rocky places, where it did not have much soil. It sprang up quickly, because the soil was shallow. But when the sun came up, the plants were scorched, and they withered because they had no root. Other seed fell among thorns, which grew up and choked the plants. Still other seed fell on good soil, where it produced a crop—a hundred, sixty or thirty times what was sown. He who has ears, let him hear."

(Matthew 13:3–9)

Afterwards, Jesus explained the parable to his disciples. He said:

"Listen then to what the parable of the sower means: When anyone hears the message about the kingdom and does not understand it, the evil one comes and snatches away what was sown in his heart. This is the seed sown along the path.

(Matthew 13:18–19)

This kind of person is like the Pharisees who were always criticizing and opposing Jesus. They did not understand God's word, even though they studied and taught it constantly. In fact, that very day they had been so misguided as to charge that Jesus was an ally of Satan! (Matthew 12:22–24).[1]

The next group of people who Jesus described in his parable started well, but ended badly. As Jesus put it:

"The one who received the seed that fell on rocky places is the man who hears the word and at once receives it with joy. But since he has no root, he lasts only a short time. When trouble or persecution comes because of the word, he quickly falls away."

(Matthew 13:20–22)

Earlier that day, Jesus' mother and brothers tried to get Jesus to become this kind of person. Seeing the danger to someone they loved, they tried to get him to stop following God's plan for his life. But Jesus resisted this temptation (Mark 3:20–22,31–34). He said, "My mother and brothers are those who hear God's word *and* put it into practice" (Luke 8:21 (emphasis added)). So despite the trouble and persecution Jesus faced, he did not fall away.

Some troubles or persecutions can be massive, like the risk of being crucified. However, I think that often it's the little troubles and persecutions that wear us down. Our adrenaline gets up for the big problems, but the routine discouragements of life drain our energy and resolve.

I often think of this when I am jogging.

I do pretty good refusing to let "the big troubles and persecutions" of jogging stop me. I dress warmly when it's cold. I run early in the day and stop to cool off and get a drink when it's hot. I warm up well to overcome aching, tired muscles. I take my glasses off when they become so covered with rain that I can't see through them. And I wear my reflecting vest in the dark so cars can see me.

All these troubles and persecutions of jogging just make me more stubborn and determined to keep on putting one aching foot ahead of the other aching foot. But the thing that comes closest to making me stop and give up is the littlest thing of all: my shoe laces keep coming untied.

I have a terrible time tying my shoes. Maybe it's because I'm left-handed, but my mother taught me how to tie my shoes right-handed. Or maybe it's just because I'm naturally clumsy. But again and again when I'm walking, I have to ask people to stop while I tie my shoes.

And sometimes when I'm jogging, I'll stop four or five times within a mile to retie my running shoes. As I crouch to tie my running shoes, I feel the cold or heat much more intensely. If it's raining, the shoe laces get wet and then it's even harder to tie them. I worry about whether a car can see me when I'm such a small, low object. But the worst thing is that my leg muscles tighten up as I crouch. They ache while I'm tying my running shoes. And it's hard to get my legs going again when I stand up to resume jogging.

Furthermore, this littlest of problems helps cause a big problem. The constant tightening of my muscles and the strain of getting them going again occasionally leads to muscle pulls that keep me from jogging for several days until they heal.

So it's the littlest problem that is most likely to make me give up jogging. And I suspect this is true in much of life—that it is the little, nagging "troubles and persecutions" that make us "fall away" from following God's words.

It's the snow in the driveway or being tired Sunday morning that keeps us from getting to church—not a potential concentration camp or firing squad if we are caught going to church. It's being cut off in traffic or coming home tired from work that gets us to lose our temper—not being spat upon because we are a Christian.

But there is another danger that we face. Even if we do not fall away from following God's ways because of troubles and persecutions, we may not implement God's ways in our lives. We may not produce the good fruit of the Holy Spirit in our lives and in our world: love, joy, peace, patience, kindness, goodness, faithfulness, gentleness and self-control. We may not bless all peoples in the Promised Land.

For people who do not produce the fruit of the Holy Spirit, Jesus had these words of warning:

> "The one who received the seed that fell among the thorns is the man who hears the word, but the worries of this life and the deceitfulness of wealth choke it, making it unfruitful."
>
> (Matthew 13:22)

These kinds of concerns also prompted Jesus' family to try to stop his preaching earlier that day. The crowd that gathered around Jesus was so great "that he and his disciples were not even able to eat" (Mark 3:20). I'm sure his family also worried about how Jesus was going to support himself financially—if he escaped the plots to kill him long enough to need the money! "Why," they wondered, "can't Jesus just come home and work as a carpenter again like he used to? This is madness to continue being a preacher despite so many problems and risks!"

Jesus refused to let such worries or the deceitfulness of wealth stop him from doing God's will. As a carpenter, he well knew the importance of being a wise man who builds the house of his life on a firm foundation. And the firmest foundation possible is to follow the advice Jesus gave in the Sermon on the Mount (Matthew 7:24–27).

During that sermon, Jesus explained why we must not let worries stop us from doing what we know is right. He said:

> "Therefore I tell you, do not worry about your life, what you will eat or drink; or about your body, what you will wear. Is not life more important than food, and the body more important than clothes? Look at the birds of the air; they do not sow or reap or store away in

barns, and yet your heavenly Father feeds them. Are you not much more valuable than they? Who of you by worrying can add a single hour to his life?

"And why do you worry about clothes? See how the lilies of the field grow. They do not labor or spin. Yet I tell you that not even Solomon in all his splendor was dressed like one of these. If that is how God clothes the grass of the field, which is here today and tomorrow is thrown into the fire, will he not much more clothe you, O you of little faith? So do not worry, saying, 'What shall we eat?' or 'What shall we drink?' or 'What shall we wear?' For the pagans run after all these things, and your heavenly Father knows that you need them. But seek first his kingdom and his righteousness, and all these things will be given to you as well. Therefore, do not worry about tomorrow, for tomorrow will worry about itself. Each day has enough trouble of its own."

(Matthew 6:25–34)

Once again, I have learned the wisdom of what Jesus taught by applying his teachings to sports—only this time the sport is golf instead of jogging. Considering how poorly I golf, it's scary to think that I draw any lessons for life from things I've learned while playing golf. But in sports as in life, the best lessons often come from our biggest mistakes.

One of the things I've learned from playing golf so poorly is that it's very important not to worry while you're playing. You must keep concentrating solely on the golf swing you're making at that moment. You can't start thinking about how good or bad your last swing was. And you can't start worrying about how difficult the next hole will be.

To paraphrase Jesus: "Do not worry about the next golf swing, for the next golf swing will worry about itself. Each golf swing has enough trouble of its own."

I often remind myself about this wisdom while I'm driving to work in the morning. I start worrying about all the things I have to do at work and all the things that can go wrong at work.

I start panicking. How can I ever get all these things done? It's impossible!

But then I calm myself down, remembering that all I have to worry about is today. Each day has enough trouble of its own. And tomorrow will worry about itself.

To calm myself further and gain more courage, I also sometimes think back to a practice for overcoming worry that I learned when I was a student at Houghton College. A guest speaker told us to think about the 23rd Psalm when we're worrying. It will always give us hope.

And it's true. If I'm feeling scared and overwhelmed, I remember:

The LORD is my shepherd, I shall not
    be in want.
He makes me lie down in green
    pastures . . .
Even though I walk
    through the valley of the shadow of
        death,
I will fear no evil,
    for you are with me . . .

(Psalm 23:1–2,4)

Another good piece of advice comes from someone who counseled a number of United States Presidents. He'd learned that the most important thing to give a President was *confidence*. Confidence that the President could make a difference for good. Confidence that he could find a way to survival and victory through the nightmares of the Cold War. This adviser said that all the Presidents were very aware of the risks and obstacles they faced. So what he tried to give them was the courage and hope that they could succeed.

And that is why worrying hurts our ability to produce good fruit. In order to be "good soil" that produces a bountiful harvest of good works "yielding a hundred, sixty or thirty times what was sown" (Matthew 13:8,23), we must not worry about what can go wrong or about how wealthy we want to be.

We must seek first the Kingdom of God and his righteousness—the Promised Land where all peoples will be blessed. We must "hear God's word *and* put it into practice" (Luke 8:21 (emphasis added)), worshiping the LORD in spirit and in truth. We must overcome our worries by hoping in the LORD.

Furthermore, we must apply the wisdom of this Parable of the Sower to each aspect of our life. People like to think about those aspects of their lives that already bear good fruit. But if we are really going to make progress in our spiritual pilgrimage so that we live more and more like Jesus, we must think about those aspects of our lives where we are not bearing good fruit.[2]

That way—instead of puffing ourselves up with pride like a Pharisee by thinking about how good we are—we will see ways that we need to change our lives to become a better person.

In some of those aspects of our lives—perhaps in visiting those in prison—we are like the path where the seed of God's word does not take root in our lives at all.

In other aspects of our lives—perhaps in loving our spouses—we are like rocky soil. We start our marriage with deep love for each other, but because our love has no "root" (no deep commitment to each other and to following God's ways in our marriage) our joy lasts only a short time. When "trouble or persecution" hits our marriage, we quickly fall away from each other.

In other areas of our lives—such as working for justice for exploited people—we do not do all that we should do because we are worried about risking our wealth and popularity by helping poor and unpopular people.

We must also apply the wisdom of this Parable of the Sower to every aspect of every group of people. There are always ways that our family—and any family—can become more fruitful in applying God's word to our lives and to our relationships with each other. There are always ways that our church—and any church—can become more fruitful in applying God's word to our lives and to our relationships with each other. There are always ways that the United States—and any nation—can become more fruitful in applying God's word to our lives and to our relationships with each other. And there are always ways that all Humanity can become more fruitful in applying God's word to our lives and to our relationships with each other.

Because any group of people will do better if they put into practice these words of Jesus—his Golden Rule from the Sermon on the Mount: "[I]n everything, do to others what you would have them do to you" (Matthew 7:12).

PART FOUR

Jesus Tells His
Disciples
He Is the Messiah

Jesus Feeds Five Thousand People

Perhaps Jesus knew so much about the problem of worrying because he had so much to worry about. Yet he never let his worries stop his ministry.

His family's worst fears were now justified. Their relative, John the Baptist, was dead—executed by Herod.

I can almost hear Mary, Jesus' mother, telling Jesus: "I told you so! Jesus, if you don't stop this madness you're going to get yourself killed just like your cousin John!"

But when Jesus heard the news of John's death, he did not let it stop his ministry. Jesus' heart was not like the "rocky places" in the Parable of the Sower. Jesus was not the kind of

> man who hears the word and at once receives it with joy. But since he has no root, he lasts only a short time. When trouble or persecution comes because of the word, he quickly falls away.
>
> (Matthew 13:20–21)

Nor was Jesus going to be distracted from his ministry by worrying that the same fate that had just befallen his cousin John was destined to befall him too. Jesus was not the kind of "man who hears the word, but the worries of this life . . . choke it, making it unfruitful" (Matthew 13:22).

139

Nevertheless, Jesus was deeply moved and grieved by the news of John's death. This is the clear implication of the comment that "[w]hen Jesus heard what had happened [to John], he withdrew by boat privately to a solitary place" (Matthew 14:13).

I assume that Jesus had known John well when they were growing up. The Bible does not go into enough detail to make this certain. However, it is a reasonable inference based on several things the Bible tells us.

We know that Mary went to see John's mother, Elizabeth, when Mary became pregnant with Jesus (Luke 1:39–56). So it's reasonable to assume that Mary kept in touch with Elizabeth as they raised their sons.

Furthermore, John the Baptist must have already known Jesus well when Jesus came to the Jordan to be baptized. Otherwise, what basis did John have for saying to Jesus: "I need to be baptized by you, and do you come to me?" (Matthew 3:13–15).

The teachings of the two men also had much in common. In theory, they could have developed their views independently of each other. But it seems far more likely that they had brainstormed together about God's ways. Because the preaching and teaching of John the Baptist and Jesus were remarkably similar.

For example, John sounded like Jesus denouncing Pharisees and other hypocrites when John said:

> "You brood of vipers! Who warned you to flee from the coming wrath? Produce fruit in keeping with repentance . . . . The ax is already at the root of the trees, and every tree that does not produce good fruit will be cut down and thrown into the fire."
>
> (Luke 3:7–10)

Furthermore, John's teachings at the Jordan River sound like Jesus' teachings in the Sermon on the Mount. When the crowd asked John what they should do, John answered: "The man with two tunics should share with him who has none, and the one who has food should do the same" (Luke 3:10–11).

So when Jesus learned that John was dead, he naturally wanted to spend some time alone, grieving and remembering. And I'm sure that Jesus' grief and anger grew as he pondered the despicable circumstances of John's death.

Herod threw John in prison for telling the truth—it was wrong for Herod to marry his brother's wife, called Herodias. Indeed, "Herod wanted to kill John, but he was afraid of the people, because they considered him a prophet" (Matthew 14:3–5).

But Herodias was not content with leaving John in prison. She was furious that John the Baptist had denounced her marriage to Herod as incestuous. So she plotted to have John executed.

Herod's birthday party gave Herodias the chance to hatch her scheme. Herodias had her daughter dance for Herod and his dinner guests. Her dancing pleased Herod very much—presumably because it was very erotic. So Herod swore an oath to grant Herodias' daughter whatever she asked for (Matthew 14:6–7). With the prompting of her mother, the girl asked for the head of John the Baptist on a platter. Rather than break his oath in front of his dinner guests, Herod ordered John's execution (Matthew 14:8–10). His severed head was duly delivered to the party "on a platter and given to the girl, who carried it to her mother" (Matthew 14:11).

As he reflected on these grizzly details of John's death, Jesus could have no illusions about the fate that awaited him as he preached the truth and lived a life of integrity—*execution*!

Herod is typical of those with power. He cared more for lies than for the truth. He cared more for watching erotic dancers than for seeing justice done. And he cared more for saving face in front of his dinner guests than for saving the life of a righteous person.

Herod and Herodias are perfect examples of the people in the Parable of the Sower who rejected God's word because it "fell along the path, and the birds came and ate it up" (Matthew 13:4). When such a person hears the message about the kingdom, he does not understand it and "the evil one comes and snatches away what was sown in his heart" (Matthew 13:19).

The only seed that bears fruit in such people is the seed of wickedness. Think of the lessons Herodias taught her daughter. Use sex as a weapon to get what you want in life. Do whatever is necessary to suppress the truth. Kill anyone who gets in your way.

So Jesus had plenty to worry about that night as he grieved alone in a solitary place for John. And worries are not always groundless. Sometimes the things you worry about really do happen. For example, just as Herod was manipulated into executing John the Baptist rather than disappointing his dinner guests, Pilate was manipulated into executing Jesus rather than disappointing the mob that shouted, "Crucify him!" (Matthew 27:15–26).

The essence of being courageous—of being "good soil" that yields a crop "a hundred, sixty or thirty times what was sown" (Matthew 13:23)—is to follow God's word despite such worries. Like Jesus, we must let our hope in the LORD overcome our worries.

Another good way to overcome the paralysis of worry and the anguish of grief is to get back to work—to resume the ministry that God has given us. And that's exactly what Jesus did now: "[w]hen Jesus . . . saw a large crowd, he had compassion on them, because they were like sheep without a shepherd. So he began teaching them many things and [healing] their sick" (Mark 6:34 plus Matthew 14:14). Indeed, Jesus ministered so long and so hard that day that he performed one of his most memorable miracles—one of the few events of his life that is recorded in all four Gospels—the Feeding of the Five Thousand.

As evening approached, the disciples began to worry. The huge crowd was hungry. There was no place nearby to get food. How could this huge crowd find food? The disciples went to Jesus and said, "This is a remote place, and it's already getting late. Send the crowds away, so they can go to the villages and buy themselves some food" (Matthew 14:15).

Jesus decided to teach the disciples and the crowd that they did not need to worry about food. God would satisfy their hunger. As Jesus emphasized in the Parable of the Sower, such worries were not only unnecessary—they choked off the fruitfulness of God's word in people's lives.

Perhaps that very day Jesus retold the Parable of the Sower. Like candidates running for President of the United States, Jesus must have repeated the same message again and again as he traveled. Such repetition would have been even more essential 2,000 years ago when a speech could not be broadcast on TV and radio.

With people worrying about where they would get food—and with the execution of John the Baptist fresh in his mind—Jesus might well have told the crowd these words from the Parable of the Sower:

"[Some people,] like seed sown among thorns, hear the word; but the worries of this life, the deceitfulness of wealth and the desires for other things come in and choke the word, making it unfruitful."

(Mark 4:18–19)

It was time for Jesus to show the disciples and the crowds that these teachings were more than nice sounding words. They were truths that people could live (and eat) by.

So perhaps that very day, Jesus repeated these teachings from the Sermon on the Mount:

"No one can serve two masters. Either he will hate the one and love the other, or he will be devoted to the one and despise the other. You cannot serve both God and Money.

"Therefore I tell you, do not worry about your life, what you will eat or drink . . . . Is not life more important than food . . . ? Look at the birds of the air; they do not sow or reap or store away in barns, and yet your heavenly Father feeds them. Are you not much more valuable than they? Who of you by worrying can add a single hour to his life?

". . . So do not worry, saying, 'What shall we eat?' or 'What shall we drink?' . . . . For the pagans run after all these things, and your heavenly Father knows that you need them. But seek first his kingdom and his righteousness, and all these things will be given to you as well."

(Matthew 6:24–27,31–33)

Jesus must have decided that now was a good time to show his disciples and the crowds that, if they sought first the Kingdom of God and his righteousness, God would give them the food they needed—both physical food and, most importantly, spiritual food.

Therefore, Jesus refused to send the crowds away, even though the disciples were urging him to send the people to nearby villages to buy food. Instead, "Jesus replied, 'They do not need to go away. You give them something to eat.'" (Matthew 14:15–16).

The disciples must have been dumbfounded. What was Jesus thinking of? Didn't Jesus realize how many people there were and how little money they had? Didn't Jesus realize that they were in a remote place—far from any McDonald's?

But Jesus knew that he had to train the disciples not to worry about such limitations when they were ministering to other people's needs. Jesus "said to Philip, 'Where shall we buy bread for these people to eat?' He asked this only to test him, for he already had in mind what he was going to do" (John 6:5–6). I suspect that Philip's voice and body language showed some exasperation and desperation as he answered Jesus: "Eight months' wages would not buy enough bread for each one to have a bite!" (John 6:7).

What follows is one of the most inspiring moments in the Bible. And since the disciple Andrew played a key role in it, it was one of the reasons that I gave my son the name "Andrew."

In the midst of Philip's despair over how to feed so many people, "Andrew . . . spoke up, 'Here is a boy with five small barley loaves and two small fish, but how far will they go among so many?'" (John 6:8–9).

I suspect that Andrew's voice and body language were full of doubt as he told Jesus about this boy's willingness to share his food. However, I suspect Andrew's voice was also tinged with hope. Perhaps Jesus could make use of this child's generosity?

In my imagination, I hear the other disciples scorning such optimism. They focused on the problems instead of the possibilities. (Since they had never seen Star Trek, they had never had the benefit of Mr. Spock's encouraging insight: "There are always possibilities.") They complained to Jesus that "We have here only five loaves of bread and two fish" (Matthew 14:17).

Despite their doubts, Jesus showed no discouragement or hesitation. He knew that "there are always possibilities" if we hope in the Lord—no matter how bleak the circumstances may be. Therefore,

Jesus said, "Have the people sit down." There was plenty of grass in that place, and the men sat down, about five thousand of them. Jesus then took the loaves, gave thanks, and distributed to those who were seated as much as they wanted. He did the same with the fish.

When they had all had enough to eat, he said to his disciples, "Gather the pieces that are left over. Let nothing be wasted." So they gathered them and filled twelve baskets with the pieces of the five barley loaves left over by those who had eaten.

(John 6:10–13)

Whenever I'm discouraged, this story gives me hope.

I often feel like the boy with "five small barley loaves and two small fish" (John 6:9). In comparison with the challenges and problems that I face, I feel hopelessly inadequate.

But then I remember that all the boy had to do was give the little bit that he had to Jesus. Jesus did the rest.

Starting with the five small loaves and two small fish that the boy gave, Jesus fed "about five thousand men, besides women and children" (Matthew 14:21). And God still works the same way today. If I give God everything I have—no matter how little it may be—God will use it to produce a crop of righteousness far greater than I could ever produce if I kept my gifts to myself. I will bless all peoples in the Promised Land.

That's why I must not "quickly fall away" when "trouble or persecution come." That's why I must not let "the worries of this life, the deceitfulness of wealth and the desires for other things come in and choke the word" of God to me, "making it unfruitful." I must be "good soil" like that boy who did not worry about feeding himself—like that boy who worshiped the Lord in spirit and in truth by giving *everything* he had to help Jesus feed others. Then I will "hear the word, accept it, and produce a crop—thirty, sixty or even a hundred times what was sown" (Mark 4:17–20). I will bless all peoples in the Promised Land.

In a sermon at Pearce Memorial Church, Senior Pastor Art Brown gave an illustration that helped me grasp this truth as I was mulling over what I would write about the Feeding of the Five Thousand. He told stories about two different people.

One person spent his life being a financial adviser. He constantly explained to people the value of discipline in investing. He always insisted on making decisions based on a careful analysis of "the numbers."

One day the man's doctor told him that he had cancer. The doctor told him the odds of survival. "The numbers" were very bleak. So the man gave up. He said, "I've spent my whole life living by 'the numbers' and I can't change now." Within a short time, he was dead.

The other person was Mother Teresa. She won a Nobel Peace Prize for her work ministering to the millions of poor people in Calcutta. Somebody once visited her and came away with this insight. If Mother Teresa had calculated the odds against ever being able to feed and clothe all the destitute people in Calcutta, she would have known it was impossible and never even have bothered to try.

But Christians never count the odds against them! Christians do not follow "the numbers"! Christians follow Jesus!

And so Mother Teresa—like that small boy with five small loaves and two small fish—gave everything she had to helping others even though "the numbers" showed that the task was hopeless. And because she was faithful in a hopeless situation she brought food, clothing and hope to millions of people in Calcutta and around the world. She blessed all peoples in the Promised Land.

Jesus performs such miracles in many ways. And, indeed, you may be aware that there are two differing understandings of how Jesus succeeded in feeding five thousand men, plus women and children, with five small loaves and two small fishes.

One understanding is that Jesus performed a *spiritual* miracle. According to this understanding, the hearts of the people were changed by Jesus' teachings that day and by the example of the boy sharing everything he had to help others. The assumption is that—like the boy—many people still had food with them. However, they were hoarding their food instead of sharing it. Once they shared what they had, there was more than enough for everybody.

Another understanding is that Jesus performed a *physical* miracle. According to this understanding, Jesus miraculously multiplied the physical amount of food so that there was more than enough to feed the large crowd.

One reason supporting this understanding is that the crowd was amazed at what happened. Why would they have been amazed if they knew that the food came from people sharing food that already existed? The amazed people must have concluded that Jesus miraculously increased the physical amount of food that was available.

Another reason supporting this understanding is that the crowd was *not* transformed spiritually that day into generous people. Instead, as we'll see in the rest of this chapter and in the next chapter, many people drew the wrong conclusion from what Jesus was teaching. Indeed, Jesus became angry with them because of their selfishness materialism.

Perhaps the correct answer is that a faithful few were inspired to share their food. So everybody was fed, even though most of the people remained selfish.

Frankly, I think it is good that there is some uncertainty and ambiguity about how Jesus performed this miracle. Because I believe that God performs both kinds of miracles.

Sometimes God accomplishes miracles by changing people's hearts. And sometimes God accomplishes miracles by changing physical realities.

For example, there is the same uncertainty and ambiguity about how God made Mother Teresa's ministry so fruitful. I believe that part of the reason for her success was because God miraculously stretched her physical resources. And even more important was the miraculous stretching of the hearts of those who followed Mother Teresa's example by giving everything they had to help others.

Despite such miracles, we should never expect quick results—even from the most spectacular miracles and the best teachings. It takes months for a crop of corn to grow. And it can take many years for a crop of righteousness to grow from our lives and teachings.

For example, the crop that Jesus planted 2,000 years ago is still growing and bearing fruit today. But even his spectacular miracle of Feeding the Five Thousand did not bring any good results immediately. In fact, it brought Jesus more problems.

Even after Jesus taught the people all day, they were not inspired to go forth serving God by doing unto others what they would want others to do for them. Instead, the people decided to do something completely the opposite of what Jesus wanted them to do:

> After the people saw the miraculous sign that Jesus did, they began to say, "Surely this is the Prophet who is to come into the world."

147

[So] Jesus, knowing that they intended to come and make him king by force, withdrew again to a mountain by himself [to pray].

(John 6:14–15)1

Once again, Jesus was alone.

He started the day alone, grieving for John the Baptist.

And, after working hard all day—teaching and performing miracles that produced results that were exactly the opposite of what he wanted—Jesus went to be alone again to pray.

I often marvel at how Jesus found the courage and discipline to carry on his ministry. Certainly, he faced more trouble, persecution, and worries than I face. How did he find the wisdom to keep hoping in the LORD despite all these problems?

I'm convinced that we see here one of the keys to overcoming troubles, persecutions and worries: Jesus withdrew from the fray long enough to pray. In solitude and prayer, he renewed his hope in the LORD.

Jesus experienced this truth from Isaiah:

[T]hose who hope in the LORD
will renew their strength.
They will soar on wings like eagles;
they will run and not grow weary,
they will walk and not be faint.

(Isaiah 40:31)

So whenever we face grief or disappointments, we need to have the discipline to take time to pray.

Like Jesus, we need to withdraw from the fray long enough to pray.

That is the way to renew our hope in the LORD.

In times of solitude and prayer, the LORD will renew our strength—the strength to live fruitful lives despite every trouble, persecution and worry that comes our way. The strength to bless all peoples in the Promised Land.

Jesus Blesses Peter

Huge crowds continued to follow Jesus after his miraculous Feeding of the Five Thousand, even though Jesus refused to let the people "come and make him king by force" (John 6:15).[1]

It would be normal human nature for Jesus to tell these crowds what they wanted to hear. Most politicians would be careful to craft their statements with an eye to the most recent public opinion polls.

But Jesus was not a politician. He refused to compromise his principles for what he knew was right. He did not hesitate to tell the people the truth, even when they didn't want to hear it. That's the only way to heal the Promised Land: teach people how to worship the LORD in spirit and in *truth*.

Therefore, when Jesus spoke to the crowds who kept following him after the Feeding of the Five Thousand, he did not flatter them in order to solidify his base of support. Instead, he told them the truth, even though he must have known that the truth would not be welcome. Jesus told the crowds, "I tell you the truth, you are looking for me, not because you saw miraculous signs but because you ate the loaves and had your fill" (John 6:26).

Jesus knew that, although these hypocrites pretended that they cared about seeking God's ways, they really were like the pagans he described in the Sermon on the Mount. They were always worrying, "'What shall we eat?' or 'What shall we drink?' or 'What shall we wear?'" (Matthew 6:31). Therefore, the crowds were like "the pagans [who] run after all these things" (Matthew 6:32).

As Jesus warned in the Parable of the Sower, such people were like seed sown among thorns. They "hear the word, but the worries of this life, the deceitfulness of wealth and the desires for other things come in and choke the word, making it unfruitful" (Mark 4:18–19).

Jesus did not want a large group of followers who were really pagans at heart. Such hypocrites were not truly following him. Therefore, Jesus did not encourage their hypocrisy with comforting lies. Instead, Jesus challenged them with the truth.

As Jesus observed in the Sermon on the Mount: "You cannot serve both God and Money" (Matthew 6:24). There is no comfortable middle ground where people can have "the best of both worlds." "No one can serve two masters. Either he will hate the one and love the other, or he will be devoted to the one and despise the other" (Matthew 6:24).

Despite their hypocritical veneer of spirituality, the crowds following Jesus hated and despised God. Greed was destroying their Promised Land. Lies would hasten the destruction of their Promised Land. Therefore, Jesus knew that the only way he could heal the Promised Land of these spiritual lepers was to touch them with the truth: if they didn't stop serving Money, their doom was certain. Because, as Jesus warned in the Sermon on the Mount, people who worry about Money are like foolish people who build their houses on sand. When the storms and floods of life beat on such people, they fall with a great crash (Matthew 7:26–27).

To avoid this fate, Jesus insisted that his followers "seek first [God's] kingdom and his righteousness" (Matthew 6:33). Only such people can survive the storms of life without falling (Matthew 7:24–25).

Therefore, Jesus told the crowds, "Do not work for food that spoils, but for food that endures to eternal life, which the Son of Man will give you. On him God the Father has placed his seal of approval" (John 6:27).

The crowds squirmed this way and that way looking for an excuse to avoid doing what Jesus asked.

Initially, the crowds tried to avoid seeking first the kingdom of God and his righteousness by asking distracting questions. They asked Jesus, "What must we do to do the works God requires?" (John 6:28).

Hypocrites love to ask questions that make it sound as if they want to do God's will. But their insincere questions are merely excuses for inaction.

Since it's easier to *talk* about doing something than to *do* something, hypocrites pretend that they don't have enough intellectual knowledge to do God's will. No hypocrite wants to be like Jesus and actually touch lepers.

Jesus refused to get distracted by such insincere questions. He'd already told the crowds the kinds of things that God wanted them to do. The trouble was that the crowds were refusing to do what Jesus had already taught them to do. They were questioning and rejecting his authority to require them to live such holy lives.

Jesus went right to the heart of the matter. Jesus affirmed with unshakable conviction that he had the authority to require people to follow him and his teachings. Jesus told the people, "The work of God is this: to believe in the one he has sent" (John 6:29).

In response, the people asked another distracting question. In order to challenge Jesus' authority over them, "they asked him, 'What miraculous sign . . . will you give that we may see it and believe you? What will you do?'" (John 6:30).

Notice how cleverly the crowds changed the subject.

This confrontation began with Jesus commanding the *crowds*: "Do not work for food that spoils, but for food that endures to eternal life, which the Son of Man will give you" (John 6:27). The crowds never answered whether they would do what Jesus commanded. And now the crowds were asking *Jesus* to do something!

As I learned in a 2-day training session on negotiating,[2] such distracting questions are a classic negotiating tactic.

Next, the crowd chose another classic negotiating tactic—setting a phony "performance standard." This tactic involves belittling the value of what the other party is offering by setting irrelevant, unrealistically high performance standards that must be met. For example, when you're trading in a 3-year old car, the car dealer may claim that he can't give you the "normal" trade-in on the car because the paint has a few scratches.

In this case, the crowd asked Jesus (the other party to the "negotia-tions") to meet a phony "performance standard" that they claimed had been met by Moses. As you may remember, when Moses led the Israel-ites through the wilderness, the people ate manna for 40 years. So the people countered Jesus' command that they believe him with this mock-ing counterproposal: "What will *you* do? Our forefathers ate the manna in the desert; as it is written: 'He gave them bread from heaven to eat.'" (John 6:30–31 (emphasis added)).

There were several clever features to this phony "performance stan-dard" as a negotiating tactic.

First, by referring to this feeding of an entire nation for 40 years, the people belittled Jesus' recent miracles: feeding "only" 5,000 people on one day and "only" 4,000 people on another day (Mark 6:30–44; Mark 8:1–9).

It was like having a car dealer look at the car you're going to trade in. In order to pay you as little as possible for your car, he's *determined* to find fault with it. He'll keep looking until he can find something bad to say about it.

The crowd was *determined* to find fault with Jesus! They kept look-ing for bad things to say about him.

There was another aspect to this "performance standard" that made it a clever negotiating tactic. Jesus couldn't meet this "performance stan-dard" in less than 40 years. This gave the crowds plenty of time to delay their decision whether to meet Jesus' performance standard of touching lepers.

And, of course, by the end of the 40 years they would have found some other excuse to delay their decision whether to obey Jesus' com-mand: "Do not work for food that spoils, but for food that endures to eternal life, which the Son of Man will give you" (John 6:27).

Jesus was in no mood to negotiate with these hypocrites. Their "per-formance standard" missed the key point. *Moses* didn't feed the people! *God* fed the people!

So Jesus said, "I tell you the truth, it is not Moses who has given you the bread from heaven, but it is my Father who gives you the true bread from heaven" (John 6:32).

Getting back to the point, Jesus again affirmed his authority to com-mand the crowds: "Do not work for food that spoils, but for food that endures to eternal life, which the Son of Man will give you" (John 6:27). He explained, "[T]he bread of God is he who comes down from heaven and gives life to the world" (John 6:33).

Rather than accept Jesus' authority, the people set a different performance standard. Instead of following Jesus' command that they *work* for food that endures to eternal life, they gave Jesus something else to do. "'Sir,' they said, 'from now on give us this bread.'" (John 6:34).

No problem! This was an easy "performance standard" for Jesus to meet. "Jesus declared, 'I am the bread of life. He who comes to me will never go hungry, and he who believes in me will never be thirsty.'" (John 6:35).

Jesus was a tough negotiator. He gave the crowds no more options.

They must choose whether Jesus had the authority to command them: "Do not work for food that spoils, but for food that endures to eternal life, which the Son of Man will give you" (John 6:27). They must agree that "God the Father has placed his seal of approval [on Jesus]" (John 6:27).

At this point, the people "began to grumble about [Jesus] because he said, 'I am the bread that came down from heaven.'" (John 6:41). Just like that car dealer, they had to find fault with what Jesus was offering.

And to find fault, they fell back on a familiar line of argument. They said, "Is this not Jesus, the son of Joseph, whose father and mother we know? How can he now say, 'I came down from heaven'?" (John 6:42). This was the same argument that the people in Jesus' hometown of Nazareth used when they rejected Jesus and tried to kill him (Luke 4:14–30).

There are always ways to find fault with Jesus or to find distractions to keep from doing what Jesus commands. One of these distractions is the error of Anti-Semitism—the error of always looking for ways to find fault with Jews. Therefore, I want to discuss a potential misunderstanding caused by the fact that this passage in the Gospel of John describes the people who argued with Jesus as "the Jews."

The text describes the crowd's reaction to Jesus (who was himself a Jew) by saying that "the Jews began to grumble about [Jesus]" and "the Jews began to argue sharply among themselves" (John 6:41,52). Unfortunately, Anti-Semites like to use such references to "the Jews" here (and elsewhere in the Bible) to condemn Jews today.

Such a conclusion is exactly the opposite of what we should learn from this story and from the Bible. Because we will miss the whole point of this story and of the Bible if we apply it to other people instead of applying it to ourselves.

Such an Anti-Semite is seeking a distraction from obeying what Jesus commands us to do just as the crowds 2,000 years ago kept seeking a distraction from following Jesus' command: "Do not work for food that spoils, but for food that endures to eternal life, which the Son of Man will give you" (John 6:27).

Because it's always easier to condemn other people than to touch lepers.

So to apply this story properly to people today, the term "the Jews" should be translated as "the Church-Goers."

The point is that the people listening to Jesus 2,000 years ago were familiar with God's teachings just as Church-Goers are today. The problem was that these people were not like the "good soil" in the Parable of the Sower that bears a bountiful crop. Instead, they were like the people in the Parable of the Sower who never matured spiritually because of troubles, persecutions, worries, the deceitfulness of wealth, and desires for other things (Mark 4:16–20).

Think how many people who attend church today are just like "the Jews" who are condemned in this story.

The Church-Goers seek every possible excuse to evade Jesus' commands such as: "Do not work for food that spoils, but for food that endures to eternal life, which the Son of Man will give you" (John 6:27) and "in everything, do to others what you would have them do to you" (Matthew 7:12).

The Church-Goers fail to mature spiritually because of troubles, persecutions, worries, the deceitfulness of wealth, and the desire for other things (Mark 4:16–20).

Just like "the Jews" that Jesus had to argue with that day, "the Church-Goers" perpetually think up questions that must be answered (such as reconciling religion and science, or reconciling free will and predestination) before they do things such as touching physical and spiritual lepers.

Just like "the Jews" that day, "the Church-Goers" set phony performance standards that God must reach (such as making them popular or making them rich) before they will believe that God really wants them to touch lepers.

And just like "the Jews" that day, "the Church-Goers" always find something to grumble about (from the color of the carpet to the content of the sermon) because they'd rather grumble than touch lepers.

When the story is applied this way, I realize that I am often like "the Church-Goers" who argued with Jesus that day. Because I've never touched a leper. And I'll look for almost any distraction or excuse to avoid touching physical or spiritual "lepers." So, if I condemn "the Jews," I must condemn "the Church-Goers" such as me far more.

Furthermore, if I condemn "the Jews," I am disobeying Jesus' command: "Do not judge, or you too will be judged. For in the same way you judge others, you will be judged, and with the measure you use, it will be measured to you" (Matthew 7:1–2).

Considering how many times I seek distractions to evade doing what God wants me to do, I cannot condemn "the Jews" without having Jesus say to me, "Why do you look at the speck of sawdust in your brother's eye and pay no attention to the plank in your own eye?" (Matthew 7:3).

And considering how many times Christians have shamefully persecuted and ridiculed Jews, Moslems and other non-Christians instead of doing to them in everything what we would have them do to us (as the Law, the Prophets and Jesus command us to do), we cannot condemn non-Christians without having Jesus say to us, "You hypocrite, first take the plank out of your own eye, and then you will see clearly to remove the speck from your brother's eye" (Matthew 7:5).

Because bigotry and prejudice against other people are just another type of distraction that keeps us grumbling instead of doing what Jesus commands. And there are always plenty of excuses for such grumbling.

For example, the people that day "began to grumble about [Jesus] because he said, 'I am the bread that came down from heaven.'" (John 6:41). Just like the people in Jesus' hometown of Nazareth, they began to scoff at any such claim, saying, "Is this not Jesus, the son of Joseph, whose father and mother we know? How can he now say, 'I came down from heaven'?" (John 6:42).

In the face of such scoffing, Jesus did not back down a bit on these astounding claims about who he was. "'Stop grumbling among yourselves,' Jesus answered . . . . . 'I am the living bread that came down from heaven. If anyone eats of this bread, he will live forever. This bread is my flesh, which I will give for the life of the world.'" (John 6:43,51).

At this explanation of who he was and how important he was, the people "began to argue sharply among themselves, 'How can this man give us his flesh to eat?'" (John 6:52).

I doubt that this was a sincere question.

In the way that I envision this confrontation with Jesus, people did not ask this question in the tone of voice of someone who sincerely wondered "How can this man give us his flesh to eat?"

Instead, people said these words in a sarcastic, disgusted tone of voice that ridiculed and rejected Jesus. It was the same kind of nasty, condescending put-down as when they said, "Is this not Jesus, the son of Joseph, whose father and mother we know?" (John 6:42).

The real motive in these nasty statements of the people was that they did not want to face the issue of whether Jesus' statements were true. So they ridiculed Jesus rather than sincerely thinking about whether Jesus' life and teachings warranted his claim to be "he who comes down from heaven and gives life to the world" (John 6:33).

The people knew that Jesus was not literally telling them to eat his flesh with a fork and knife when he said, "I am the living bread that came down from heaven. If anyone eats of this bread, he will live forever" (John 6:51). In the context, it was clear that Jesus was speaking figuratively about the need to follow him and do what he taught people to do—not about the need to become cannibals!

I believe the people were deliberately and in bad faith trying to misunderstand Jesus on this point.

Their response reminds me of Nicodemus' effort to twist Jesus' words about being "born from above" by being "born again" (John 3:1–8). I believe that Nicodemus—like these people—knew that Jesus did not intend the words to be taken literally.

But Nicodemus—like these people—tried to evade the profound *spiritual truth* that Jesus was teaching by giving the words a *nonsensical physical interpretation*. In the case of Nicodemus, he scoffed at Jesus as if Jesus was telling him to re-enter his mother's womb to be born again a second time physically. And, in the case of these people, they scoffed at Jesus as if he was telling them to become cannibals by cutting up his physical flesh and eating it.

Such foolish misinterpretations of what Jesus taught were not made in good faith. They were one more example of a distraction—such as prejudices and worries—that people indulge in to avoid becoming "good soil" that accepts God's words for their lives and puts God's words into practice so that they produce a bountiful crop of righteousness.

Jesus emphasized how much better the spiritual bread was that he offered compared to the physical bread that the people craved. He said, "This is the bread that came down from heaven. Your forefathers ate manna and died, but he who feeds on this bread will live forever" (John 6:58).

Instead of accepting the good news that Jesus offered them better "food" than the manna that their forefathers received from Moses, the people continued to prefer feeding their stomachs instead of "feeding" their hearts and minds.

Instead of accepting Jesus' claims about who he was, the people rejected Jesus. Indeed, even many of Jesus' hard-core supporters rejected him. As the Gospel of John tells us, "On hearing it, many of his disciples said, 'This is a hard teaching. Who can accept it?'" (John 6:60).

What was the "it" that these disciples heard and had such trouble accepting? To some extent, it was a theological, intellectual "it." But primarily the "it" that these people could not accept was the claim of Jesus to have authority over how they lived.

The Bible mentions several times that the people were amazed at Jesus because he taught with authority (Mark 1:21–28; Luke 4:31–37).[3] For example, when Jesus had finished the Sermon on the Mount, "the crowds were amazed at his teaching, because he taught as one who had authority, and not as their teachers of the law" (Matthew 7:28–29). And when Jesus healed a paralyzed man and forgave his sins, the crowd was "filled with awe; and they praised God, who had given such authority to men" (Matthew 9:1–8).

The question of Jesus' authority was becoming more and more critical as the times became more dangerous—as it cost more and more to be a disciple of Jesus.

Powerful political and religious leaders were plotting to kill Jesus (Matthew 12:14; Mark 3:6; Luke 6:11; John 5:16–18). And it was clear that such plots must be taken seriously. John the Baptist himself had recently been beheaded (Matthew 14:1–12; Mark 6:14–29; Luke 9:7–9). Accordingly, there were enough troubles and persecutions to tempt any but the most hardy (or most *fool*hardy!) of souls to fall away from following Jesus.

People often do not like to admit the true reasons for their actions. Often they do not even admit the truth to themselves.

So rather than admit that they were scared to follow Jesus anymore, the people focused on questions about who Jesus claimed to be. Because anyone's authority is always an intertwining of two factors: the persuasiveness of what they say and who they are.

In Jesus' case, this meant that his authority flowed from two intertwining sources: (1) the truth of his teachings; and (2) his special status as someone on whom "God the Father has placed his seal of approval" because he is "the bread of God . . . who comes down from heaven and gives life to the world" (John 6:27,33).

A police officer is an example of how authority flows from this intertwining of the truth of our message and our special status.

If the police officer tells us that we were driving too fast and we should slow down for our safety and the safety of the public, part of the authority of his message depends on its truth. Our logic and experience tell us that the police officer is right. So we tend to acknowledge the authority of his advice and to follow his advice in the future.

But the other reason we acknowledge the police officer's authority is simply because of who he is—someone given special powers to enforce speed limits by giving us tickets.

The authority of Jesus also flows both from our perception that his teachings are true and because of who he is. Some people lean more toward accepting Jesus' authority because they've pondered his teachings intellectually and believe based on logic and experience that Jesus is right. Other people lean more toward accepting Jesus' authority based on recognizing his special status and power to enforce his commands.

Furthermore, the same person may change their basis for recognizing Jesus' authority as they mature.

For example, when we are immature, we tend to accept someone's authority based primarily on our recognition of the *power* of the person giving the command. We tend to operate on the principle that "might makes right."

Such Christians may tend to follow Jesus based primarily on their acceptance of the theological truth that Jesus is the Son of God—fully God and fully human. As the Gospel of John puts it, Jesus (who is referred to as "the Word of God") is fully God because "[i]n the beginning was the Word, and the Word was with God, and the Word was God" (John 1:1). And Jesus is fully human because "[t]he Word became flesh and made his dwelling among us" (John 1:14).

But, as we mature, we tend to accept someone's authority based primarily on our personal belief that what they are commanding is *true* and *good*. We tend to operate on the principle that "right makes might."

Such Christians may tend to follow Jesus based primarily on their moral conviction—after much thought and reflection—that his teachings are true and good. As the Gospel of John puts it, in Jesus "was life, and that life was the light of [Humanity]. The light shines in the darkness . . . . The true light that gives light to every [person] . . ." (John 1:4–5,9). So, if you hold to Jesus' teachings—if you are *really* his disciples—"you will know the truth, and the truth will set you free" (John 8:31–32).

The critical thing is to accept Jesus' authority for whatever reasons are most compelling to you.

For example, the most important thing when taking a trip on an airplane is to accept its power to fly through the air to get you to where you want to go.

Very few people fully understand how a plane works. And nobody—not even an engineer who builds and designs planes—understands every detail of every piece of the plane. Despite such a lack of complete knowledge and understanding, people can climb into the plane and get to where they need to go.

But, if someone doesn't believe in the power of the airplane to fly—if they don't have faith in the plane—they'll never climb into the plane and get to where they need to go.

Similarly, very few people understand every nuance of Christian doctrines such as the Doctrine of the Trinity.

This is not surprising when you realize how few people understand every nuance of theories about the way that the physical universe operates. How many people can truthfully say that they understand completely quantum theory, the General Theory of Relativity, and the Special Theory of Relativity?

We'd expect the explanation of how the spiritual universe operates to be even more complicated and difficult to grasp. And even those who do have a basic understanding of the Doctrine of the Trinity cannot possibly understand every detail about the interrelationships between Jesus, God the Father, the Holy Spirit, humans, and the physical universe.

Fortunately, we do not need to understand every detail of these complicated theological issues in order to live the way Jesus commanded us to live—to touch lepers.

It's very simple to light a room. Just flip the light switch.

It works even though the full explanation of why it works is too complicated and difficult for most people to understand completely.

How many people can truthfully say that they completely understand how nuclear plants, coal-powered plants, and hydro-electric plants were constructed and how they work? About the same number of people who can truthfully say that they completely understand the origins of God and the universe, and how they work.

How many people can truthfully say that they completely understand how electricity is transmitted over the power grid and into our homes? About the same number of people who can truthfully say that they completely understand how God sustains the universe and communicates with people.

How many people can truthfully say that they completely understand how electricity passing through the filament in a light bulb generates light? About the same number of people who can truthfully say that they completely understand how God lights the world by changing people's hearts.

How many people can truthfully say that they completely understand how white light consists of every color of the rainbow? About the same number of people who can truthfully say that they completely understand how one God can be three persons—God the Father, God the Son, and God the Holy Spirit.

How many people can truthfully say that they completely understand how light exists as both a particle (the photon) and as a wave? About the same number of people who can truthfully say that they completely understand how God can be all-powerful, yet can give us free will to choose whether to follow God and God's ways.

Even though we do not completely understand all of these complicated things about light, we can still light our homes. All we have to do is flip the light switch.

And even though we do not completely understand all of these complicated things about God, we can still light our lives and our world. All we have to do is "Believe in the Lord Jesus, and [we] will be saved" (Acts 16:31). This flips the light switch in our hearts!

All we have to do is have enough faith to "get on the plane" by accepting Jesus' authority and following him!

Because to do some things, having the faith to follow Jesus is the *only way* to go.

Some trips can be made without a plane. For example, we can get to California from New York by driving a car. We can go many good places and do many good things throughout North and South America by driving a car.

Driving so far is not as easy or as fast as flying. But it can be done.

Similarly, other "religions" than "having the faith to follow Jesus Christ" can get us lots of good places and do lots of good things. Not as easily or as fast as following Jesus. But they can do it.

In contrast, if we start driving a car in New York, we can *never* reach Hawaii. A car can *never* cross the ocean that separates us from Hawaii—our ultimate, best destination.

Similarly, having the faith to follow Jesus Christ is the *only way* that we can reach our ultimate, best destination. Because following Jesus is the *only way* to cross the ocean of Sin that separates us from our ultimate, best destination.

What is our ultimate, best destination? *The* Promised Land: *Jesus'* Promised Land where we establish the work of our hands because we do not work for food that spoils but for food that endures; Jesus' Promised

Land where we worship the Lord in spirit and in truth; and Jesus' Promised Land where we bless all peoples by doing for them what we want them to do for us.

Therefore, we can *never* reach the Promised Land by following any "religion," but only by following Jesus. (See Appendix A: *"Force Majeure*: Does God Forgive Non-Christians?")

Because having the faith to follow Jesus Christ is the only way to cross the ocean of Sin that separates us from God—the only way to heal the Promised Land. ***Following Jesus is the only way to reach the Promised Land!***

Unfortunately, it's hard to accept the full authority of Jesus in our lives—whether it was 2,000 years ago or yesterday.

It's so hard to do to others what we would have them do to us. To turn the other cheek. To love our enemies.

It's so easy to look at others lustfully. To serve Money and despise God. To worry about food, drink and clothes. To run after all these material things like pagans do. To judge others more harshly than we judge ourselves. To fall away from doing good when troubles and persecutions befall us.

It's so illogical to believe that the same Jesus who was a carpenter's son also existed in the beginning with God and is God.

Therefore, like those early disciples, we often say that Jesus' teachings are too hard and we fall away.

Perhaps we still come to church every Sunday, sing songs, and pretend we're following Jesus. But in fact, we have rejected Jesus by not accepting who he is and by not doing what he wants us to do. In our hearts and minds and lives, we are grumbling just like those early disciples: "This is a hard teaching. Who can accept it?" (John 6:60).

Such grumbling infected those who wanted to kill Jesus. They "tried all the harder to kill him [because] not only was he breaking the Sabbath, but he was even calling God his own Father, making himself equal with God" (John 5:18). Just as Ancient Israel (the original Promised Land) was destroyed by greed, lies and violence, these sinners were going to destroy Jesus (the new Promised Land) because of their greed, their lies, and their violence.

Those who wanted to kill Jesus because of what he taught about the Sabbath rejected him based on a rejection of his teachings. And those who wanted to kill Jesus because he called God his own Father, making himself equal with God, rejected Jesus based on who he said he was.

In both cases, they rejected Jesus' authority over their own lives and over the world.

Because, in the aftermath of Feeding the Five Thousand, it became clearer and clearer that Jesus meant what he said about working for food that endures to eternal life instead of working for food that spoils. And, as if this wasn't difficult enough to accept, Jesus kept insisting that God had placed his seal of approval on him and that Jesus was the bread of God who came down from heaven to give life to the world.

Since these teachings were too hard for many of Jesus' disciples to accept, "[f]rom this time many of his disciples turned back and no longer followed him" (John 6:66).

These disciples were not the twelve disciples who we usually refer to today as "the Disciples." The disciples who no longer followed Jesus belonged to a larger group of followers who were not in the same inner circle as "the Twelve."

Jesus now turned to his closest supporters—the Twelve—and asked them: "You do not want to leave too, do you?" (John 6:67).

There were several tones of voice in which Jesus could have asked this question.

If it had been me, I probably would have said these words angrily. My anger would have been caused by my fears and insecurities.

What would happen to me? Where had I gone wrong? Why were all these people—even my disciples—leaving me?

The ingrates! After all I'd done for them, now they were deserting me!

But Jesus would not have let such fears and insecurities govern his actions or his words. So I do not think that he used an angry tone of voice when he said, "You do not want to leave too, do you?"

If it had been me, I might have asked the question in a fearful tone of voice. Depressed and scared, I might have convinced myself that the Twelve would leave me too.

But Jesus would not have let such depression and fear govern his actions or his words. So I do not think that he used a fearful tone of voice when he said, "You do not want to leave too, do you?"

Instead, I think Jesus asked the question in an encouraging tone of voice. Because Jesus always does his best to bring hope to discouraged people.

And the Twelve must have needed hope. How could they not be discouraged, fearful, insecure and depressed? John the Baptist was executed! And now most of Jesus' followers were deserting him!

Jesus did not want the Twelve to fall away due to these troubles and persecutions. Jesus did not want worrying to choke the fruitfulness of their lives. So I think that Jesus used an *encouraging* tone of voice when he said, "You do not want to leave too, do you?"

And Jesus got the answer he was looking for. Peter said, "Lord, to whom shall we go? You have the words of eternal life. We believe and know that you are the Holy One of God" (John 6:68–69).[4]

In this answer, Peter wove together the reasons for accepting the authority of Jesus that we have been discussing.

Regarding the unique authority of Jesus' teachings, Peter said, "You have the words of eternal life." And regarding the unique status of Jesus as a person, Peter said, "We believe and know that you are the Holy One of God."

Peter knew that Jesus was a unique person based on what Jesus taught and what Jesus did. Indeed, Peter knew that Jesus was so unique that there was no one else to follow *except* Jesus.

So Peter said, "Lord, to whom shall we go?"

At about this same time (and perhaps during the same conversation), Jesus decided to pin down Peter and the rest of the disciples about exactly who they thought he was. Jesus asked the twelve disciples, "Who do the crowds say I am?" (Luke 9:18).[5]

This was a nonthreatening way to raise the topic. The disciples weren't being asked what they believed personally. They merely had to repeat what others were saying.

Since they'd heard many ideas about who Jesus was, they replied, "Some say John the Baptist; others say Elijah; and still others, that one of the prophets of long ago has come back to life" (Luke 9:19).

Now Jesus asked his disciples the hard question. What did they believe personally?

With the disciples 2,000 years ago—just as with us today—the key question is not what we hear *other people* saying about Jesus. The key question is what *we* believe about Jesus.

As Jesus put it: "But what about you? . . . Who do you say I am?" (Luke 9:20).

We are not told how long it took the disciples to answer this simple—yet key—question.

In my imagination, I see them seated around Jesus. They started fidgeting uneasily—like school children who aren't sure what answer they're supposed to give their teacher.

The awkward silence continued for a few seconds. Then Peter blurted out his answer: "You are the Christ, the Son of the living God" (Matthew 16:16).

In my mind's eye, I see an instant of silence. All the fidgeting stopped. Every eye was fixed on Jesus. All the disciples wondered: "Will Jesus claim he is the Christ—the Messiah—or not!"

Once Jesus had their full attention he confirmed that Peter was right. Jesus really was "the Christ, the Son of the living God."

Jesus expressed his pleasure the way any teacher expresses their pleasure when a student has answered a hard question well. Jesus praised his star student, Peter.

However, the words of praise that Jesus used to praise Peter were different from any words you ever heard from your teachers.

> "Jesus replied, 'Blessed are you, Simon son of Jonah, for this was not revealed to you by man, but by my Father in heaven. And I tell you that you are Peter, and on this rock I will build my church, and the gates of Hades will not overcome it. I will give you the keys of the kingdom of heaven; whatever you bind on earth will be bound in heaven, and whatever you loose on earth will be loosed in heaven.'"
> (Matthew 16:17–19)

As you probably recognize, these words of praise that Jesus gave Peter have been the subject of bitter controversies between Protestants and Catholics for centuries. Catholics use these words as support for the Pope's authority over all Christians. Protestants (and Orthodox Christians) reject this interpretation.[6]

I do not want to rehash centuries of arguments. However, since I am a Protestant rather than a Catholic, I'll summarize a few key reasons why I do not believe these verses support the Pope's authority over all Christians.

First of all, the passage is very brief and ambiguous—especially if its purpose was to set forth the need to have one church hierarchy that all Christians must follow.

In comparison, consider how much of the Old Testament was devoted to establishing the priesthood of Ancient Israel and to describing the practices and powers of the priests. Virtually the entire book of Leviticus was devoted to this subject. And large portions of the books of Exodus, Numbers, 1 and 2 Chronicles, and Ezra were consumed with the subject (Exodus 24–40; Numbers 3–9,16–19; 1 Chronicles 15–17,22–29; 2 Chronicles 2–7,15,24,29–31,34–35; Ezra 1–3,6,8).

In contrast, the New Testament has very few references to how the church is to be run in a *bureaucratic sense*. Indeed, Jesus' statement praising Peter for declaring that Jesus is the Christ, the Son of the Living God, appears *only* in the Gospel of Matthew. The writers of the gospels of Mark, Luke and John evidently did *not* feel the statement was important enough to be included in their gospels!

Furthermore, where the subject of the clergy comes up in the New Testament, the emphasis is on the *conduct* of the clergy far more than on the *authority* of the clergy over other Christians—the emphasis is on how the church is to be run in a *spiritual sense*. For example, Paul gave Timothy this advice about choosing an "overseer"—a word that traditionally was translated from the Greek as "bishop."[7]

> Here is a trustworthy saying: If anyone sets his heart on being an overseer, he desires a noble task. Now the overseer must be above reproach, the husband of but one wife, temperate, self-controlled, respectable, hospitable, able to teach, not given to drunkenness, not violent but gentle, not quarrelsome, not a lover of money. He must manage his own family well and see that his children obey him with proper respect. (If anyone does not know how to manage his own family, how can he take care of God's church?) He must not be a recent convert, or he may become conceited and fall under the same judgement as the devil. He must also have a good reputation with

166

outsiders, so that he will not fall into disgrace and into the devil's trap.

(1 Timothy 3:1–7)

Of course, as the word "overseer" implies, a bishop or other member of the clergy is expected to exert some kind of authority within the church. And as with all authority, their authority flows from an intertwining of what they teach and what position they hold.

But the authority of the clergy flows far more from the fact that their teachings and actions are good than from the mere fact that they hold the position of the clergy or even of a bishop.

That's why, when Paul wrote to Titus about selecting overseers, he emphasized the personal qualities that overseers must have rather than the authority that overseers automatically exercise by virtue of their position in the church. Paul wrote:

> Since an overseer is entrusted with God's work, he must be blameless—not overbearing, not quick-tempered, not given to drunkenness, not violent, not pursuing dishonest gain. Rather he must be hospitable, one who loves what is good, who is self-controlled, upright, holy and disciplined. He must hold firmly to the trustworthy message as it has been taught, so that he can encourage others by sound doctrine and refute those who oppose it.
>
> (Titus 1:7–9)

Therefore, when we have leaders of the Christian church who exemplify such righteous lives—such as Mother Teresa, Pope John Paul II and Billy Graham—I am happy to acknowledge their "authority" over me and over all who follow Jesus Christ. And I praise them just as Jesus praised Peter for declaring that Jesus is "the Christ, the Son of the living God" (Matthew 16:16).

But as a Protestant, I also recognize the sad truth that from time to time leaders of the Church (including leaders of Protestant churches) do not live the kind of lives that Jesus and Paul required for church leadership. Sometimes leaders do not teach the things that Jesus and Paul taught. Sometimes leaders do not exercise their authority in the manner that Jesus and Paul required.

In such tragic circumstances, we must choose between following the kind of authority exerted by a position and the kind of authority exerted by good teaching and a good life. As a Protestant, I believe that we must choose to follow the authority of good teaching and a good life, instead of following the authority of a position that someone holds.[8]

The history of God's people is filled with such courageous decisions to follow the authority exerted by what is *right* instead of the authority exerted by who holds a *position* of power.

For example, Jesus continually defied the authority of the Pharisees and teachers of the law by healing on the Sabbath. Jesus did this because it is more important to treat other people as our neighbors by doing to them what we would have them do to us than to obey any other law, rule or authority.

And, ultimately, Jesus was crucified for following God and God's ways instead of yielding to the authority of religious and political leaders.

Similarly, the apostles followed God and God's ways instead of yielding to the authority of "the Sanhedrin—the full assembly of the elders of Israel" (Acts 5:21). The Sanhedrin ordered the apostles to stop teaching in the name of Jesus. But the apostles refused to obey this order. They told the Sanhedrin: "We must obey God rather than men!" (Acts 5:29).

The Protestant Reformation was sparked because Christians at that time, such as Martin Luther, were determined to follow what they believed was right instead of following leaders who were doing what was wrong.

And my own denomination, the Free Methodists, was founded out of the conviction that it was more important to take a stand against slavery than to obey authorities within the Methodist Church who were willing to let Christians practice slavery.

Therefore, Protestants and Catholics continue to disagree over the inferences to be drawn from Jesus telling Peter: "[Y]ou are Peter, and on this rock I will build my church, and the gates of Hades will not overcome it. I will give you the keys of the kingdom of heaven; whatever you bind on earth will be bound in heaven, and whatever you loose on earth will be loosed in heaven" (Matthew 16:18–19).

But the most important message in these words is something that all Christians—Roman Catholic, Orthodox and Protestant—can agree with. It is a message of hope. Jesus Christ promised us that "I will build my church, and the gates of Hades will not overcome it" (Matthew 16:18).

No matter how dark the circumstances may be, Jesus Christ will still build his Church. Even though John the Baptist is dead and most of the disciples are deserting Jesus, this hope remains unshaken.

And the Church is not on the *defensive*. The Church is on the *offensive*.

The gates of Hades are under attack. The forces of evil are besieged. And their gates—the defenses of their Evil City—will not withstand the assault of the Church that Jesus Christ is building (Matthew 16:18).

This was another way to express the ancient truth proclaimed by Isaiah: there is always hope when we hope in the LORD.

The Church will always renew its strength. The Church will soar on wings like eagles. The Church will run and not grow weary. The Church will walk and not be faint (Isaiah 40:31).

All we must do is flip the light switch in our heart by believing in the Lord Jesus and we will be saved (Acts 16:31). The gates of Hades will not withstand our attack. All we must do is join Peter and all other Christians by declaring our Faith that: "[Jesus is] the Christ, the Son of the living God" (Matthew 16:16). Then we will share the hope and the victory of the Church that the Messiah, Jesus Christ, is building.

Jesus Tells His Disciples He Must Die

I think that Peter is one of the people in the Bible who I would most like to meet. He has such exuberance and enthusiasm. I think it would be a lot of fun to have Peter around.

I also take comfort from the fact that Peter could make big mistakes yet Jesus still loved him and used Peter to accomplish great things for the Church. I need this reassurance because—like Peter—I have such a wonderful talent for saying and doing the wrong thing.

In this chapter we see a classic example of how Peter's exuberance and enthusiasm got him into trouble from time to time.

The setting of the story is soon after a high point in Peter's life. Jesus has just praised Peter for declaring that "[Jesus is] the Christ, the Son of the living God" (Matthew 16:16–19).

Then Jesus "warned his disciples not to tell anyone that he was the Christ" (Matthew 16:20). Jesus evidently wanted time to explain fully to his disciples what it meant to be "the Christ" before the news became public.

What Jesus told his disciples must have been a shock to them. They evidently assumed (as did the other Jews of their time) that "the Christ" would be the Messiah who would deliver Israel from all of its problems by being a combination of King David and King Solomon. Therefore, they would have expected that Jesus would win great military victories like David did and that they would share a wonderful life with Jesus in a palace grander than Solomon built. Indeed, they must have assumed that Jesus would *surpass* all of their expectations.

Instead, Jesus completely *contradicted* all of their expectations. Jesus did not predict that things would go *well* for his disciples and him because he was the Messiah. Jesus emphasized how *difficult* things were going to be! "From that time on Jesus began to explain to his disciples that he must go to Jerusalem and suffer many things at the hands of the elders, chief priests and teachers of the law, and that he must be killed and on the third day be raised to life" (Matthew 16:21).

Good old Peter decided to set Jesus straight. Perhaps Peter thought that Jesus was depressed by all the difficult times they'd been going through recently.

Who wouldn't be depressed and gloomy? John the Baptist was dead. Most of the disciples had recently deserted Jesus after the Feeding of the Five Thousand because Jesus insisted that he was "the bread of God . . . who comes down from heaven and gives life to the world" (John 6:33).

So like any good (if somewhat bossy) friend, Peter decided to cheer Jesus up. "Peter took [Jesus] aside and began to rebuke him. 'Never, Lord!' he said. 'This shall never happen to you!'" (Matthew 16:22).

Peter must have been shocked by Jesus' reaction. "Jesus turned and said to Peter, 'Get behind me, Satan! You are a stumbling block to me; you do not have in mind the things of God, but the things of men.'" (Matthew 16:23).

Instead of thanking Peter for trying to cheer him up, Jesus vehemently rejected Peter's pep talk!

Then Jesus let Peter and the other disciples know in no uncertain terms just how high the cost is to be a follower of Jesus. Jesus said, "If anyone would come after me, he must deny himself and take up his cross and follow me. For whoever wants to save his life will lose it, but whoever loses his life for me will find it" (Matthew 16:24–25).

As Jesus made clear in the Parable of the Sower, his followers must not let troubles, persecutions, worries, the deceitfulness of wealth, or the desire for any other thing hinder them from following him.

At first blush, this cost seems far too high to pay. But Jesus made it clear that any other way of life is far more costly:

"What good will it be for a man if he gains the whole world, yet forfeits his soul? Or what can a man give in exchange for his soul?"
(Matthew 16:26)

Therefore we must pay any price and bear any cross as we follow Jesus in doing for others what we would have them do for us. No matter the cost and the suffering, we must follow Jesus to the Promised Land.

PART FIVE

Jesus Trains His Disciples How to Be Great

Jesus Tells His Disciples To Be Like Little Children

It did not take hundreds of years for Christians to start arguing about who is the greatest. The arguing began while Jesus still walked among us. In fact, perhaps Jesus' praise for Peter when Peter declared that Jesus was "the Christ, the Son of the living God" (Matthew 16:16–19) is what got the other disciples jealous.

Whatever the precise cause, we are told that "[a]n argument started among the disciples as to which of them would be the greatest" (Luke 9:46). Evidently, the argument began as they were walking along the road to Capernaum. So when they got to the house in Capernaum, Jesus "asked them, 'What were you arguing about on the road?'" (Mark 9:33).

The disciples must have known that Jesus wouldn't approve of their arguing about who would be the greatest. So—just like a bunch of guilty children with their hands caught in the cookie jar—"they kept quiet because on the way they had argued about who was the greatest" (Mark 9:34).

Jesus knew their thoughts. And he knew that he needed to impress upon them what true greatness is. So "[s]itting down, Jesus called the Twelve and said, 'If anyone wants to be first, he must be the very last, and the servant of all.'" (Mark 9:35).

Then Jesus used the perfect illustration to make his point. "He called a little child and had him stand among them. And he said: 'I tell you the truth, unless you change and become like little children, you will never enter the kingdom of heaven. Therefore, whoever humbles himself like this child is the greatest in the kingdom of heaven.'" (Matthew 18:2–4).

Several things about Jesus' teaching must have shocked the Twelve.

They must have been upset that someone other than "the Twelve" could be considered the greatest in the kingdom of heaven. They thought they'd already "made the cut" to be at *least* among the twelve greatest. Now Jesus was making clear that they were not necessarily even in the top twelve.

Worse yet, they might not enter the kingdom of heaven at all! Jesus told them that unless they changed and became like little children, they would never even enter the kingdom of heaven. And before you think that this was an idle threat, remember that Judas Iscariot—the traitor who betrayed Jesus—was one of the Twelve.

Imagine how Judas Iscariot and the other disciples must have had their view of themselves and the kingdom of heaven turned upside down when Jesus told them, "[W]hoever humbles himself like this child is the greatest in the kingdom of heaven" (Matthew 18:4).

I know that such thoughts always challenge my instinctive ideas about who must be the greatest at church. My first thoughts turn to those who preach the best, sing the best, or give the most money. But this is wrong. The most important people in the church are the children. They're the ones who can best teach us how to be great.

I remember Senior Pastor Gary Walsh making this point several times a year at Pearce Memorial Church. During the children's sermon, he'd tell the children gathered at the front of the church (and all the rest of us listening from the pews): "Do you know that you children are the most important people here? You are! Because Jesus told us that we're all supposed to be becoming just like you. Usually, we grownups get it exactly wrong. We keep telling you to act like us. But really, we big people are the ones who need to learn how to act from you!"

In the hustle and bustle of the church and of life, children are often overlooked. But not by Jesus.

In fact, he urged the Twelve to welcome children. "Taking [a little child] in his arms, he said to them, 'Whoever welcomes one of these little children in my name welcomes me (Mark 9:36–37); and whoever welcomes me welcomes the one who sent me. For he who is least among you all—he is the greatest.'" (Luke 9:48).

Jesus made the hard things so simple.

What is God like? How should we welcome him?

We don't need hard, lengthy prayers! We don't need gigantic churches! We don't need elaborate rituals! And we don't need to know very much!

We merely need to know how to welcome a little child.

Few scenes are as touching in the Bible as Jesus taking a little child in his arms. And few are more profound.

Yet there is nothing hard about it.

We can all do it.

All that stands in our way are our pretensions to greatness—our reluctance to be the least of all by serving others.

So stop arguing about who is the greatest.

Start living like the greatest people in the kingdom of God.

Become like little children.

And take little children in your arms—the way I loved to take my children and hold them in my arms when they were little.

Jesus Blesses the Little Children

The poor disciples! It seemed as if they never could learn what Jesus wanted them to do!

Just a short time before, Jesus had impressed upon them that they must change and become like little children in order to enter the kingdom of heaven.

Indeed, Jesus had taught them that whoever humbles himself like a little child is the greatest in the kingdom of heaven. And Jesus specifically told them that, "[W]hoever welcomes a little child . . . in my name welcomes me" (Matthew 18:3–5).

But when the disciples had a chance to welcome little children, they flunked the test.

Little children were being "brought to Jesus for him to place his hands on them and pray for them" (Matthew 19:13). If the disciples had put Jesus' recent teachings into practice, they would have welcomed the children as if they were welcoming Jesus himself. But instead "the disciples rebuked those who brought them" (Matthew 19:13).

"When Jesus saw this he was indignant" (Mark 10:14). He knew the disciples needed a refresher course on how important children are. Jesus told the disciples, "Let the little children come to me, and do not hinder them, for the kingdom of God belongs to such as these. I tell you the truth, anyone who will not receive the kingdom of God like a little child will never enter it" (Mark 10:14–15).

Then follows one of those scenes that teaches us more about who Jesus is, what God is like, and how we should live than volumes of theological speculations or hundreds of pages of my writings: Jesus "took the children in his arms, put his hands on them and blessed them" (Mark 10:16).

Jesus Tells the Rich, Young Ruler How to Follow Him

Since it's so simple to do what God wants, why do we find it impossible to do it? Why aren't we always welcoming little children, taking them in our arms, putting our hands on them, and blessing them?

For many of us, the stumbling block to doing what God wants is what the Parable of the Sower calls "the deceitfulness of wealth" (Mark 4:19). Too often we are "like seed sown among thorns[. We] hear the word [of God]; but . . . the deceitfulness of wealth . . . come[s] in and choke[s] the word, making it unfruitful" (Mark 4:18–19).

Such a person came to Jesus "[a]s Jesus started on his way" (Mark 10:17) after taking the children in his arms, putting his hands on them and blessing them. This person had obviously been touched by Jesus' teachings—and perhaps by observing the tenderness with which Jesus held the little children. So the "man ran up to [Jesus] and fell on his knees before him" (Mark 10:17).

A conversation began between this eager, earnest young man and Jesus. "'Good teacher,' he asked, 'what must I do to inherit eternal life?'" (Mark 10:17).

Like most good teachers,[1] Jesus responded to a question with another question. "'Why do you call me good?' Jesus answered. 'No one is good—except God alone.'" (Mark 10:18).

I suspect that Jesus had several motives for asking this question.

One motive was to get the man thinking about who Jesus was. Was Jesus really "just" a man? Or was Jesus something more? Was Jesus God himself?

And I think the other motive was to get the man thinking about what there was about Jesus that made the young man think that Jesus was "good."

Was it the moral content of what Jesus taught? Was it the way Jesus treated children?

Because whatever the young man believed made Jesus "good" was what the young man should start believing and doing if he wanted to "inherit eternal life" (Mark 10:17).

Apparently, the man was stumped by this question. Or at least his answer is not recorded for us.

So—again like a good teacher—Jesus reminded the man of something he already knew in order to help him answer the question. Jesus said, "If you want to enter life, obey the commandments" (Matthew 19:17).

"'Which ones?' the man inquired" (Matthew 19:18). He wanted Jesus to answer his specific, initial question: "[W]hat good thing must I do to get eternal life?" (Matthew 19:16).

Jesus replied by referring to major commandments that must have been well known to the man: "'Do not murder, do not commit adultery, do not steal, do not give false testimony, honor your father and your mother,' and 'love your neighbor as yourself.'" (Matthew 19:18–19).

"Teacher," he declared, "all these I have kept since I was a boy" (Mark 10:20). "What do I still lack?" (Matthew 19:20).

I hear anguish and frustration in the young man's voice. He's sincerely done the best he can do. He's kept all these commandments. And yet—deep in his heart—he knows he still lacks something.

Now he's desperate to hear from Jesus how to fill this void in his life. He's looking—like so many people, but especially like so many earnest, enthusiastic young people—to find out what good thing he must do to set everything right.

In the face of such earnest desperation, "Jesus looked at him and loved him" (Mark 10:21).

It's hard to look at someone and truly love them when they come seeking help. In our hearts, we tend to be like Pharisees, eager to make ourselves look good and the other person look bad. Or we tend to get side-tracked into theological issues designed to show our superior intellect and erudition.

But Jesus always loves anyone who sincerely seeks to find out what their life lacks. And since Jesus loves us, he always tells us the truth—even when it's not what we want to hear.

With this young man, Jesus confirmed: "One thing you lack" (Mark 10:21). Then Jesus told him the one thing he didn't want to hear: "Go, sell everything you have and give to the poor, and you will have treasure in heaven" (Mark 10:21).

Jesus followed this difficult command with the most wonderful invitation the young man would ever receive: "Then come, follow me" (Mark 10:21). "At this the man's face fell. He went away sad, because he had great wealth" (Mark 10:22). The deceitfulness of wealth had claimed another victim! "Jesus looked around and said to his disciples, 'How hard it is for the rich to enter the kingdom of God!'" (Mark 10:23).

I assume that Jesus' voice was full of sadness as he saw the young man walk away. Because Jesus was not trying to be nasty when he asked the man to give away everything to the poor. The man himself knew that his life lacked something. Jesus agreed. So Jesus was trying to help the man see that the deceitfulness of wealth was keeping him from the life he wanted.

The man needed to stop hoping in his money and start hoping in the LORD.

The disciples were amazed that Jesus thought that it was hard for a rich man to enter the kingdom of God (Mark 10:24). In their culture, it was felt that riches were a blessing from God showing that a person was living a good life. So Jesus' observation conflicted with the popular assumption that *rich* people were *righteous* people.

Despite the disciples' amazement, Jesus did not retract or modify his statement. Instead, "Jesus said again, 'Children, how hard it is to enter the kingdom of God! It is easier for a camel to go through the eye of a needle than for a rich man to enter the kingdom of God.'" (Mark 10:24–25).

Now "[t]he disciples were even more amazed, and said to each other, 'Who then can be saved?'" (Mark 10:26).

Who has not asked that question when confronted with how Jesus requires us to live. If Jesus isn't asking us to sell everything we own, then he's asking us to do other "impossible things" such as touching lepers and loving our enemies.

Whether it's troubles, persecutions, the worries of this life, the deceitfulness of wealth, or the desire for other things, Jesus demands that we rid our lives of *all* such things that hinder us from running the race that is set before us—the race to follow Jesus to the Promised Land (Hebrews 12:1–3). Anyone who is honest with themselves must despair of ever being good enough to follow Jesus. Like the disciples, we wonder "Who then can be saved?"

Fortunately, Jesus gives us the same answer he gave the disciples: "With man this is impossible, but not with God; all things are possible with God." (Mark 10:27).

If we hope in ourselves, we will fail.

Our lives will always lack the one thing we most want. We will go away sadly from Jesus instead of accepting his invitation to follow him.

But if we hope in the LORD, we will succeed.

We will live fruitful lives that lack nothing of importance. We will follow Jesus faithfully regardless of how often we face troubles, persecutions, the worries of this life, the deceitfulness of wealth, and the desire for other things.

Hoping in the LORD is the good thing we must do to get eternal life—the good thing we must do to follow Jesus across the ocean of Sin to the Promised Land.[2]

The Good Samaritan

As the time approached for him to be taken up to heaven, Jesus resolutely set out for Jerusalem (Luke 9:51). I always feel a chill when I read these words. Even though Jesus knew that he must soon die for our sins, he did not turn back from the path that God wanted him to take. Despite the cost, he "resolutely set out for Jerusalem" (Luke 9:51).

The very first incident on the way to Jerusalem must have made him wonder if he'd been wasting his time teaching his disciples for the last few years. On the way to Jerusalem, Jesus and his disciples passed through Samaria. Jesus "sent messengers on ahead, who went into a Samaritan village to get things ready for him" (Luke 9:52). Unfortunately, the people in the Samaritan village "did not welcome [Jesus], because Jesus was heading for Jerusalem" (Luke 9:53).

The Jews and the Samaritans hated each other for a variety of reasons stretching back almost 1,000 years. The reasons included religious differences, racial differences, and national differences—the same kind of differences that cause so much hatred and violence throughout the world today.

How did Jesus deal with such differences? How did Jesus act when he was the victim of discrimination and prejudice based on religion, race and national origin?

Not the way most people do! And not the way the disciples wanted to!

The disciples showed their "true colors" by their reaction. "[T]he disciples James and John . . . asked, 'Lord, do you want us to call fire down from heaven to destroy them?'" (Luke 9:54).

Obviously, James and John had not been paying attention when Jesus taught them: "Love your enemies and pray for those who persecute you" (Matthew 5:44). And obviously they totally misunderstood what Jesus meant by commanding his disciples: "[I]n everything, do to others what you would have them do to you" (Matthew 7:12).

So "Jesus turned and rebuked them, and they went to another village" (Luke 9:55–56).

The first step in teaching his disciples how to respond in the face of discrimination and prejudice was to avoid using violence to retaliate. Such a violent response of anger and hatred feeds the cycle of anger, hatred and violence. To prove this, we need look no further than places such as Northern Ireland, Bosnia and the Middle East.

But Jesus wants far more from his disciples than merely avoiding violence in the face of discrimination and prejudice. Jesus wants us to love other people, regardless of all the reasons we have to hate them.

Jesus made this point in a story about a Samaritan that he told a short time after his disciples wanted to burn down the Samaritan village. He told this famous story of "the Good Samaritan" in response to some questions by "an expert in the law [who] stood up to test Jesus" (Luke 10:25).

This "expert" started by asking Jesus a question similar to the question of the rich young ruler in the previous chapter: "Teacher, . . . what must I do to inherit eternal life?" (Luke 10:25).

Jesus responded with the questions: "What is written in the Law? . . . How do you read it?" (Luke 10:26).

The legal expert quoted the laws: "'Love the Lord your God with all your heart and with all your soul and with all your strength and with all your mind'; and, 'Love your neighbor as yourself.'" (Luke 10:27).

Jesus agreed with the legal expert, replying: "You have answered correctly . . . . Do this and you will live" (Luke 10:28).

So far the conversation had gone pretty much the way it did with the rich young ruler. In each case, the person questioning Jesus knew what commandments they needed to keep to inherit eternal life.

But here the conversations diverged.

The rich young ruler came to Jesus on his knees begging to learn what he needed to do to fill the lack he felt in his life. Jesus challenged him to give his riches to the poor and come follow Jesus.

In contrast, this legal expert stood up to test Jesus. He showed no sign that he thought that he lacked anything in his life. Instead, "he wanted to justify himself" (Luke 10:29).

"[S]o he asked Jesus, 'And who is my neighbor?'" (Luke 10:29).

By asking this question, he was using his legal training to trivialize what Jesus was teaching him. Like any skilled lawyer, he decided to quarrel over the exact definition of a word in the law. And he tried to define the word in a manner that would make it easy to comply with the law.

In this case, the key word was "neighbor." The legal expert wanted to define "neighbor" to include as *few people* as possible so that it would be easier to keep the law: "Love your neighbor as yourself" (Luke 10:27).

In response, Jesus defined the term "neighbor" to include as *many people* as possible by telling the story of the Good Samaritan.

I assume that the story is familiar to you. A man was attacked by robbers as he traveled from Jerusalem to Jericho. "They stripped him of his clothes, beat him and went away, leaving him half dead" (Luke 10:30).

The first two people to pass by refused to help the man. This would be contemptible enough even if they were just ordinary people. But they were clergy—a priest and a Levite—people who should be committed to modeling God's ways in their lives.

We are not told exactly why these two people refused to stop and help. Perhaps they were in too much of a hurry. Perhaps they were afraid the robbers would return and attack them. Either reason would be a poor excuse for not helping someone.

But probably the biggest reason that these clergy wouldn't help the man was a religious reason—they didn't want to become ceremonially unclean by touching an injured person. That's why Jesus stressed that both clergy "passed by on the other side" when they saw the man (Luke 10:31–32).

If they became ceremonially unclean, they couldn't perform their role as clergy until enough time had passed and they had performed the necessary rituals. This was the type of hypocritical religiosity that most infuriated and angered Jesus.

It was the attitude of a typical Pharisee. Worrying more about themselves than about other people. Caring more about *keeping rules* than about *helping people*.

In contrast, the Good Samaritan acted the way Jesus wants us to act. As the Samaritan traveled, he "came where the man was; and when he saw him, he took pity on him" (Luke 10:33).

Jesus always prefers pity to piety.

The Samaritan's compassion is all the more remarkable and commendable because the Samaritan had plenty of excuses for hating the man. Based on the religious, racial and national prejudices of the Samaritans, he easily could have thought to himself, "Good! That Jew got what he deserved. I hope he dies. The only good Jew is a dead Jew!"

Jesus' own disciples had such hate in their hearts when they wanted to destroy a Samaritan village with fire from heaven.

Fortunately, instead of being motivated by the hatred that his culture taught, the Samaritan was motivated by the kind of love that Jesus taught. He helped the person.

Furthermore, the Samaritan didn't merely use a cellular phone to call for help like we might do today. We'd feel we were "saints" if we were willing to spend a dollar on a phone call and were willing to interrupt listening to the radio in order to help a stranger.

The Samaritan "wasted" a considerable amount of time and money to help this stranger who his culture taught him to hate. As Jesus told the legal expert:

> "He went to him and bandaged his wounds, pouring on oil and wine. Then he put the man on his own donkey, took him to an inn and took care of him. The next day he took out two silver coins and gave them to the innkeeper. 'Look after him,' he said, 'and when I return, I will reimburse you for any extra expense you may have.'"
> (Luke 10:34–35)

Now Jesus was ready to get back to debating with the legal expert what the word "neighbor" meant. Jesus asked him, "Which of these three do you think was a neighbor to the man who fell into the hands of robbers?" (Luke 10:36).

At least this legal expert was smart enough to know he'd met a better lawyer than he was. And he was honest enough to answer Jesus truthfully. So the legal expert replied: "The one who had mercy on him" (Luke 10:37).

We are not supposed to define "neighbor" narrowly to include as few people as possible. We are supposed to look as hard as we can every day to find people who we can treat as "neighbors." Even if the person is someone who we have good reason to hate, we still must love them as our neighbor.[1]

Furthermore, Jesus isn't content with us merely having the correct intellectual understanding of what it means to love our neighbor as ourselves. Jesus demands that we put love into action.

And so Jesus told the legal expert the same thing that he tells each of us today: "Go and do likewise" (Luke 10:37). Go follow Jesus, being a Good Samaritan, a good neighbor, who blesses *all* peoples in the Promised Land.

Mary and Martha

This is one of my favorite stories in the Bible because it's so true to life.

Jesus and his disciples were on their way toward Jerusalem. A woman named Martha graciously opened her home to Jesus. There was a great deal of work involved cleaning and cooking for so many guests. But Martha's sister, Mary, did not help Martha with all the cleaning and cooking. She plopped down at Jesus' feet listening to him. So Martha got mad at Mary for not helping with all the housework.

I am constantly in trouble with my wife for the same reason that Mary was in trouble with Martha. I'm off doing things that I want to do instead of doing the housework that my wife wants me to do. (Of course, my excuses for not helping with the housework are not as good as Mary's reason—I'm not sitting at Jesus' feet listening to him.)

Martha went to Jesus for help. She said, "Lord, don't you care that my sister has left me to do the work by myself? Tell her to help me!" (Luke 10:40).

This request seemed only fair. And you'd think that Jesus would tend to support Martha who (after all) was kind enough to invite Jesus into her home. But Jesus knew that the best way to repay Martha for her kindness was to tell her the truth rather than to do what she wanted him to do. Jesus had seen that "Martha was distracted by all the preparations that had to be made" (Luke 10:40). So he knew that Martha had to learn better time management and better prioritizing of her activities.

Therefore, Jesus told her: "Martha, Martha, . . . you are worried and upset about many things, but only one thing is needed. Mary has chosen what is better, and it will not be taken away from her" (Luke 10:41–42).

Like any good house guest, Jesus was letting Martha know that she should relax. He didn't mind if the house wasn't perfectly clean and if the food wasn't perfectly prepared. He wanted Martha to sit down and visit with him. After all, that was why he'd come to be a guest in her home.

This comment by Jesus was a real life application of the Parable of the Sower. Jesus was reminding Martha that "the worries of this life . . . come in and choke the word, making it unfruitful" (Mark 4:19). Jesus wanted her to stop being worried and distracted by housework so that she could become "like . . . good soil, hear[ing] the word, accept[ing] it, and produc[ing] a crop—thirty, sixty or even a hundred times what was sown" (Mark 4:20).

This lesson is important for both men and women to learn. Men can get too worried and distracted by their golf game and their career to take the time to learn from Jesus. And, especially now that women have careers as well as housework to keep them busy, women have to take time to learn from Jesus.

However, I think that this story has a special importance for women. Jesus treated women with respect. Jesus believed that women should do more than merely do housework. Jesus believed that women were intellectually and spiritually able to learn about the most important things in life—to worship the LORD in spirit and in truth. In Jesus' Promised Land, all peoples will be blessed, including women. Because Jesus still encourages women to come, sit at his feet, and learn from him.

The Rich Fool

Jesus told the story of the Rich Fool "when a crowd of many thousands had gathered, so that they were trampling on one another" (Luke 12:1). As Jesus was teaching, someone in the crowd interrupted by saying: "Teacher, tell my brother to divide the inheritance with me" (Luke 12:13).

I find it fascinating that Martha asked Jesus to help her get her sister to divide the housework with her. And now a man was asking Jesus to help get his brother to divide the inheritance with him.

In each case, Jesus did not give the answer that the person wanted. Martha was told to stop worrying. The man was told to stop being greedy.

Martha had to be reminded that "the worries of this life . . . [can] come in and choke the word, making it unfruitful" (Mark 4:19). This man had to be reminded that "the deceitfulness of wealth . . . [can] come in and choke the word, making it unfruitful" (Mark 4:19).

Jesus rebuffed the man's rude interruption by replying, "Man, who appointed me a judge or an arbiter between you?" (Luke 12:14). Then Jesus said to the crowd, "Watch out! Be on your guard against all kinds of greed; a man's life does not consist in the abundance of his possessions" (Luke 12:15).

Obviously, Jesus did not agree with the bumper stickers that say: "He who dies with the most toys wins." To make this point as strongly as possible, Jesus told the crowd the Parable of the Rich Fool.

The "problem" began when "[t]he ground of a certain rich man produced a good crop" (Luke 12:16). Instead of enjoying his good fortune, this rich fool simply worried more than ever. "He thought to himself, 'What shall I do? I have no place to store my crops.'" (Luke 12:17).

It is very easy for money to become a source of worry instead of a source of joy. I've noticed this same tendency in me and many other people. The more money we save, the more we worry about our money and the more we fear that we may lose it.

Plus, it's easy to waste incredible amounts of time investing money. One reason I put my money in mutual funds instead of actively trading stocks and bonds is to prevent such wheeling and dealing from wasting my time.

Nevertheless, I often find myself worrying about whether my 401(k) is building up fast enough for me to retire. I often find my thoughts wandering to which investments I should have my money in. And, despite my exhaustion at the end of the week, I love to watch Louis Rukeyser and his guests discuss Wall Street on Friday nights instead of resting or spending time with my family.

When I catch myself thinking about such things, I get angry with myself. Because I realize I'm becoming a "rich fool." The more money I get, the more I worry about losing it! And the busier I get, the more time I find myself wasting to get even more money! Such is "the deceitfulness of wealth!"

Two thousand years ago, they didn't have mutual funds or 401(k) funds. So the rich fool in Jesus' parable couldn't increase his stock market investments with all his extra money.

Instead, he said to himself: "This is what I'll do. I will tear down my barns and build bigger ones, and there I will store all my grain and my goods. And I'll say to myself, 'You have plenty of good things laid up for many years. Take life easy; eat, drink and be merry'" (Luke 12:18–19).

I once heard someone comment that one of the key signs this man was a fool was that all these thoughts were in the future tense. He "will do" a number of things and only then "will he" be happy.

In fact, as this person pointed out and as I have observed again and again, these kind of people *never* "Take life easy; eat, drink and be merry."

After all, there was no reason that this rich fool couldn't start enjoying his money *immediately*. But instead, he fooled himself into thinking that he needed even *more* money before he could start enjoying himself.

As some fabulously wealthy man is reported to have said when asked how much more money he wanted, he answered, "Always just a little bit more than I have!" This is part of the deceitfulness of wealth that Jesus spoke of in the Parable of the Sower.

That's one reason why I always reject the thought that I should put off doing something "until I retire." Or for that matter, that's why I always reject putting off doing *anything* because there's some excuse for not doing it today.

What I've noticed about most retired people is that they live the same way *after* they retire as they did *before* they retired. If they were active and enjoyed life, they stay active and enjoy life. But if they always found excuses for not doing things before they retired, they'll keep right on finding excuses for not doing things after they retire.

Every day going and coming from work I drive by the cemetery where my Grandmother and Grandfather Harner are buried on the southern edge of the Village of Spencerport in Fairfield Cemetery. And sometimes, when I'm wondering whether to do something like take my kids to Disney World *again*, or go to Paris with my wife to celebrate our wedding anniversary, I "ask" my grandparents, "Should I do it?" Because there are always multitudes of reasons for *not* doing something!

And my grandparents always "remind" me from their graves: "Yes! Do it! Sure there are risks that things can go wrong. But the only certainty is that you'll end up dead like us! So do everything you want to do *now* while you still have time!"

I often reflect as well that "It's not quite true that 'We can't take it with us.' We can't take physical possessions with us. But we *can* take our memories with us." So if my wife and I spend a romantic week in Paris, we'll always have those memories to cheer us throughout all eternity.

The rich fool in Jesus' parable did not understand this. He probably sincerely thought that *someday* he'd enjoy himself.

God intruded on this self-deception with stark reality. "God said to him, 'You fool! This very night your life will be demanded from you. Then who will get what you have prepared for yourself?'" (Luke 12:20).

We aren't told what killed the rich fool. But I'm inclined to think that he died of a heart attack or a stroke brought on by worrying about what to do with all his money.

Such things do happen. I remember hearing a story about a man who was a very successful stock market investor. He started with $5,000 and turned it into a fortune. But when he was about 60 his health collapsed. As he told a friend shortly before he died: "I ruined my health with so much fretting and stress. It was the stupidest thing I've ever done."

And the rich fool wasn't just unlucky. He wouldn't have been proven wise if he'd only lived longer. Jesus said, "This is how it will be with anyone who stores up things for himself but is not rich toward God" (Luke 12:21).

Since we all die, it is foolish for any of us to store things up for ourselves. Because one night—no matter how long we live—God will tell us our time is up. And then we will face with despair the question: "[W]ho will get what you have prepared for yourself?" (Luke 12:20).

Therefore, the only way to live wisely is to live the way Jesus told us to live in the Sermon on the Mount. Indeed, he repeated part of that advice to conclude this Parable of the Rich Fool. Jesus said:

> "Therefore I tell you, do not worry about your life, what you will eat; or about your body, what you will wear. Life is more than food, and the body more than clothes . . . . .
>
> . . . . And do not set your heart on what you will eat or drink; do not worry about it. For the pagan world runs after all such things, and your Father knows that you need them. But seek his kingdom, and these things will be given to you as well."
>
> (Luke 12:22–31)

Jesus Welcomes Sinners

Why did Jesus "resolutely set out for Jerusalem" (Luke 9:51) even though he knew that a shameful, agonizing death on a cross awaited him there?

As with any question "Why?" there are many different perspectives from which to answer it. But I believe that the best answer is that Jesus loved sinners so much that he was willing to pay any price to save them—even if the price was a shameful, agonizing death on a cross.

Jesus' immense love for sinners shines through the three stories that are the subject of this chapter. The setting for these three stories was that "the tax collectors and 'sinners' were all gathering around to hear [Jesus]. But the Pharisees and the teachers of the law muttered, 'This man welcomes sinners and eats with them.'" (Luke 15:1–2).

I'm sure that Jesus was exasperated and angry at this attitude of the Pharisees and the teachers of the law. They should have been rejoicing that people were willing to change their lives and follow God. Instead, all they could do was criticize, condemn and find fault. They were the kind of people who always love to be "muttering" something bad about somebody.

Jesus told three stories to illustrate how happy we should be when "tax collectors and sinners" gather around to hear Jesus teach them how to change their lives.

199

In the first story, someone has 100 sheep and loses one of them. The person seeks the lost sheep until he finds it. "And when he finds it, he joyfully puts it on his shoulders and goes home" (Luke 15:5–6).

The person's joy is so great that he can't contain himself. When he gets home "he calls his friends and neighbors together and says, 'Rejoice with me; I have found my lost sheep'" (Luke 15:6).

Jesus has the same reaction toward people who are lost and wandering from God. He will search for that person until he finds him or her. And when Jesus joyfully carries that person back "home" to the way their life should be (back home to the Promised Land), he knows that "there will be more rejoicing in heaven over one sinner who repents than over ninety-nine righteous persons who do not need to repent" (Luke 15:7).

In the second story, a woman loses one of her ten silver coins. Frantically, she lights a lamp, sweeps the house, and searches carefully until she finds it. "And when she finds it, she calls her friends and neighbors together and says, 'Rejoice with me; I have found my lost coin'" (Luke 15:9).

In the same way, Jesus searches diligently for each lost sinner. And when he finds one and restores that person to the kind of life they should enjoy, Jesus knows "there is rejoicing in the presence of the angels of God over one sinner who repents" (Luke 15:10).

In the third story (well-known as the story of the Prodigal Son), a father's younger son demanded that his father give him his share of the inheritance even before the father is dead. The father honored the request and gave the son his inheritance. The son took the entire inheritance, "set off for a distant country and there squandered his wealth in wild living" (Luke15:13).

It was fun while it lasted. Then the son faced the harsh realities of life. "After he had spent everything, there was a severe famine in that whole country, and he began to be in need" (Luke 15:14). In his desperation, he took one of the most disgusting, demeaning jobs imaginable (especially for a Jew): he fed pigs. He became so hungry that "[h]e longed to fill his stomach with the pods that the pigs were eating, but no one gave him anything" (Luke 15:16).

At last, "he came to his senses" (Luke 15:17). He finally realized his wickedness and foolishness. He'd run far away from a father who gave him everything to a distant land where nobody gave him anything. He said to himself: "How many of my father's hired men have food to spare, and here I am starving to death!" (Luke 15:17).

He decided to go back to his father and tell him: "Father, I have sinned against heaven and against you. I am no longer worthy to be called your son; make me like one of your hired men" (Luke 15:18–19).

He did more than think about changing his life. He took the first steps toward putting his life back together again: "he got up and went to his father" (Luke 15:20).

Now we come to another one of those word pictures that tells us more about who God is, what God is like, and how God wants us to live than volumes of books about religion or hundreds of pages of my writings.

In the chapter titled "Jesus Blesses The Little Children," the word picture was of Jesus taking small children in his arms, putting his hands on them, and blessing them (Mark 10:16).

This time the word picture is of the father welcoming his wayward son home: while the returning son "was still a long way off, his father saw him and was filled with compassion for him; he ran to his son, threw his arms around him and kissed him" (Luke 15:20).

That is the kind of father I want to be. And so in my first letters to my children (written in the Bibles that I gave them as their first present after their birth) I let them know that I'd always welcome them home and love them no matter what they did.

In Sarah's letter I wrote: "[T]ake comfort from this assurance: no matter what you do or say, both your Heavenly Father and your earthly Father will always forgive you (if you ask for mercy and are merciful to others) and will always love you (even if you do not ask for love or mercy)."

In Andy's letter I wrote: "[I]f you do wrong, remember that: Blessed are the merciful for they will be shown mercy. (Matthew 5:7). No matter what you have done, you can always be forgiven by, and reconciled with, your Father on Earth and your Father in Heaven. You can always come Home."

And what a homecoming repentant sinners get!

In Jesus' story, the father did not rebuke his son. He did not sit down and complain about all the money that had been wasted.

The returning son asked only to be forgiven and to become a servant of his father. He knew he was no longer worthy to be called his son.

But his father quickly affirmed that his son was still his *son*—not a *servant*.

Instead of dwelling on the past, the father was going to celebrate the present. "[T]he father said to his servants, 'Quick! Bring the best robe and put it on him. Put a ring on his finger and sandals on his feet. Bring the fattened calf and kill it. Let's have a feast and celebrate. For this son of mine was dead and is alive again; he was lost and is found.'" (Luke 15:22–24).

That is the kind of joyous welcome we can always expect from God whenever we come home to the Promised Land. Because—as impossible as it seems—God loves us even more than we love our children.

The Proud Pharisee and the Humble Sinner

Once again, Jesus ran into some people "who were confident of their own righteousness and looked down on everybody else" (Luke 18:9). To show them how far they were from being truly righteous, Jesus told them a story about a Pharisee and a tax collector who went up to the temple to pray.

The Pharisee was a legend in his own mind. He stood up (the normal posture for praying in that culture) and prayed: "God, I thank you that I am not like other men—robbers, evildoers, adulterers—or even like this tax collector" (Luke 18:11).

In the guise of "thanking" God for making him so "good," he tried to make himself look good by making everybody else look bad. He worshiped the LORD in rules and in boasts, instead of in spirit and in truth. Therefore, the Pharisee was careful to explain to everyone listening what made him so good: "I fast twice a week and give a tenth of all I get" (Luke 18:12). A Pharisee always thinks that being righteous enough to live in the Promised Land means *following rules* instead of *blessing people*.

Pharisees are always looking for ways to sacrifice. This Pharisee was, therefore, proud that he sacrificed food and money for God. But, as Jesus told some Pharisees on another occasion, "[G]o and learn what this means: 'I desire mercy, not sacrifice.'" (Matthew 9:13).

No wonder tax collectors and other "sinners" loved to be around Jesus. They longed to find the mercy that they knew they needed for their sins.

And so, the tax collector who went to the temple in Jesus' story "stood at a distance. He would not even look up to heaven, but beat his breast and said, 'God, have mercy on me, a sinner.'" (Luke 18:13).

I'm sure that the people listening "who were confident of their own righteousness and looked down on everybody else" were angry when Jesus told them that the tax collector, rather than the Pharisee, "went home justified before God. For everyone who exalts himself will be humbled, and he who humbles himself will be exalted" (Luke 18:14). People who ask God for mercy will heal their Promised Land.

To apply this story of the Pharisee and the tax collector today, I think it is best to think of the Pharisee as a "Church-Goer." Because, as Church-Goers, we must be ever vigilant to prevent the errors of the Pharisee from slipping into our thoughts and actions.

One error of the Pharisee that afflicts Church-Goers is spending our time thinking up rules of do's and don'ts. Don't make up a list of things you will sacrifice. Because God desires mercy not sacrifice.

Another error of the Pharisee that afflicts Church-Goers is spending our time comparing ourselves to other people who we think aren't as good as us. These other people can be people who don't come to church at all. Or these other people can be like the tax collector. They come to church, but stand "at a distance." They don't measure up to our ideas about how people should act.

Instead of wasting time thinking how bad other people are, spend time thinking how you can become better. Then put your thoughts into action.

Become great by humbling yourself like a little child. Welcome children. Receive the kingdom of God by becoming like a little child yourself. Let Jesus take you in his arms, put his hands on you, and bless you. Do not let the deceitfulness of wealth stop you from following Jesus. Love your neighbor as yourself. Help people who are hurting. Do not let the worries of life distract you from living a fruitful life. Guard against all kinds of greed. Do not be a rich fool. Rejoice when people who are lost come Home. Do not look down on anybody else. Beg God to have mercy on you, a sinner.

Become more than merely a Church-Goer. Become a fully-trained disciple of Jesus Christ. Heal your Promised Land. Worship the LORD in spirit and in truth. Bless all other peoples in the Promised Land.

PART SIX

*Jesus Sacrifices
Himself
to Save Others*

Jesus Raises Lazarus from the Dead

We do not usually think about Jesus having good friends. But he did!

Among his best friends were the family of Mary, Martha and Lazarus. They were siblings who lived in Bethany, a town less than two miles from Jerusalem. Since this was a reasonably short walk to Jerusalem and its temple, Jesus apparently stayed in Bethany quite often (Mark 11:11).

We met Mary and Martha in a previous chapter. While Jesus was a guest at Martha's house, Martha complained that Mary was sitting at Jesus' feet listening to him instead of helping her with all the housework. Jesus replied, "Martha, Martha, . . . you are worried and upset about many things, but only one thing is needed. Mary has chosen what is better, and it will not be taken away from her" (Luke 10:38–42).

The Gospel of John tells us that "Jesus loved Martha and her sister and Lazarus" (John 11:5). So when Lazarus became gravely ill, "the sisters sent word to Jesus, 'Lord, the one you love is sick.'" (John 11:1,3).

Nevertheless, Jesus waited several days before setting out to see Lazarus.

His disciples probably assumed that Jesus was afraid to go near Jerusalem—even to see his sick friend, Lazarus. Because, when Jesus told his disciples that they were going to Bethany, they objected on the grounds that it was too dangerous. They said, "But Rabbi, . . . a short while ago the Jews tried to stone you, and yet you are going back there?" (John 11:7–8).

Jesus refused to be intimidated by such fears. He told the disciples: "Are there not twelve hours of daylight? A man who walks by day will not stumble . . ." (John 11:9).

Then Jesus "told them plainly, 'Lazarus is dead, and for your sake I am glad I was not there, so that you may believe. But let us go to him.'" (John 11:14–15).

Now the disciples *really* must have doubted the wisdom of returning to Bethany. Perhaps it was worth running such risks if Lazarus still lived. Then they could visit him and Jesus could heal him. But what was the point of risking death to see somebody who was already dead!

Despite such doubts, Thomas (who later became famous as "Doubting Thomas" because, at first, he doubted that Jesus had risen from the dead) "encouraged" the disciples to follow Jesus with this gloomy comment: "Let us also go, that we may die with him" (John 11:16).

It is to the credit of the disciples that they continued following Jesus despite the dangers that they faced. We often criticize the disciples for deserting Jesus when he was arrested in the Garden of Gethsemane. But how many of us would have had the courage and faithfulness to follow him that long?

Would we have had the faith of a Doubting Thomas? When we recognize the perils into which Jesus is leading us and when we doubt the wisdom of what Jesus is asking us to do, do we still have the courage and faithfulness to say: "Let us also go, that we may die with him."?

Burdened by such gloomy, discouraging thoughts, Jesus and the disciples arrived at Bethany. By then, "Lazarus had already been in the tomb for four days . . . and many Jews had come to Martha and Mary to comfort them in the loss of their brother" (John 11:17–19). This scene must have depressed everyone even more.

"When Martha heard that Jesus was coming, she went out to meet him, but Mary stayed at home" (John 11:20). Martha greeted Jesus with words that expressed her frustration at his late arrival—and maybe carried an implied rebuke: "Lord, . . . if you had been here, my brother would not have died" (John 11:21).

Perhaps something in Jesus' eyes gave her hope, however. Perhaps she realized that it is never too late for Jesus to come and help us. Because she added, "But I know that even now God will give you whatever you ask" (John 11:22).

Jesus gave her hope. He said, "Your brother will rise again" (John 11:23). Martha answered: "I know he will rise again in the resurrection at the last day" (John 11:24). I suspect that in her tone of voice there was an unspoken plea for Jesus to do more than tell her to wait for "the last day" to see her brother again. Why else would she have told Jesus that she knew "that even now God will give you whatever you ask"? (John 11:22).

Jesus responded with this astounding claim: "I am the resurrection and the life. He who believes in me will live, even though he dies; and whoever lives and believes in me will never die. Do you believe this?" (John 11:25–26).

"'Yes, Lord,' she told him" (John 11:27).

With this brief reply expressing her faith in Jesus, Martha became far more than a busy housekeeper distracted by worry. Her brother's death had taught her just how trivial such matters were. Now—like Mary—she chose what was better, and it would not be taken away from her (Luke 10:42). It *could* not be taken away from her because Jesus is Lord.

In the face of death, Martha latched onto the face of Jesus. She told him: "I believe that you are the Christ, the Son of God, who was to come into the world" (John 11:27).

"[A]fter she had said this, she went back and called her sister Mary aside" (John 11:28). She told Mary that Jesus was asking for her (John 11:28). "When Mary heard this, she got up quickly and went to him" (John 11:29).

Many of the people who were comforting Mary followed her. They assumed that she was going to the tomb to mourn. So there were many witnesses to what happened next (John 11:19,31).

"When Mary reached the place where Jesus was and saw him, she fell at his feet . . ." (John 11:32). And "[w]hen Jesus saw her weeping, and the Jews who had come along with her also weeping, he was deeply moved in spirit and troubled" (John 11:33).[1]

Jesus asked, "Where have you laid him?" (John 11:34). When they answered, "Come and see, Lord" (John 11:34), Jesus could not hold back his tears.

"Jesus wept" (John 11:35).

And so we come to another picture that tells us more about who God is, what God is like, and how God wants us to live than volumes of books about religion or hundreds of pages of my writings.

Jesus comes to us when things go wrong. Jesus comforts us in our grief and despair. Jesus weeps with us.

In the same way, we should come to people when things go wrong in their lives. We should comfort them in their grief and despair. We should weep with them.

Those who saw Jesus weeping said, "See how he loved him!" (John 11:36). But some of them complained: "Could not he who opened the eyes of the blind man have kept this man from dying?" (John 11:37).

Who has not felt a similar frustration in the face of death? On the one hand, we sense God's love in the ways he comforts us. But on the other hand, we feel frustration—and even anger—that God didn't stop this terrible thing from happening.

Fortunately, Mary and Martha did not have to wait long to see how God used this tragedy to bring a triumph. "Jesus, once more deeply moved, came to the tomb. It was a cave with a stone laid across the entrance" (John 11:38). At this scene of ultimate despair, Jesus brought hope. He said, "Take away the stone" (John 11:39).

Martha started worrying. Ever the compulsive housekeeper, she worried about the bad smell from the decaying body. She objected, "But, Lord, . . . by this time there is a bad odor, for he has been there four days" (John 11:39).[2]

Jesus needed to remind Martha of her earlier confidence that he was the Messiah and that God would do whatever he asked. Jesus said, "Did I not tell you that if you believed, you would see the glory of God?" (John 11:40).

We often need similar reminders. In the face of the tombs of despair in our lives, we forget who Jesus is. We forget our confidence that God can do anything. At such moments, we need to be reminded that we can always find hope in the LORD.

Despite the foolishness of Jesus' request and the likelihood that there would be a bad odor, "they took away the stone" (John 11:41). I'm sure that none of them had enough faith *really* to believe that Jesus was about to raise Lazarus from the dead. Fortunately, they didn't need that much faith. All they needed was enough faith to do what Jesus asked them to do—take the stone away from the tomb. Jesus did the rest.

"Jesus called in a loud voice, 'Lazarus, come out!'" (John 11:43).

Imagine the look on Mary and Martha's tear-streaked faces as they looked at the tomb to see if Jesus could raise their brother from the dead. They didn't have to wait long. "The dead man came out, his hands and feet wrapped with strips of linen, and a cloth around his face" (John 11:44).

As their tears of sorrow turned into tears of joy, Jesus thought of Lazarus. How typical of Jesus. If I had just raised someone from the dead, I'd be distracted by thinking about how great I was. I'd probably start making a speech about how great I was. But not Jesus. Jesus always thought about helping others instead of about helping himself.

That was why Jesus was the one who realized that Lazarus still was not totally freed from the shackles of death. He was still wrapped in strips of linen with a cloth around his face. Instead of boasting, Jesus quickly thought about how to make Lazarus comfortable. He said: "Take off the grave clothes and let him go" (John 11:44).

That is how Jesus restores hope to us. He doesn't merely take care of the big things such as calling forth our "dead dreams" from the tombs where they've been buried. He takes care of the little details such as the "grave clothes" that bind our movements and blind our sight.

Because Jesus is "the resurrection and the life" (John 11:25). Even though we've never seen him resurrect someone from the dead, we can be certain that he will always resurrect our hopes and dreams from the tombs where they've been buried. Jesus won't merely weep with us in our despair. Jesus will bring hope back to our lives in the midst of our despair. And Jesus will give us life after death, calling each of us by name as he reunites us with those we love.

Caiaphas Tells the Sanhedrin That Jesus Must Die

For every action there is a reaction.

Jesus had just performed an amazing miracle—raising Lazarus from the dead. Now the reaction set in. The religious leaders decided they must kill Jesus!

The chief priests and the ruling religious body (called the Sanhedrin) quickly learned about Jesus raising Lazarus from the dead. They also learned that "many of the Jews who had come to visit Mary, and had seen what Jesus did, put their faith in him" (John 11:45). They learned these things because some of those who had been there "went to the Pharisees and told them what Jesus had done" (John 11: 46).

Upon hearing these tidings, "the chief priests and the Pharisees called a meeting of the Sanhedrin" (John 11:47). The Sanhedrin was the name given to "the ruling council of the Jews in Jesus' time. It was made up of seventy men, and the leader was the high priest."[1] The Sanhedrin was a cherished remnant of autonomy and self-rule among the Jews. Even though their land was occupied and ruled by the hated Romans, the Jews could still decide for themselves many matters based on Jewish laws and customs.

The chief priests and Pharisees were so upset by the news about many people putting their faith in Jesus that they called a meeting of the Sanhedrin to discuss the matter. Or perhaps it would be more accurate to say that they called a meeting of the Sanhedrin to rubber stamp the decision that the powerful inner clique had already made—Jesus must die!

The meeting began with people wringing their hands over the problem Jesus represented. "What are we accomplishing?" they asked. "Here is this man performing many miraculous signs. If we let him go on like this, everyone will believe in him, and then the Romans will come and take away both our place and our nation" (John 11:47–48).

In a narrow sense, "the place" they were worrying about losing was the temple.[2] But in a broader sense, these politicians were primarily worried about losing their "place" of power and prestige. Therefore, this story warns us against allowing the love of power and prestige to influence our motives or our actions.

This is not to say that the fears of the squirming politicians in the Sanhedrin were groundless. History itself showed that their fears were justified. They well remembered that—about 600 years before—the Babylonians destroyed the temple and carried the Ancient Israelites into exile. And, a generation after Jesus was crucified, the Romans destroyed Jerusalem and its temple, forcing the Jews into an exile that lasted almost 2,000 years—until the creation of modern Israel after World War II in the wake of the horrors of the Nazi Holocaust.[3]

But the cynical politicians who guided the Sanhedrin in Jesus' time totally misunderstood how to save their "place" and their nation. For example, Caiaphas, who was high priest that year, said, "You know nothing at all! You do not realize that it is better for you that one man die for the people than that the whole nation perish" (John 11:49–50).

Caiaphas said these words the way a cynical politician would say them. He was proud that he would stop at nothing to maintain his power. Even if it meant murdering an innocent man. He'd sneer at anybody who hesitated to take such strong measures to stay in power.

Many a politician has followed Caiaphas in such Machiavellian schemes throughout the ages. As a result, many an innocent person has been undermined, betrayed and destroyed.

But God is not mocked. God is all powerful. God turns the schemes of the wicked against them.

And so, writing years later, John saw the irony in Caiaphas' cynical statement. Caiaphas had been right! But not in the way *Caiaphas hoped!* Caiaphas was right in the way that *Jesus hoped* and foresaw! Because "as high priest that year [Caiaphas] prophesied that Jesus would die for the Jewish nation, and not only for that nation but also for the scattered children of God, to bring them together and make them one" (John 11:51–52)—to bless all peoples in the Promised Land.

Caiaphas—like many a wicked schemer through the ages—did not realize that for every action there is a reaction. Caiaphas did not realize that the betrayal and murder of Jesus would lead to a new birth of love and life that will ultimately triumph over Caiaphas and anyone who thinks and acts like him. Such wicked schemers will lose their places of power and prestige to everyone for whom Jesus died—to everyone who hopes in the LORD—as Jesus brings us together and makes us one in the Promised Land.

Jesus Tells Judas Iscariot to Leave Mary Alone

The danger to Jesus' life was now extremely high.

For quite some time, Jesus' life had been in danger. Early in his ministry he was nearly killed by people from his hometown when he dared to preach in their synagogue that God cared for people who were not Jews and that a prophet is never accepted in his hometown (Luke 4:16–30). On a later occasion, some "Pharisees went out and plotted how they might kill Jesus" after he healed on the Sabbath (Matthew 12:9–14).

Now the plot to kill Jesus reached the highest level of the Jewish political and religious leadership. In the wake of reports that Jesus raised Lazarus from the dead, these leaders feared that Jesus' growing popularity would be the spark that would lead to the Romans destroying the temple and destroying the Jewish nation. To prevent this disaster, the high priest himself, Caiaphas, declared that Jesus must die. "So from that day on they plotted to take his life" (John 11:49–50,53).

Jesus was aware of the danger. "Therefore Jesus no longer moved about publicly among the Jews. Instead he withdrew to a region near the desert . . . where he stayed with his disciples" (John 11:54).

"When it was almost time for the Jewish Passover, many went up from the country to Jerusalem . . ." (John 11:55). These visitors to Jerusalem wondered whether Jesus would dare to come to Jerusalem for the Passover. There was no television coverage about Jesus' whereabouts or intentions. People "kept looking for Jesus, and as they stood in the temple area they asked one another, 'What do you think? Isn't he coming to the [Passover] Feast at all?'" (John 11:56).

Jesus was popular with many of these people visiting Jerusalem—as would be proven when they gave him such a warm, triumphal entry to Jerusalem on "Palm Sunday" (John 12:12–14). Unfortunately, the people visiting Jerusalem were not the only ones looking for Jesus. The religious leaders were also looking for Jesus so they could kill him. Indeed, "the chief priests and Pharisees had given orders that if anyone found out where Jesus was, he should report it so that they might arrest him" (John 11:57).

The chief priests and Pharisees could not have imagined how well their efforts to learn Jesus' whereabouts would succeed. One of Jesus' inner circle of twelve disciples, Judas Iscariot, would betray Jesus so they could arrest him and kill him.

The event that triggered Judas' betrayal happened just outside Jerusalem in the "suburb" of Bethany where Jesus' good friends, Mary, Martha and Lazarus lived. Judas and the other disciples were guests at a dinner given in Jesus' honor—perhaps to thank Jesus for raising Lazarus from the dead a short time before.[1]

As seems typical of the two sisters, Mary and Martha, Martha was serving dinner while Mary was paying more attention to Jesus than to the housework (John 12:2–3).2 "Lazarus was among those reclining at the table with [Jesus]. Then Mary took about a pint of pure nard, an expensive perfume; she poured it on Jesus' feet and wiped his feet with her hair. And the house was filled with the fragrance of the perfume" (John 12:2–3).

We are not told why Mary poured this expensive perfume on Jesus' feet and wiped his feet with her hair. One obvious reason was to thank Jesus for raising her brother, Lazarus, from the dead. It also may be that she was worried about all the plots to kill Jesus so she wanted to do something very nice to Jesus as a gesture of support and sympathy at this difficult and dangerous time.

Judas Iscariot "objected, 'Why wasn't this perfume sold and the money given to the poor? It was worth a year's wages.'" (John 12:4–5).

A number of other disciples also complained about this "waste" of valuable perfume (Matthew 26:8–9; Mark 14:4–5).3 Some of those present—presumably including Judas Iscariot—"rebuked her harshly" (Mark 14:5).

Perhaps some of those present sincerely cared about "the poor." Even so, you would think they would be hesitant to criticize someone who was doing something nice for Jesus. They were awfully quick to say that using the perfume on Jesus was a "waste."

Furthermore, Judas Iscariot's objections were not based on any love for the poor. His objection was not "because he cared about the poor but because he was a thief; as keeper of the money bag, he used to help himself to what was put into it" (John 12:6).

Jesus jumped to Mary's defense. "'Leave her alone,' said Jesus. 'Why are you bothering her? She has done a beautiful thing to me. The poor you will always have with you, and you can help them any time you want. But you will not always have me. She did what she could. She poured perfume on my body beforehand to prepare for my burial.'" (Mark 14:6–8).

Presumably, this rebuke by Jesus played a key role in convincing Judas to betray him. Judas had not heeded the warning Jesus gave during the Sermon on the Mount: "No one can serve two masters. Either he will hate the one and love the other, or he will be devoted to the one and despise the other. You cannot serve both God and Money" (Matthew 6:24). Judas loved Money, despising Jesus. Therefore, Judas betrayed Jesus.

Remember this whenever you find yourself loving Money. You cannot serve both God and Money. If you love Money, you will despise Jesus. You will betray Jesus.

Jesus Drives the Merchants Out of the Temple

The religious leaders already feared Jesus enough to kill him. Imagine their fear and desperation when an enthusiastic crowd welcomed Jesus to Jerusalem as if he was Israel's king—as if he was the eagerly anticipated Messiah who would free Israel from Roman rule.

The scene has captured people's imaginations throughout the ages. We celebrate it every Palm Sunday. When "the great crowd that had come for the [Passover] Feast heard that Jesus was on his way to Jerusalem [, t]hey took palm branches and went out to meet him, shouting,

'Hosanna!'

'Blessed is he who comes in the name
   of the Lord!'

'Blessed is the King of Israel!'"

(John 12:12–13)

No one seeing the crowds and hearing their cries of adoration could doubt that Jesus was popular enough to pose a threat to the religious leaders. The cries of the crowd were encouraging Jesus to declare that he was Israel's king.

223

Jesus did not discourage these cries of the crowd. Indeed, Jesus deliberately chose to fulfill a prophecy concerning the arrival of the Messiah—the king who would be "righteous and having salvation," who would "proclaim peace to the nations," and whose "rule will extend from sea to sea . . . to the ends of the earth" (Zechariah 9:9–10). To fulfill this prophecy that the Messiah would come to Jerusalem peacefully riding a young colt, "Jesus found a young donkey and sat upon it, as it is written,

'Do not be afraid, O Daughter of Zion;
    see, your king is coming,
gentle and riding on a donkey,
    on a colt, the foal of a donkey.'"

(John 12:14–15 & Matthew 21:5,
referring to Zechariah 9:9)

The crowd gladly treated Jesus as their king. "As he went along, people spread their cloaks on the road" (Luke 19:36). "When he came near the place where the road goes down the Mount of Olives, the whole crowd of disciples began joyfully to praise God in loud voices for all the miracles they had seen:

'Blessed is the king who comes in the name of the Lord!'

'Peace in heaven and glory in the highest!'"

(Luke 19:37–38)

All this praise for Jesus was more than the Pharisees could stand. Furthermore, letting the crowds treat Jesus like a king had immense religious and political significance. The crowds were expressing their hope that Jesus was the true king of Israel, arriving at last in fulfillment of ancient prophecies about the Messiah.

It would be similar to having someone who condemned the President arrive at Washington, D.C. and be greeted by a huge crowd shouting that he or she was the *real* President. Naturally, the "powers that be" would react with fear to this challenge to their power.

And so "[s]ome of the Pharisees in the crowd said to Jesus, 'Teacher, rebuke your disciples!'" (Luke 19:39). Jesus flatly refused to restrain the crowd's enthusiasm. Nor was Jesus willing to contradict the crowd's shouts that he was "the king who comes in the name of the Lord" (Luke 19:38). Instead, Jesus affirmed the crowd's reaction to his arrival in Jerusalem. "'I tell you,' he replied [to the Pharisees], 'if they keep quiet, the stones will cry out.'" (Luke 19:40).

Imagine Caiaphas' consternation at the crowd's enthusiasm for Jesus. Imagine Caiaphas' fear when he learned that Jesus refused the Pharisees' request to rebuke his disciples when they openly proclaimed that Jesus was "the king who comes in the name of the Lord" (Luke 19:38). These events must have confirmed the conclusion of Caiaphas and his cronies after hearing about Jesus raising Lazarus from the dead: "If we let [Jesus] go on like this, everyone will believe in him, and then the Romans will come and take away both our place and our nation . . . . [Therefore,] it is better . . . that [Jesus] die for the people than that the whole nation perish" (John 11:48, 50).

It must also have been clear to Caiaphas and his cronies that all their plotting to kill Jesus had been futile. Jesus successfully eluded their plots after raising Lazarus from the dead by staying in a region near the desert (John 11:53–54). And following his triumphal entry, Jesus left Jerusalem to spend the night with his friends in Bethany (Mark 11:11) where Caiaphas and his cronies evidently could not find Jesus and arrest him.

The need to intensify their plotting became even clearer to Caiaphas and his cronies the next day when "Jesus entered the temple area and began driving out those who were buying and selling there. He overturned the tables of the money changers and the benches of those selling doves, and would not allow anyone to carry merchandise through the temple courts" (Mark 11:15–16). Such actions by Jesus threatened the financial interests of Caiaphas and his cronies.

Moreover, Jesus did not stop with mere actions. His teachings made clear his condemnation of all those responsible for the way the temple was being perverted and exploited for financial gain. Jesus condemned Caiaphas and his cronies as he taught the crowds in the temple area, saying, "Is it not written:

> "'My house will be called
> a house of prayer for all nations.'"?
>
> But you have made it a "den of robbers.'""
>
> (Mark 11:17)

The crowd loved this. Caiaphas and his cronies hated it. "The chief priests and the teachers of the law heard this and began looking for a way to kill him, for they feared him, because the whole crowd was amazed at his teaching" (Mark 11:18).

The crowd was also amazed at the miracles Jesus performed. Jesus did not perform some kind of a miraculous stunt to "prove" he was the Messiah—at the very beginning of his public ministry three years earlier he'd overcome the temptation to jump from the highest point of the temple and summon angels to catch him (Matthew 4:5–7). Instead of performing such self-aggrandizing miracles, Jesus performed miracles that helped other people. When "[t]he blind and the lame came to him at the temple, . . . he healed them" (Matthew 21:14).

Children were wise enough to understand that these healings were wonderful and that Jesus was indeed the Messiah. The children shouted, "Hosanna to the Son of David," just as the people had during the triumphal entry of Jesus into the city. (By calling Jesus the Son (or descendant) of David, Israel's greatest king, the people were proclaiming that Jesus should be their king, their Messiah.)

But Caiaphas and his cronies lacked this wisdom of children. They were blinded by greed, cynicism and fear. "[W]hen the chief priests and the teachers of the law saw the wonderful things [Jesus] did and the children shouting in the temple area, 'Hosanna to the Son of David,' they were indignant" (Matthew 21:15).

Once again—as during Jesus' triumphal entry—they tried to get Jesus to silence the shouts of the children praising Jesus and proclaiming him king. Jesus reminded them about the psalm that says:

> "'From the lips of children and infants
> you have ordained praise'"
>
> (Matthew 21:16, referring to Psalm 8:2)

Once again—as during his triumphal entry—Jesus flatly refused to restrain his supporters' enthusiasm. Nor was Jesus willing to contradict the children as they rejoiced and proclaimed that Jesus was their king, their Messiah.

Once again—for the moment at least—Jesus evaded the plotting of Caiaphas and his cronies to kill him. Jesus "left them and went out of the city to Bethany, where he spent the night" (Matthew 21:17) among the relative safety of his friends.

Never become like Caiaphas and his cronies. *Blinded* by greed, cynicism and fear so that you can no longer see Jesus at work in our lives and in our world. *Driven* by greed, cynicism and fear so that you oppose the work of Jesus in our lives and in our world—as Caiaphas and his cronies opposed Jesus when his ways threatened their power and money.

Instead, always be like a child at heart. Be quick to rejoice when Jesus comes to heal us and our world. Be enthusiastic to welcome Jesus into our lives and into our world. Be eager to proclaim that Jesus is the one true king—the Messiah.

Jesus Defeats Caiaphas' Cronies

Caiaphas and his cronies "were trying to kill [Jesus]. Yet they could not find any way to do it, because all the people hung on his words" (Luke 19:47–48). They "looked for a way to arrest him immediately, because they knew he had spoken . . . against them. But they were afraid of the people" (Luke 20:19).

Caiaphas and his cronies knew, however, that there is more than one way to skin a cat. If the direct approach of arresting Jesus and killing him wouldn't work, they'd try to find an indirect way to destroy him. "[T]he Pharisees went out and laid plans to trap him in his words" (Matthew 22:15). "Keeping a close watch on him, they sent spies, who pretended to be honest. They hoped to catch Jesus in something he said so that they might hand him over to the power and authority of the governor" (Luke 20:20).

These spies started by flattering Jesus: "Teacher, we know you are a man of integrity. You aren't swayed by men, because you pay no attention to who they are; but you teach the way of God in accordance with the truth" (Mark 12:14).

Then the spies sprung their trap. They asked, "Is it right to pay taxes to Caesar or not? Should we pay or shouldn't we?" (Mark 12:14–15).

The spies thought they'd cornered Jesus with this question. They hoped that he would say that they *should not* pay taxes to Caesar. Then they would turn him in to the Romans as a troublemaker who was fomenting rebellion by telling people not to pay their taxes. But even if Jesus answered that people *should* pay taxes to the Romans, at least it would hurt his popularity with the people. It is never popular to tell people to pay taxes. Moreover, in this case, it would make Jesus look unpatriotic because the taxes were paid to the hated Romans who were occupying Israel.

The spies hoped that Jesus would lower his guard because of their flattering remarks about Jesus being a man of integrity who wasn't swayed by men but who taught the way of God in accordance with the truth. However, "Jesus knew their hypocrisy" (Mark 12:15). He asked the spies, "Why are you trying to trap me?" (Mark 12:15).

Then Jesus found the perfect way to escape the trap while teaching the truth. He said, "'Bring me a denarius and let me look at it.' They brought the coin, and he asked them, 'Whose portrait is this? And whose inscription?'" (Mark 12:15–16). Like many coins today, this Roman coin had a picture of a person on it. There was only one possible answer to Jesus' question. "'Caesar's,' they replied" (Mark 12:16). "Jesus said to them, 'Give to Caesar what is Caesar's and to God what is God's.'" (Mark 12:17). This wise answer affirmed both the duty to *pay taxes* the way the Romans wanted and the duty to *live life* the way God wanted.

"When [the spies] heard this, they were amazed. So they left him and went away" (Matthew 22:22). The spies were gone, but the effort of Caiaphas and his cronies to discredit Jesus continued. The next group of questioners tried to make Jesus look stupid. These questioners were Sadducees—a group who said "there is no resurrection" (Mark 12:18). To prove how silly it was for Jesus to believe that there is life after death, they asked him to answer an extremely unlikely hypothetical.

The Sadducees started by noting that according to the Mosaic law, "if a man's brother dies and leaves a wife but no children, the man must marry the widow and have children for his brother" (Mark 12:19). There was no dispute between the Sadducees and Jesus that the Mosaic law contained this requirement to marry a brother's widow if the dead brother had no children. The reason the Sadducees mentioned this law was to pose the following quandary for Jesus to answer:

"Now there were seven brothers. The first one married and died without leaving any children. The second one married the widow, but he also died, leaving no child. It was the same with the third. In fact, none of the seven left any children. Last of all, the woman died too. At the resurrection whose wife will she be, since the seven were married to her?"

(Mark 12:20–23)

Jesus refused to be cowed by the "intellectual sophistication" of his questioners. Instead of being defensive and uncertain in his response, Jesus immediately went on the offensive, belittling their lack of knowledge and faith. "Jesus replied, 'Are you not in error because you do not know the Scriptures or the power of God?'" (Mark 12:24).

Next, Jesus dismissed their silly hypothetical about whose wife the widow would be after death. He said, "When the dead rise, they will neither marry nor be given in marriage" (Mark 12:25).

On the key question of whether there is life after death, Jesus relied on the Scriptures as authoritative. Jesus said, "Now about the dead rising—have you not read in the book of Moses, in the account of the bush, how God said to him, 'I am the God of Abraham, the God of Isaac, and the God of Jacob'? He is not the God of the dead, but of the living. You are badly mistaken!" (Mark 12:26–27, quoting Exodus 3:6).

In giving this reply, Jesus showed immense confidence in the accuracy with which the text of the Scriptures has been preserved through the ages. Because Jesus' response relied on the accuracy of the verb tense recorded in the Scriptures centuries earlier.

Abraham, Isaac and Jacob had died hundreds of years before God spoke these words to Moses at the burning bush. So if Abraham, Isaac and Jacob were no longer living after their physical deaths, God would have said, "I *was*" the God of Abraham, Isaac and Jacob. But since God told Moses "I *am*" the God of Abraham, Isaac and Jacob, it proved that they were still alive hundreds of years after their physical deaths.

When Jesus replied to the next question he also relied on the power of God and the authority of the Scriptures. This question came from one of the teachers of the law who heard the Sadducees debating Jesus about whether there is life after death. "Noticing that Jesus had given them a good answer, he asked him, 'Of all the commandments, which is the most important?'" (Mark 12:28).

In reply, Jesus gave the answer that lay at the heart of the Jewish faith. It was a reply that affirmed monotheism—that God is one—and that affirmed we must love God and our neighbors. Jesus quoted Moses and said:

> "The most important [commandment] . . . is this: 'Hear, O Israel, the Lord our God, the Lord is one. Love the Lord your God with all your heart and with all your soul and with all your mind and with all your strength.' The second is this: 'Love your neighbor as yourself.' There is no commandment greater than these." (Mark 12:29–31, quoting Deuteronomy 6:4–5 & Leviticus 19:18)

By affirming that "[T]he Lord our God, the Lord is one," Jesus affirmed that there is nothing inconsistent between this core belief of Jews that there is only one God and the core belief of Christians that Jesus is the incarnate Son of God who is fully human *and* fully God. To be sure, exactly how this works remains a mystery after two thousands years of much thought and reflection by Christians. But the arguments against the Doctrine of the Trinity are much like the arguments of the Sadducees against life after death. They rely on complicated hypotheticals to make the Doctrine of the Trinity—that God is three persons in one—look silly. In reality, however, these skeptics do not know the power of God or the Scriptures.

Because the power of God knows no limits. With God, **_ALL_** things are possible, even being three persons in one.

Furthermore, the Scriptures clearly teach that Jesus, the Word of God, is fully God because "[i]n the beginning was the Word, and the Word was with God, and the Word was God" (John 1:1). *And* the Scriptures clearly teach that Jesus is fully human because "[t]he Word became flesh and made his dwelling among us" (John 1:14).

Another key aspect of Jesus' reply was that he showed his ability to stay focused on what was essential. Faced with plots to kill him and beset by brilliant debaters, Jesus never lost sight of his core teachings. We must love God. (We must worship the Lord in spirit and in truth.)

And we must love all other people. (We must bless all peoples in the Promised Land.)

Therefore, the teacher of the law who asked Jesus what was the most important commandment was impressed by Jesus' answer. "'Well said, teacher,' the man replied. 'You are right in saying that God is one and there is no other but him. To love him with all your heart, with all your understanding and with all your strength, and to love your neighbor as yourself is more important than all burnt offerings and sacrifices.'" (Mark 12:32–33). "Jesus saw that he had answered wisely" (Mark 12:34). So Jesus praised this teacher of the law by saying to him: "You are not far from the kingdom of God" (Mark 12:34).

"[F]rom then on no one dared ask [Jesus] any more questions" (Mark 12:34). And no wonder! Caiaphas and his cronies gained their power and wealth because people came to the temple to make burnt offerings and sacrifices. The last thing Caiaphas and his cronies wanted was for people to worship by loving God with all their heart, understanding and strength and by loving their neighbors as themselves—instead of by spending money making burnt offerings and sacrifices in the temple!

Never ask Jesus questions out of impure motives. Ask Jesus questions only when you sincerely want to follow Jesus and his wisdom. Then Jesus will give you the wisdom to see through hypocritical questions by reminding hypocrites to give to God what is God's. Then Jesus will give you the wisdom to answer silly, distracting hypotheticals by affirming the power of God and by relying on the accuracy and authority of the Scriptures. Then Jesus will give you the wisdom to proclaim that the most important thing in life is to love God and all people (James 1:5).

Judas Betrays Jesus for Thirty Silver Coins

A s Jesus continued teaching in the temple, he denounced people who behaved like Caiaphas and his cronies. Jesus said, "Watch out for the teachers of the law. They like to walk around in flowing robes and be greeted in the marketplaces, and have the most important seats in the synagogues and the places of honor at banquets" (Mark 12:38–39).

If such vain, pompous people had merely been arrogant showoffs, it would have been bad enough. But there was a dark side to their vanity. They obtained the money for such ostentatious displays by oppressing the poor. As Jesus said, "They devour widows' houses and for a show make lengthy prayers" (Mark 12:40). Jesus warned, "Such men will be punished most severely" (Mark 12:40).

Taking a breather from his public teaching in the temple, "Jesus sat down opposite the place where the offerings were put and watched the crowd putting their money into the temple treasury" (Mark 12:41). Apparently, there was little or no privacy when donating money to the temple. Because Jesus and the disciples could tell that "[m]any rich people threw in large amounts. But a poor widow came and put in two very small copper coins, worth only a fraction of a penny" (Mark 12:41–42).

Jesus saw a perfect opportunity for teaching his disciples the proper perspective on money—and for emphasizing how wicked it was for rich people to devour widows' houses while showing off by making lengthy prayers. "Calling his disciples to him, Jesus said, 'I tell you the truth, this poor widow has put more into the treasury than all the others. They all gave out of their wealth; but she, out of her poverty, put in everything—all she had to live on.'" (Mark 12:43–44).

All this was too much for Judas Iscariot!

A few days before, Jesus rebuked Judas in front of the other disciples when Judas criticized Mary for "wasting" expensive perfume on Jesus instead of selling the perfume and giving the money to the poor. Although pretending to be concerned about the poor, Judas was actually "a thief; as keeper of the money bag, he used to help himself to what was put into it" (John 12:6). In short, Judas was the type of greedy hypocrite who Jesus condemned—someone who "devour[s] widows' houses and for a show make[s] lengthy prayers" (Mark 12:40).

Now Jesus was praising a poor widow instead of the wealthy donors who could fill the money bag with coins that Judas could steal! Furthermore, Jesus kept predicting his death. If Jesus was going to die, Judas wanted to be on the winning side—the side where the money was!

At last, Judas decided to betray Jesus. Judas must have heard that Caiaphas and his cronies would pay handsomely for information enabling them to arrest Jesus quietly when no crowd was present. Judas wanted that reward. And so, Judas looked for a chance to communicate with Caiaphas and his cronies.

It would have been fairly easy to slip away for a short time. "Each day Jesus was teaching at the temple . . ." (Luke 21:37). Caiaphas and his cronies were nearby. As keeper of the money bag, Judas could find an excuse to go away to buy something—then make a "detour" to earn his reward.

Furthermore, a pattern had developed in Jesus' movements that would enable Caiaphas to arrest Jesus quietly if he became aware of it. "[E]ach evening [Jesus] went out to spend the night on the hill called the Mount of Olives" (Luke 21:37).

Judas correctly surmised that Caiaphas and his cronies would pay handsomely for his information. This information was valuable because "the chief priests and the elders of the people . . . [were] plott[ing] to arrest Jesus in some sly way and kill him" (Matthew 26:3–4). The only thing stopping them was Jesus' popularity with the crowds. As they warned each other, they must not arrest Jesus "during the Feast . . . or there may be a riot among the people" (Matthew 26:5). Therefore, they needed to arrest Jesus quietly away from the crowds. The Mount of Olives at night was the perfect place.

Imagine the look of glee on Caiaphas' face when Judas came to him and asked, "What are you willing to give me if I hand him over to you?" (Matthew 26:15). Negotiations began. "Judas . . . discussed with them how he might betray Jesus" (Luke 22:4). Perhaps Judas bragged about how easily he could outwit Jesus and turn him in. Perhaps Judas was cagey—not wanting to reveal too much about Jesus' whereabouts until he felt his reward in his hands. Whatever Judas told Caiaphas and the officers of the temple guard, it was just what they wanted to hear. "They were delighted . . ." (Luke 22:5).

We are not told what excuses Judas concocted for his betrayal. Perhaps Judas claimed to sympathize with Caiaphas' concern that things were getting out of hand so that, as a patriot and as a lover of the temple, Judas had to betray Jesus lest "the Romans . . . come and take away both our place and our nation" (John 11:48).[1] Perhaps Judas told such lies. Perhaps Judas even half-deceived himself into believing that he was motivated by patriotism and by love for the temple.

But whatever lies Judas told himself and Caiaphas about his motives, Caiaphas saw through the lies. Whatever Caiaphas' other faults, he was a good judge of character. He knew that nothing but death could stop Jesus from doing good deeds and teaching in the temple. And he knew that Judas would do *anything* for enough money. So Caiaphas and his cronies "agreed to give [Judas] money" (Luke 22:5).

The only remaining question was how much money it would take. Caiaphas knew how to win over a greedy person such as Judas. He had the money counted out right in front of Judas' eyes. He let Judas hear the clink of each silver coin. "[T]hey counted out for him thirty silver coins" (Matthew 26:15). That was all it took! "[Judas] consented, and watched for an opportunity to hand Jesus over to them when no crowd was present" (Luke 22:6).

What a contrast with the poor widow putting her two tiny copper coins into the temple treasury! Picture her face as she gave God everything she had to live on. Imagine how her eyes glowed with joy.[2] Then picture Judas' face as he counted his thirty silver coins. Imagine how his eyes glowed with greed.

Decide which face you want. And live that way.

The Last Supper

I wonder how well Judas could hide the look of greed and betrayal on his face when he rejoined Jesus and the other disciples. Apparently, Judas could fool the other disciples. But, as we shall see, he could not fool Jesus.

"When the hour came, Jesus and his apostles reclined at the table. And he said to them, 'I have eagerly desired to eat this Passover with you before I suffer. For I tell you, I will not eat it again until it finds fulfillment in the kingdom of God.'" (Luke 22:14–16).[1]

This was a bleak way to begin the meal that has come to be known as "the Last Supper." Usually, we begin meals with some kind of upbeat comment to put everybody in the mood to enjoy good food and good conversation. But Jesus began the meal by saying he was glad to eat before he suffered.

Jesus knew that he was about to be betrayed and crucified. Indeed, when the Apostle Paul wrote about these events, he did not refer to them as happening during "the Last Supper"—but as happening during "the night [Jesus] was betrayed" (1 Corinthians 11:23).

Jesus also knew the significance of the suffering he was about to endure. That was why he said that he would not eat the Passover "again until it finds fulfillment in the kingdom of God" (Luke 22:16). Jesus knew that his crucifixion and resurrection would "fulfill" the Passover.

To understand why this was so, let's review briefly the events that the Passover commemorated. The events surrounding "the Passover" took place while Moses was trying to free the Hebrews from slavery to the Egyptians. Despite a series of plagues, Pharaoh stubbornly refused to let the Hebrews go free. As the final plague, the LORD passed through Egypt striking down every firstborn—both men and animals—thereby bringing judgment on all the gods of Egypt. However, God promised to "pass over" and spare anyone who sacrificed a lamb and put the blood on the doorpost of their house. After this plague, Pharaoh freed God's people from their slavery (Exodus 11:1–12:51, see especially Exodus 12:12–13).

In a similar way, Jesus saw that God's people were slaves to sin. Jesus was determined to be the sacrificial "lamb" whose blood would cause death to "passover" God's people, setting God's people free from their slavery to sin.

To express this truth, Jesus performed two simple acts at the Last Supper:

[H]e took bread, gave thanks and broke it, and gave it to them, saying, "This is my body given for you; do this in remembrance of me."

In the same way, after the supper he took the cup, saying, "This cup is the new covenant in my blood, which is poured out for you."
(Luke 22:19–20)

I'm sure Jesus wanted a serene, contemplative Passover celebration with his disciples so he could perform these two simple acts and explain their significance. But Jesus had no better luck than I usually did when I tried to teach my children something profound. There were constant disruptions and distractions.

For example, "a dispute arose among [the Twelve] as to which of them was considered to be greatest" (Luke 22:24).

Once before when such a dispute arose, Jesus told the Twelve, "If anyone wants to be first, he must be the very last, and the servant of all" (Mark 9:35). Jesus, being a great teacher, knew that a tangible illustration of this abstract truth was necessary. So Jesus took a little child and had him stand among them. Taking him in his arms, he said to them, "Whoever welcomes one of these little children in my name welcomes me; and whoever welcomes me does not welcome me but the one who sent me (Mark 9:36–37). For he who is least among you all—he is the greatest."

(Luke 9:48)

Jesus must have been disappointed and discouraged that the Twelve had learned so little of what he had taught them. Time was running out to teach them such truths.

Jesus quickly offered a refresher course. Jesus told them:

"The kings of the Gentiles lord it over them; and those who exercise authority over them call themselves Benefactors. But you are not to be like that. Instead, the greatest among you should be like the youngest, and the one who rules like the one who serves."

(Luke 22:25–26)

Jesus looked for a tangible illustration of this abstract truth. This time there was no little child to stand among them. Instead, the illustration that occurred to Jesus was the idea of serving at a supper. Jesus told them, "For who is greater, the one who is at the table or the one who serves? Is it not the one who is at the table? But I am among you as one who serves" (Luke 22:27).

Jesus illustrated this truth by his own actions. He had no doubt about his own status as the greatest in the Kingdom of God. "Jesus knew that the Father had put all things under his power, and that he had come from God and was returning to God" (John 13:3).

Any normal person (like me) would start boasting that "the Father had put all things under his power." But not Jesus. Jesus knew true greatness. And to teach us true greatness, Jesus served instead of boasting.

Jesus "got up from the meal, took off his outer clothing, and wrapped a towel around his waist" (John 13:4). Jesus voluntarily assumed the role of a slave—he voluntarily became "the very last, and the servant of all" (Mark 9:35). Jesus "poured water into a basin and began to wash his disciples' feet, drying them with the towel that was wrapped around him" (John 13:5).

241

When Jesus came to Peter, he questioned Jesus' actions. Always the impetuous, boisterous disciple, Peter said, "Lord, are you going to wash my feet?" (John 13:6).

"Jesus replied, 'You do not realize now what I am doing, but later you will understand.'" (John 13:7). With this answer, Jesus was doing his best to reassure Peter that—despite Peter's doubts—Peter could relax. Jesus did indeed know what he was doing. And Jesus was letting Peter know that—despite Peter's cocky belief that he had everything figured out—Peter still didn't fully understand what Jesus was doing.

But cocky Peter refused to take the "hint." In fact, instead of merely questioning the wisdom of Jesus abasing himself as a slave, Peter flatly rejected the whole idea. "'No,' said Peter, 'you shall never wash my feet.'" (John 13:8).

Peter's cockiness left Jesus with no choice but to give Peter this clear warning: "Unless I wash you, you have no part with me" (John 13:8).

Peter loved Jesus deeply. Indeed, it was partly because of his great love for Jesus that he couldn't stand to see Jesus humiliating and abasing himself by acting like a slave. Now that Jesus had made Peter understand that his feet must be washed by Jesus, Peter quickly agreed.

But being impetuous, boisterous Peter, he went overboard the other way! Instead of agreeing to let Jesus do precisely what Jesus asked to do, Peter replied, "Then, Lord . . . [wash] not just my feet but my hands and my head as well!" (John 13:9).

Jesus reassured Peter that this was not necessary. Peter's "whole body" was clean. It was just his feet that needed washing (John 13:10).

In contrast, Jesus warned that one of the Twelve was not clean. "For he knew who was going to betray him, and that was why he said not every one was clean" (John 13:11.)

Indeed, perhaps Jesus made this warning at the very moment he was washing the feet of Judas Iscariot. We are not told what transpired when Jesus washed Judas' feet. But it surely must have been a dramatic moment.[2]

Did the two men look each other in the eye? We don't know. My best guess is that Jesus tried to look Judas in the eye, and Judas looked away—unable to face directly the close companion and good, kind person who he was betraying.

Did the two men say anything to each other? We don't know. But I suspect not. The Bible records what Jesus said to Peter while he washed his feet, what Jesus said about his betrayal after he was done with the footwashing, what Jesus and Judas said to each other quietly when Jesus confirmed that he knew that Judas would betray him, what Jesus said to Judas when he left the meal to betray Jesus, and what Jesus and Judas said to each other when Jesus was arrested in the Garden of Gethsemane. So I suspect that one of the Gospels would tell us what, if anything, Jesus and Judas said while Jesus washed Judas' feet.

Furthermore, Jesus' actions spoke far louder and more eloquently than any words he could say. Jesus was still willing to help Judas—still willing to clean him from the sin of betrayal.

And what did Judas' face look like while Jesus washed his feet, begging him by deed and attitude to confess his sin and remain loyal to Jesus? Judas must have been very good at hiding his inner thoughts and feelings. Because none of the other disciples discerned that Judas was a traitor. However, I suspect that a keen observer of character such as Jesus who knew the truth could discern a slight look of contempt on Judas' face.

Judas was now so devoted to Money that I believe he could no longer do anything but despise Jesus and the ways of God. As Jesus taught Judas in the Sermon on the Mount:

> "No one can serve two masters. Either he will hate the one and love the other, or he will be devoted to the one and despise the other. You cannot serve both God and Money."
>
> (Matthew 6:24)

The astounding thing about Jesus is that he could serve Judas as a slave by washing his feet even though he knew Judas despised him and was betraying him.

The wonderful thing about Jesus is that he could wash the feet of Peter even though he knew that Peter was about to run away and deny he even knew Jesus.

That is why I believe that Jesus washing the feet of his disciples is another one of those pictures that teaches us more about who Jesus is, what God is like, and how we should live than volumes of theological speculations or hundreds of pages of my writings.

And Jesus certainly hoped that we would go and do likewise. That instead of disputing which of us is greatest we would busy ourselves with serving each other by "washing each other's feet." Therefore,

> [w]hen [Jesus] had finished washing their feet, he put on his clothes and returned to his place. "Do you understand what I have done for you?" he asked them. "You call me 'Teacher' and 'Lord,' and rightly so, for that is what I am. Now that I, your Lord and Teacher, have washed your feet, you also should wash one another's feet. I have set you an example that you should do as I have done for you . . . . . Now that you know these things, you will be blessed if you do them."
> (John 13:12–17)

Perhaps Jesus wanted to return to the theme of why he eagerly desired to eat this Passover with them before he suffered. Perhaps Jesus wanted to explain the ways that the Passover would be "fulfilled" by Jesus giving his broken body and pouring out his blood so that the consequences of sin would "passover" their lives. Perhaps Jesus wanted to explain how dying for us was the ultimate way he would wash our feet and wash the sins from our lives.

But Jesus became too "troubled in spirit" (John 13:21) to continue with such thoughts. He told the disciples, "I tell you the truth, one of you is going to betray me—one who is eating with me" (John 13:21; Mark 14:18).

This was definitely not an upbeat gathering! Jesus kicked it off by saying he was glad to eat before he suffered. Now he told his closest companions and followers—the Twelve—that one of the Twelve who was eating with him was going to betray him.

"They were saddened, and one by one they said to him, 'Surely not I?'" (Mark 14:19). The greedy traitor, Judas, must have been a great actor to deceive the other disciples by pretending to be saddened by this news. How could Judas find the gall to say to Jesus, "Surely not I?"?

But Jesus knew the truth. "'It is one of the Twelve,' he replied, 'one who dips bread into the bowl with me.'" (Mark 14:20).

Jesus had told the disciples just moments before that his betrayal would "fulfill the scripture: 'He who shares my bread has lifted up his heel against me.'" (John 13:18). Jesus then said, "I am telling you now before it happens, so that when it does happen you will believe that I am He" (John 13:19).

Jesus did not want to create the impression that he was somehow excusing Judas' betrayal by noting that it would "fulfill the scripture." Jesus said, "The Son of Man will go just as it is written about him. But woe to that man who betrays the Son of Man! It would be better for him if he had not been born" (Mark 14:21).

Judas must have realized that this dire warning was directed at him. Perhaps Jesus even looked him in the eye as he said it. Because "[t]hen Judas, the one who would betray him, said [quietly to Jesus], 'Surely not I, Rabbi?'" And "Jesus answered [quietly], 'Yes, it is you.'" (Matthew 26:25).[3]

The rest of the people at the table must not have heard (or at least must not have understood) this quick interchange between Judas and Jesus. Because the "disciples stared at one another, at a loss to know which of them he meant" (John 13:22).

As we would expect, Peter could not wait quietly wondering who Jesus meant would betray him. Peter motioned to John (who was reclining next to Jesus) and said, "Ask him which one he means" (John 13:23–24).[4] (Remember that in that culture people did not sit in chairs to eat the way we do today—they reclined on couches to eat). So "[l]eaning back against Jesus, [John] asked him [quietly], 'Lord, who is it?'" (John 13:25).[5]

"Jesus answered [quietly], 'It is the one to whom I will give this piece of bread when I have dipped it in the dish.' Then, dipping the piece of bread, he gave it to Judas Iscariot . . ." (John 13:26).[6]

I assume that Jesus and Judas made eye contact when Jesus gave him the piece of bread. Jesus' act of hospitality and friendship in offering bread to Judas, together with his merciful eyes, gave Judas one last chance to change his mind. Especially in that culture, it was reprehensible to betray someone with whom you'd shared a meal.

Perhaps Judas could no longer bear to look into the eyes of the good man he was betraying. Or, perhaps Judas returned Jesus' gaze with a look of contempt now that Judas no longer needed to hide how much he despised Jesus. (Because Judas now knew that Jesus knew he was a traitor.) All that the Bible tells us about this dramatic moment of betrayal is that "[a]s soon as Judas took the bread, Satan entered into him" (John 13:27).

Seeing that Judas had made up his mind to betray him, Jesus said to Judas, "What you are about to do, do quickly" (John 13:27). The others at the table heard Jesus say this to Judas, "but no one at the meal understood why Jesus said this to him. Since Judas had charge of the money, some thought Jesus was telling him to buy what was needed for the Feast, or to give something to the poor" (John 13:28–29).

None of the other disciples understood what Jesus meant. But Judas understood. "As soon as Judas had taken the bread, he went out. And it was night" (John 13:30).

The Bible does not tell us that "it was night" when Judas left to betray Jesus just so that we know what time of day it was. This detail is given to us to underscore the fact that this was a dark, depressing moment. In less than 24 hours, Jesus would be dead. And during this time of spiritual night he would suffer betrayal, denial, physical torture, crucifixion, and death.

Nevertheless, Jesus saw the glorious dawn of his resurrection that lay beyond this night of betrayal. As soon as Judas was gone, "Jesus said, 'Now is the Son of Man glorified and God is glorified in him.'" (John 13:31).

Jesus then began to prepare his disciples for the terrible events that were about to transpire. He said, "My children, I will be with you only a little longer. You will look for me, and just as I told the Jews, so I tell you now: Where I am going, you cannot come" (John 13:33).

Then—perhaps trying to get back to what he tried to teach them by washing their feet—Jesus said, "A new command I give you: Love one another. As I have loved you, so you must love one another. By this all men will know that you are my disciples, if you love one another" (John 13:34–35).

Just as Jesus was trying to develop this inspiring thought that we should all love one another, Peter interrupted. Peter wasn't interested in exploring what Jesus meant by loving each other. Peter's mind was still focusing on Jesus' statement that "Where I am going, you cannot come" (John 13:35). "Peter asked him, 'Lord, where are you going?'" (John 13:36).

Jesus must have sighed at this interruption. Time was so short! Peter *never* could seem to avoid interrupting with argumentative questions. Nevertheless, Jesus stopped teaching about why we should love one another and addressed Peter's question.

"Jesus replied, 'Where I am going, you cannot follow now, but you will follow later.'" (John 13:36).

Jesus' answer was not good enough for Peter. "Peter asked, 'Lord, why can't I follow you now? I will lay down my life for you.'" (John 13:37).

"Then Jesus answered, 'Will you really lay down your life for me? I tell you the truth, before the rooster crows, you will disown me three times!'" (John 13:38).[7]

Jesus rewarded Peter's persistent questioning with the truth. Even though Peter would not be pleased or comforted by the truth.

As Peter and the rest of the disciples were absorbing this shocking pronouncement, "Jesus told them, 'This very night you will all fall away on account of me, for it is written:

"I will strike the shepherd,
     and the sheep of the flock will be
          scattered."

But after I have risen, I will go ahead of you into Galilee.'" (Matthew 26:31–32).

Peter was not convinced by this argument that the Scriptures taught that everyone would desert Jesus. Nor did he seize upon the hope Jesus was willing to give him and the other disciples—the hope that, after they were scattered, Jesus would rise and go ahead of them into Galilee where they could join him again.

Instead of Peter hoping in the LORD, Peter wanted Jesus hoping in Peter. He "replied, 'Even if all fall away on account of you, I never will.'" (Matthew 26:33).

I'm sure that Jesus was pleased that Peter wanted to be loyal and courageous. But Jesus knew that, in fact, Peter was overconfident. Peter was boasting. Jesus answered, "I tell you the truth, . . . this very night, before the rooster crows, you will disown me three times" (Matthew 26:34).

Peter refused to accept this. "Peter insisted emphatically, 'Even if I have to die with you, I will never disown you.'" (Mark 14:31).

Peter was not alone in his overconfidence. "[A]ll the other disciples said the same" (Matthew 26:35).

Jesus knew that the terrors and despair of this coming night would overwhelm the courage and loyalty of these people he loved. So even as Jesus repeated the heart-breaking truth, he left a thought of hope for Peter and the rest to reflect upon after they all fell away.

In a voice that I believe was full of love, Jesus gently explained the truth to Peter again. No longer using the name "Peter" that means "rock"[8] (because Peter would not be strong like a rock tonight), Jesus said, "Simon, Simon, Satan has asked to sift you as wheat. But I have prayed for you, Simon, that your faith may not fail. And when you have turned back, strengthen your brothers" (Luke 22:31–32).

When I am tempted to be overconfident and boastful about my own strength to remain loyal to Jesus, I remember that Satan can sift me like wheat. Like Peter, I can fail. We all can fail. We all can fall away.

When that happens, we must grasp onto the hope that Jesus gave Peter and the other disciples that night in which he was betrayed. Even though Jesus sees through our overconfident boasting to the truth of our weaknesses and sins, he still loves us. He still prays that our faith may not fail. And he will still have a purpose for us after we have failed. He knows that we will strengthen others who have failed, too.

It is very hard to accept that we can fail. Peter couldn't accept this truth about himself. He replied to Jesus, "Lord, I am ready to go with you to prison and to death" (Luke 22:33).

"Jesus answered, 'I tell you, Peter, before the rooster crows today, you will deny three times that you know me.'" (Luke 22:34).

Whenever we try to be a rock—a "Peter"—hoping in our own strength, we will fail as Peter failed. Our only hope is to hope in the LORD.

Then, even when we fail, we can be confident that Jesus will pray that our faith will not fail. We can turn back to Jesus. We can still find purpose for our lives by strengthening others who have failed, too.

Therefore, even after we have failed, we can help others learn that they too can always hope in the LORD. With such words of encouragement, we can bless all peoples in the Promised Land.

The Garden of Gethsemane

Soon after Judas left the Last Supper to betray him, Jesus told his remaining disciples:

> "A new command I give you: Love one another. As I have loved you, so you must love one another. By this all men will know that you are my disciples, if you love one another."
>
> (John 13:34–35)

Peter interrupted Jesus' discussion of this key idea. Peter had more "important" things on his mind than loving one another. He was too curious about where Jesus was going. He was too concerned with proving that he was strong enough and brave enough to go anywhere Jesus could go. He was too upset by the allegation that he would deny Jesus.

After these interruptions, Jesus returned to the thought that we must love one another. He said, "My command is this: Love each other as I have loved you" (John 15:12). This sets an amazingly high standard for how we are *commanded* to love each other. This kind of love is not optional for disciples of Jesus Christ. We are *ordered* by Jesus to love each other the way Jesus loved: blessing children, welcoming sinners, weeping with each other, and washing each other's feet. Only with this kind of love can we worship the Lord in spirit and in truth by blessing all peoples in the Promised Land.

Then Jesus referred to the ultimate proof of his great love for us. He said, "Greater love has no one than this, that he lay down his life for his friends" (John 15:13). At that moment, the disciples did not realize that Jesus was literally going to lay down his life for them the next day. Only after Jesus died to save them would they fully understand how much Jesus loved them.

Perhaps even more amazing than that Jesus would die for his disciples was that Jesus would call them his "friends." Jesus wants to be more than merely our teacher. Jesus wants to be more than merely our Lord. Jesus wants to be our friend—our *best* friend. Jesus assured his disciples: "You are my friends if you do what I command" (John 15:14). And he reminded them a few moments later: "This is my command: Love each other" (John 15:17).

Therefore, the goal of teaching people about Jesus is not merely to give them head knowledge about Jesus. The goal is to give people a heart for living with Jesus—a heart for being friends with Jesus, walking and talking with Jesus daily. Because Jesus says to his disciples today, as he said to his disciples at the Last Supper:

> "I no longer call you servants, because a servant does not know his master's business. Instead, I have called you friends, for everything that I learned from my Father I have made known to you."
>
> (John 15:15)

A short time later, Jesus and the eleven remaining disciples left the Upper Room where they'd eaten the Last Supper. They went to an olive grove called Gethsemane to spend the night. "Judas, who betrayed him, knew the place, because Jesus had often met there with his disciples" (John 18:2). Jesus knew that Judas would show up soon with the henchmen of Caiaphas and his cronies to arrest Jesus, leading to his crucifixion.

Waiting for something terrible to happen is often the hardest thing to do. There is no action to take our mind off the impending horror. And so it was with Jesus as he waited for Judas to come and betray him. Throughout the insults and sufferings of that night and the following day, Jesus remained remarkably calm and composed. But for these few hours of inaction while he waited, Jesus agonized.

When Jesus and his disciples arrived at Gethsemane, "he said to them, 'Sit here while I go over there and pray.'" (Matthew 26:36).

At this difficult moment, Jesus wanted his closest friends—his best friends—with him. "He took Peter and the two sons of Zebedee along with him, and he began to be sorrowful and troubled" (Matthew 26:37).

Jesus knew the importance of sharing our innermost thoughts and burdens with our best friends so that they can help us through the tough times. "[H]e said to them, 'My soul is overwhelmed with sorrow to the point of death. Stay here and keep watch with me.'" (Matthew 26:38).

"Going a little farther, [Jesus] fell with his face to the ground and prayed, 'My Father, if it is possible, may this cup be taken from me. Yet not as I will, but as you will.'" (Matthew 26:39).

After spending some time in this agony over whether God *really* would require him to lay down his life for his friends, Jesus "returned to his disciples and found them sleeping" (Matthew 26:40).

Imagine how Jesus felt! If he needed an excuse not to bother laying down his life for these guys, here it was!

Jesus had told them to stay awake and pray. He had told them he needed their support because his soul was overwhelmed with sorrow to the point of death. And they fell asleep!

"'Could you men not keep watch with me for one hour?' he asked Peter" (Matthew 26:40).

Jesus wasn't making this request merely to help himself. The disciples needed to pray for strength and discipline to overcome their own weaknesses. Jesus cautioned them, "Watch and pray so that you will not fall into temptation. The spirit is willing, but the body is weak" (Matthew 26:41).

Jesus then "went away a second time and prayed, 'My Father, if it is not possible for this cup to be taken away unless I drink it, may your will be done.'" (Matthew 26:42).

There was no doubt that it was physically possible for Jesus to still avoid his suffering, crucifixion and death.

Christians often make this point by emphasizing Jesus' miraculous powers. They reason that, since Jesus could raise Lazarus from the dead, he could certainly have overpowered the crowd who came to arrest him. Or, they emphasize that Jesus could have called on legions of angels to deliver himself.

But Jesus did not need to resort to any supernatural powers to escape arrest. All he had to do was leave the Garden of Gethsemane quickly and go some place where Judas couldn't find him.

Jesus was not agonizing in prayer over his physical inability to escape suffering, crucifixion and death. The means of his deliverance was as simple as walking away.

Jesus was in agony because his "strong preference" (to put it mildly) was *not* to go through suffering, crucifixion and death. If there was *any* other way to fulfill God's purposes, Jesus wanted to try it.

As I like to say, "God is a pretty bright guy. If he could have found any way to save us other than getting himself killed, he wouldn't have gotten himself crucified. *There was no other way!*"[1]

Indeed, if you think about it, God had *already* tried every other way to save us, but they'd all failed.

God had appeared in a cloud with lightning and a loud voice at Mount Sinai. His people had immediately broken the Ten Commandments.

God had given his people great leaders such as David and Solomon. But his people (and David and Solomon themselves) had sinned.

God had sent prophet after prophet to help his people live the right way. But they'd failed. And his people had been carried into exile to Assyria and Babylon.

God had even sent Jesus as the perfect teacher—in word and in deed—to explain God's ways to people. But no one—not even his twelve closest companions, his twelve best friends—understood. And even to the extent they understood what God wanted, none of them could live the way God required. No one could meet the high standards that Jesus taught in the Sermon on the Mount.

Therefore, there was no way left except to offer Jesus as a sacrifice for people's sins. Jesus would have to put his love into action by laying down his life for his friends. Jesus would have to "fulfill" the Passover by being the sacrificial "lamb" whose blood would cause death to "passover" God's people and whose blood would set God's people free from their lives of sin.

After a while of praying in agony over God's plan for his life, Jesus went back to his friends. "[H]e again found them sleeping, because their eyes were heavy" (Matthew 26:43).

In an odd way, perhaps the very weakness of his friends helped to prove to Jesus that God the Father was right. There was *no way* that people could save themselves from their sins. They were too weak and undisciplined.

There was no other way to save Humanity than for God to sacrifice himself for us. There was no other way to save Humanity than for one of the three persons of the Trinity—Jesus, the Son of God—to die on the cross for us. As we liked to say at Kodak when I worked there summers during college: "If you want the job done right, you have to do it yourself!"[2]

Jesus "went away once more and prayed the third time, saying the same thing" (Matthew 26:44). All through these dark hours, Jesus kept praying that God the Father's will would be done, no matter what the cost to him personally.

At last, the agony of waiting was over. Jesus "returned to the disciples and said to them, 'Are you still sleeping and resting? Look, the hour is near, and the Son of Man is betrayed into the hands of sinners. Rise, let us go! Here comes my betrayer!'" (Matthew 26:45–46).

Judas was the only one of Jesus' disciples who wasn't sleepy that night. He'd been busy earning his reward. Now, "[w]hile [Jesus] was still speaking, Judas, . . . arrived. With him was a large crowd armed with swords and clubs, sent from the chief priests and the elders of the people" (Matthew 26:47).

Since there were no photographs or videos of Jesus, it was hard for the crowd with Judas to identify Jesus. In the darkness, Jesus still might have been able to slip away.

But Judas had thought of everything—everything except whether it was right to betray Jesus. Judas "had arranged a signal . . . : 'The one I kiss is the man; arrest him.'" (Matthew 26:48).

There must have been no question in Jesus' mind why Judas was there in the middle of the night with a large crowd armed with swords and clubs. After all, Jesus himself had told Judas earlier that night that he knew Judas would betray him (Matthew 26:25; John 13:21–26).

Earlier that night, Jesus and Judas had twice confronted each other. Once when Jesus washed Judas' feet. And later when Jesus handed Judas the piece of bread signifying that he knew Judas was the person who would betray him. Now came the third and final confrontation.

"[Judas] approached Jesus to kiss him, but Jesus asked him, 'Judas, are you betraying the Son of Man with a kiss?'" (Luke 22:47–48). Jesus was trying to make Judas realize the full extent of his treachery, offering him the chance even at this last moment to realize that he did *not* want to betray his best friend, Jesus.

But, as Jesus must have already realized, Judas was not going to change his mind now. "Going at once to Jesus, Judas said, 'Greetings, Rabbi!' and kissed him" (Matthew 26:49).

The Bible does not tell us what tone of voice Judas used when he said, "Greetings, Rabbi!" But in my imagination I hear Judas saying these words in a voice full of contempt for Jesus. I think he was mocking Jesus in the tone of voice in which we'd say "Greetings, sucker!" or "Greetings, fool!"

I believe that Judas despised Jesus. His attitude fulfilled Jesus' warning at the Sermon on the Mount: "You cannot serve both God and Money." Because you "will be devoted to the one and despise the other" (Matthew 6:24). And I believe that in his moment of "triumph," Judas could not resist making it clear to Jesus by the sarcasm in his voice and the mockery in his kiss, that he despised Jesus.

Judas' contemptuous attitude toward Jesus makes Jesus' response all the more remarkable. "Jesus replied, 'Friend, do what you came for.'" (Matthew 26:50). An alternative translation catches an important implication of how Jesus greeted Judas: "Friend, why have you come?"[3]

The Bible does not tell us the tone of voice in which Jesus said, "Friend, . . ."

Jesus could have filled his voice with contempt and sarcasm for this greedy traitor. But I don't think so.

I think Jesus, even now, was reaching out to Judas in sincere friendship and concern. Even though Jesus knew that Judas would not change his mind, he was still doing his best to help Judas, to love Judas, to befriend Judas.

This was the way Jesus taught us to treat people who treat us badly. As Jesus said in the Sermon on the Mount:

"You have heard that it was said, 'Love your neighbor and hate your enemy.' But I tell you: Love your enemies and pray for those who persecute you, that you may be sons of your Father in heaven"

(Matthew 5:43–45)

I believe that in his last few moments with Judas, Jesus tried to awaken him to the full horror of what he was doing. What had Judas *really* come to do? *Why* had Judas come?

These are good questions for all of us to ask ourselves as we go through life. What are we *really* doing with are lives? Are we betraying Jesus? And, if we are betraying Jesus, *why* are we betraying him? Is it because we are greedy? Because we want thirty silver coins?

Fortunately, with Jesus there is always hope that we can realize the error of our ways, confess our sins to him, and be forgiven. Jesus laid down his life for his friends. Because Jesus always wants to call us his friend.

Even when we fail to love each other the way Jesus loved us by blessing children, welcoming sinners, weeping with each other, and washing each other's feet. Even when Jesus knows we will soon deny that we are his friend. Even when we fall asleep instead of doing what Jesus wants us to do. Even when we betray Jesus. Jesus **_ALWAYS_** wants to be our friend—our best friend.

Jesus Allows Himself to Be Arrested Without a Fight

The agonizing wait in Gethsemane was over. Judas betrayed Jesus with a kiss, identifying him as the one who should be arrested. "[T]he men [with Judas] stepped forward, seized Jesus and arrested him" (Matthew 26:50). Along with the "large crowd armed with swords and clubs, sent from the chief priests" (Matthew 26:47) there was "a detachment of soldiers and some officials from the chief priests and Pharisees . . . carrying torches, lanterns and weapons" (John 18:3).

Peter did his best to help Jesus. As they arrested Jesus, "Peter, who had a sword, drew it and struck the high priest's servant, cutting off his right ear. (The servant's name was Malchus.)" (John 18:10).

When I was summarizing this story from the Bible, my first impulse was to leave out the name of the person whose ear was cut off. Why clutter the narrative with this detail?

But then I realized that it is always easier to use violence against someone if they are a faceless person without a name. Therefore, it is always important and worth remembering that each person who is hurt by violence has a name.

That is a major reason why the Vietnam Memorial on the Mall in Washington is so moving. It is "nothing" but a long black wall inscribed with the names of the over 50,000 people who died serving the United States in Vietnam. But it is almost impossible not to cry as you touch a name and realize that it is the name of a person who loved life as much as we all do.

In a similar way, the Holocaust Museum in Washington brings home the mind-numbing horror of the Holocaust. How can we ever grasp an evil so terrifying and cruel that it slaughtered millions of innocent people? By giving each visitor the name of a person who endured the Holocaust. By letting that visitor follow the story of the suffering and "crucifixion" of an innocent person with a name.

Jesus understood the cost of violence. Jesus understood that each person hurt by violence has a name. And Jesus understood that violence is not the way to usher in God's kingdom. Therefore, Jesus "commanded Peter, 'Put your sword away! Shall I not drink the cup the Father has given me?'" (John 18:11).

One reason that Jesus ordered Peter to put his sword away was Jesus' understanding that violence causes more violence. As Jesus said to Peter, "Put your sword back in its place . . . for all who draw the sword will die by the sword" (Matthew 26:52).

In this instance, violence was also unnecessary. Jesus assured Peter, "Do you think I cannot call on my Father, and he will at once put at my disposal more than twelve legions of angels? But how then would the Scriptures be fulfilled that say it must happen in this way?" (Matthew 26:53–54).

Jesus told Peter, "Shall I not drink the cup the Father has given me?" (John 18:11). Jesus had more than enough power to prevent his arrest. Instead of using this power, Jesus voluntarily and willingly submitted to his arrest and to the unmerited suffering and crucifixion that followed. Jesus put his hope in the LORD.

Jesus truly practiced what he preached. In the Parable of the Sower, he urged everyone to be "like seed sown on good soil, hear[ing] the word, accept[ing] it, and produc[ing] a crop—thirty, sixty or even a hundred times what was sown" (Mark 4:20). To be such seed, we must drink the cup the Father gives us, even when "trouble or persecution comes because of the word" (Mark 4:17). To be such seed, we must drink the cup the Father gives us, even when "the worries of this life, the deceitfulness of wealth and the desires for other things come in" and try to "choke the word, making it unfruitful" (Mark 4:19).

Jesus knew that if he drank the cup the Father gave him it would lead to suffering, crucifixion and death. Jesus chose to drink the cup anyway. Jesus still placed his hope in the LORD even when the cup of life he had to drink was so bitter and hopeless. Because, as Jesus had told some people a few days earlier, "unless a kernel of wheat falls to the ground and dies, it remains only a single seed. But if it dies, it produces many seeds. [Therefore,] [t]he man who loves his life will lose it, while the man who hates his life in this world will keep it for eternal life" (John 12:24–25).

Most followers of Jesus do not have to die literally and lose their life as martyrs. Most of us "die" symbolically by refusing to let troubles, persecutions, the worries of this life, the deceitfulness of wealth or the desires for other things prevent us from doing what God wants us to do. But, if necessary, followers of Jesus must also be willing to place their hope in the Lord and to accept suffering and death as the cost of their discipleship.

How do we know which cup God wants us to drink? We learn by studying the Scriptures, praying about their application to our life and mission, and putting their commands into practice. Then our lives will be "fulfilled" even as we "fulfill" those Scriptures that guide our specific life and ministry.

Jesus had spent a lifetime studying the Scriptures, praying about their application to his life and mission, and putting their commands into practice. Therefore, now—in the ultimate crisis of his life and ministry—Jesus knew what God wanted him to do. And—like a well-trained athlete—Jesus had the strength, endurance and discipline to do what needed to be done.

Jesus declared to the crowd as he was arrested: "Am I leading a rebellion, that you have come out with swords and clubs to capture me? Every day I sat in the temple courts teaching, and you did not arrest me. But this has all taken place that the writings of the prophets might be fulfilled" (Matthew 26:55–56).

Which Scriptures was Jesus thinking about that must be fulfilled? In the broadest sense, there was parallelism between the destruction of the original Promised Land (Ancient Israel) and the destruction of the new Promised Land (Jesus, the Messiah). As we saw in *Healing The*

Promised Land, the original Promised Land was destroyed by greed, lies and violence. Now the new Promised Land was being destroyed by the greed and lies of Caiaphas and his cronies. Now the new Promised Land was being destroyed by the greed and lies of Judas Iscariot; indeed, betrayal for a bribe is the worst form of lie and greed imaginable. Now the new Promised Land was being destroyed by violence; indeed, the crucifixion of Jesus is the most cruel, violent death imaginable.

Fortunately, the pattern of how God *heals* his Promised Land is also always the same. After the exile of God's people in Babylon, God resurrected the nation of Israel using the wisdom of Isaiah, Jeremiah, Daniel, Ezekiel, Esther, Ezra and Nehemiah. After the death of Jesus, God resurrected his suffering servant, Jesus Christ. And after the Holocaust, God resurrected his suffering servant, Israel.

In addition to this general pattern of how God uses a suffering servant to serve him—whether it is an entire nation that suffers or a single person who suffers—many Old Testament Scriptures are cited in the New Testament to prove that Jesus was the Messiah. Indeed, the application of many of these Old Testament Scriptures to Jesus' life and ministry was explained to the early disciples by Jesus himself. Because, not only before his death, but also after his resurrection, Jesus began "with Moses and all the Prophets [and] explained to them what was said in all the Scriptures concerning himself" (Luke 24:27).[1]

One such passage that may have instructed and sustained Jesus in these dark hours of unmerited suffering and condemnation came from a prophecy written centuries earlier:

> "He was led like a sheep to the
>   slaughter,
>   and as a lamb before the shearer is silent,
>   so he did not open his mouth.
> In his humiliation he was deprived of
>   justice.
>   Who can speak of his descendants?
>   For his life was taken from the
>   earth."
>   (Acts 8:32–33, quoting Isaiah 53:7,8)[2]

By letting himself be arrested without a struggle, Jesus was allowing himself to be "led like a sheep to the slaughter." During the sham judicial proceedings that followed his arrest, "as a lamb before the shearer is silent" Jesus "did not open his mouth." The result of these sham judicial proceedings was that "[i]n his humiliation Jesus was deprived of justice" and "his life was taken from the earth."

Other passages from this centuries-old prophecy were also fulfilled. This prophecy about a suffering servant of the LORD began:

> See, my servant will act wisely;
> he will be raised and lifted up and
> highly exalted.
>
> (Isaiah 52:13)

No one can dispute that Jesus acted wisely and that, ultimately, he was "highly exalted."

But the path to being "highly exalted" was not an easy one, even for this servant who "will act wisely." In words that evoke images of the mutilation and humiliation endured by one who is crucified, the prophecy foretold:

> . . . there were many who were appalled at him—
> his appearance was so disfigured
> beyond that of any man
> and his form marred beyond human likeness.
>
> (Isaiah 52:14)

The prophecy also foretold that this wise servant would be despised as Jesus was despised by greedy Judas. And this wise servant would be rejected as Jesus was rejected by the chief priests and Pharisees. As the prophet said centuries earlier:

> He was despised and rejected by men,
> a man of sorrows, and familiar with
> suffering.
> Like one from whom men hide their
> faces

263

he was despised, and we esteemed
him not.

(Isaiah 53:3)

This centuries-old prophecy also described the wise servant's role in "fulfilling" the Passover as the sacrificial "lamb" whose blood would cause death to "passover" God's people and would set God's people free from their lives of sin. As the prophet foretold:

Surely he took up our infirmities
and carried our sorrows,
yet we considered him stricken by
God,
smitten by him, and afflicted.
But he was pierced for our
transgressions,
he was crushed for our iniquities;
the punishment that brought us peace
was upon him,
and by his wounds we are healed.
We all, like sheep, have gone astray,
each of us has turned to his own
way;
and the LORD has laid on him
the iniquity of us all.

(Isaiah 53:4–6)

This wise servant "was cut off from the land of the living" (Isaiah 53:8). And this wise servant was killed unjustly. "By oppression and judgment he was taken away" (Isaiah 53:8). Surely the plotting of Caiaphas and his cronies that cut off Jesus from the land of the living fulfilled this prophecy of oppression and judgment that would take away the life of the wise servant.

The wise servant suffered this tragic death even "though he had done no violence, nor was any deceit in his mouth" (Isaiah 53:9).

In keeping with this prophecy made centuries earlier, Jesus did nothing violent. For his Triumphal Entry, Jesus entered Jerusalem as a king "gentle and riding on a donkey" (Matthew 21:5, quoting Zechariah

9:9). And when Jesus was betrayed and arrested in Gethsemane, he "commanded Peter, 'Put your sword away.'" (John 18:11).

Nor was any deceit found in Jesus' mouth. As he told Pilate during his interrogation: "[F]or this reason I was born, and for this reason I came into the world, to testify to the truth. Everyone on the side of truth listens to me" (John 18:37).[3]

Even though this wise servant of the LORD was gentle and truthful, "[y]et it was the LORD's will to crush him and cause him to suffer" (Isaiah 53:10). This perplexing punishment of an innocent servant of the LORD troubled Jesus greatly as he prayed in Gethsemane the night he was betrayed. His soul was "overwhelmed with sorrow to the point of death" (Matthew 26:38). So "he fell with his face to the ground and prayed, 'My Father, if it is possible, may this cup be taken from me.'" (Matthew 26:39). Nevertheless, despite the unmerited suffering in God the Father's plan for his life, Jesus, the Son of God, found the courage to pray as a wise, obedient servant: "Yet not as I will, but as you will" (Matthew 26:39).

Perhaps part of the reason that Jesus found the courage to remain an obedient, wise servant of the LORD in the midst of tragedy was that this same prophecy gave him hope that "in all things God [the Father] works for the good of those who love him, who have been called according to his purpose" (Romans 8:28). Jesus foresaw—as the prophet had foretold centuries earlier—that

> [even though] it was the LORD's will
>   to crush [his wise servant]
>   and cause him to suffer,
> and though the LORD makes his life
> a guilt offering,
> he will see his offspring and prolong
>   his days,
> and the will of the LORD will prosper
>   in his hand.
>
> (Isaiah 53:10)

Jesus had faith that God would resurrect him and his hopes from the dead—that God would establish the work of his hands by healing his Promised Land. As the prophet foretold:

After the suffering of his soul,
    he will see the light of life and be
        satisfied;
by his knowledge my righteous
        servant will justify many,
    and he will bear their iniquities.
Therefore I will give him a portion
        among the great,
    and he will divide the spoils with the
        strong,
because he poured out his life unto
        death,
    and was numbered with the transgressors.
For he bore the sin of many,
    and made intercession for the transgressors.

                                      (Isaiah 53:11–12)

Sustained by the hope that "[a]fter the suffering of his soul, he [would] see the light of life and be satisfied" (Isaiah 53:11), Jesus was strong and courageous enough to tell Peter: "Put your sword away! Shall I not drink the cup the Father has given me?" (John 18:11).

And, on this night in which he was betrayed, Jesus needed all the strength and courage he could find by hoping in the LORD. Because "all the disciples deserted him and fled" (Matthew 26:56).

I pray that you will always find the strength and courage to hope in the LORD and to drink the cup of life that God asks you to drink.

No matter how bitter that cup may be, drink it with hope.

Live a fulfilling life by fulfilling God's purpose for your life.

And learn God's purpose for your life by diligent study and application of the Scriptures to the circumstances in which you find yourself.

Because "in all things God works for the good of those who love him, who have been called according to his purpose" (Romans 8:28). God will establish the work of our hands by healing our Promised land even when we are "despised and rejected by [people], a [person] of sorrows, and familiar with sufferings" (Isaiah 53:3). God will heal our Promised Land even when our best friends betray us and desert us.

Jesus Tells the High Priest That He Is the Messiah

Caiaphas and his cronies won. "Those who had arrested Jesus took him to Caiaphas, the high priest, where the teachers of the law and the elders had assembled" (Matthew 26:57).

Now Caiaphas and his cronies moved quickly to gain the fruits of their victory: the death of Jesus before the crowds favorable to him could rally to his side and his cause.

After all, the whole reason for spending thirty pieces of silver to bribe Judas was so they could "arrest Jesus in some sly way and kill him" (Matthew 26:4). They had needed Judas' help so they could arrest Jesus in a quiet, out-of-the way place such as the Garden of Gethsemane in the middle of the night "when no crowd was present" (Luke 22:6) so that there would not be "a riot among the people" (Matthew 26:5). Because, especially after the enthusiastic welcome given Jesus during his Triumphal Entry into Jerusalem and the support of so many people for Jesus when he tossed the money changers and merchants out of the temple, Caiaphas and his cronies "were afraid of the people" (Luke 22:2).

Peter fled and deserted Jesus after Jesus commanded him not to fight to prevent Jesus' arrest. However, Peter "followed [Jesus] at a distance, right up to the courtyard of the high priest. He entered and sat down with the guards to see the outcome" (Matthew 26:58).

Not that there was any real doubt as to the outcome of Jesus being arrested in the middle of the night. Such a clandestine action only made sense if Caiaphas and his cronies were going to kill Jesus quickly.

And Caiaphas and his cronies were *certainly* not going to give Jesus a fair trial. After all, just a few days before, Caiaphas' cronies had worried, "If we let [Jesus] go on like this, everyone will believe in him, and then the Romans will come and take away both our place and our nation" (John 11:48). And Caiaphas had told them, "[I]t is better for you that one man die for the people than that the whole nation perish" (John 11:50).

Nevertheless, Peter lingered in the courtyard of the high priest to see and hear as best he could what would happen to Jesus. Peter's worst fears were quickly confirmed.

"The chief priests and the whole Sanhedrin were looking for false evidence against Jesus so that they could put him to death" (Matthew 26:59). So much for an impartial inquiry!

At first, "they did not find any [such evidence], though many false witnesses came forward" (Matthew 26:60). But then "two came forward and declared, 'This fellow said, "I am able to destroy the temple of God and rebuild it in three days."'" (Matthew 26:60–61).

This sounded like a promising line of inquiry. If they could accuse Jesus of wanting to destroy the temple, who wouldn't want to see such a troublemaker silenced? And, if he was claiming God-like powers to rebuild the temple in three days, they could condemn him as a blasphemer and a madman.

"[T]he high priest stood up and said to Jesus, 'Are you not going to answer? What is this testimony that these men are bringing against you?'" (Matthew 26:62). The high priest probably hoped to provoke Jesus into saying something that could be twisted against him. But Jesus refused to dignify these false witnesses with a reply. "Jesus remained silent" (Matthew 26:63). As foretold by the prophecy centuries earlier:

He was oppressed and afflicted,
    yet he did not open his mouth;
he was led like a lamb to the slaughter,

and as a sheep before her shearers is
    silent,
so he did not open his mouth.

(Isaiah 53:7)

We do not have a video of this confrontation between the high priest and Jesus. We cannot be certain of the two men's demeanor and tone of voice. However, I suspect that by this point in the confrontation, the high priest was getting agitated and angry.

The night had started well. The arrest of Jesus had gone smoothly. But now things were bogging down. He couldn't get enough credible evidence to kill Jesus. And he couldn't provoke Jesus into saying something that could be used against him.

What was a high priest to do?

This high priest decided to try the direct approach. Instead of manufacturing fake charges against Jesus, he decided to ask Jesus unequivocally whether he was the Messiah. If Jesus claimed to be the Messiah, that would be all the evidence the high priest needed.

He could justify the execution of Jesus to the Jews who would consider Jesus to be a blasphemer. And he could justify the execution of Jesus to the Romans who would consider Jesus to be a threat to their rule.

Therefore, the "high priest said to [Jesus], 'I charge you under oath by the living God: Tell us if you are the Christ, the Son of God.'" (Matthew 26:63). (The Greek word "Christ" meant the same thing as the Hebrew word "Messiah").[1]

Peter may well have been able to see and hear this decisive question as he lingered in the courtyard of the high priest. If so, Peter must have held his breathe. This was the key moment. If Jesus said he was the Messiah, Peter knew his execution was certain.

Perhaps Peter thought back to that moment when Jesus asked his disciples, "Who do you say I am?" (Matthew 16:15). Peter was the one who answered, "You are the Christ, the Son of the living God" (Matthew 16:16). Jesus immediately confirmed the truth of Peter's declaration—he was the Messiah. But Jesus also immediately "warned his disciples not to tell anyone that he was the Christ" (Matthew 16:17–20).

Jesus knew it meant certain death at the hands of the Jews or the Romans to confirm publicly that he was the Messiah.

Peter was probably saying silently to himself, "Please, Jesus! Dodge this question just one more time! Maybe you should even *deny* you are the Messiah. Perhaps then they won't kill you. Then you can live to fight another day!"

But Jesus knew that the moment had come when he must tell the truth. He must declare publicly who he really was. Even though to do so meant that he would drink the bitter cup of suffering, crucifixion and death that awaited him.

Because after agonizing in prayer for hours in Gethsemane, Jesus knew that it was the will of God the Father: Jesus, the Messiah, the Christ, the Son of the living God, must become the sacrificial "lamb" whose blood would cause death to "passover" God's people and whose blood would set God's people free from their lives of sin.

There must be no more delay. During this very celebration of the Passover, Jesus would fulfill the centuries-old prophecy:

> Surely he took up our infirmities
> and carried our sorrows,
> . . . he was pierced for our
> transgressions,
> he was crushed for our iniquities;
> the punishment that brought us peace
> was upon him,
> and by his wounds we are healed.
> . . . [because] the LORD has laid on him
> the iniquity of us all.
>
> (Isaiah 53:4–6)

Therefore, when the high priest asked Jesus "under oath by the living God" to "[t]ell us if you are the Christ, the Son of God" (Matthew 26:63), Jesus told the truth. Jesus replied, "Yes, it is as you say" (Matthew 26:64). "I am" (Mark 14:62).

Not only was this reply a clear, unequivocal declaration that Jesus was "the Christ, the Son of God." But for Jesus to say "I am" in this context was a declaration by Jesus that he himself *is* God. Because when

God spoke to Moses out of the burning bush, God told Moses that the name of God is: "I AM WHO I AM" (Exodus 3:14).

With his reply to the chief priest's question, Jesus assured his execution. I suspect that the high priest's face began to show a mixture of triumph and contempt. Triumph—because he knew he had the excuse he needed for killing Jesus. And contempt—because it was so ridiculous for this pitiful looking figure standing alone in front of him to claim that he was "the Christ, the Son of God."

Jesus wasn't done, however. Jesus knew that he would live to fight another day! (Though not in the way Peter was thinking—by escaping death after denying he was the Messiah).

As his accusers began to gloat and smirk, Jesus said with total confidence in his ultimate triumph, "But I say to all of you: In the future you will see the Son of Man sitting at the right hand of the Mighty One and coming on the clouds of heaven" (Matthew 26:64).

This statement by Jesus referred to several passages in the Scriptures that would have been well known to Caiaphas and his cronies as descriptions of the Messiah. In Psalm 110:1, the Lord says to King David's Lord (the Messiah): "Sit at my right hand until I make your enemies a footstool for your feet."[2] And a prophecy in the book of Daniel that referred to the Messiah said:

> "In my vision at night I looked, and there before me was one like a son of man, coming with the clouds of heaven. He approached the Ancient of Days and was led into his presence. He was given authority, glory and sovereign power; all peoples, nations and men of every language worshiped him. His dominion is an everlasting dominion that will not pass away, and his kingdom is one that will never be destroyed."
>
> (Daniel 7:13–14)

Caiaphas and his cronies lost all self-control when Jesus dared to proclaim that he "was given authority, glory and sovereign power [so that] all peoples, nations and men of every language [would] worship[] him" (Daniel 7:14). "[T]he high priest tore his clothes and said, 'He has spoken blasphemy!'" (Matthew 26:65).

Triumph must have spread across Caiaphas' face as he said, "Why do we need any more witnesses? Look, now you have heard the blasphemy. What do you think?" (Matthew 26:65–66).

His cronies gave the answer Caiaphas expected and demanded: "He is worthy of death" (Matthew 26:66).

Not that his cronies needed any encouragement to hate Jesus and want to see him dead. "[T]hey spit in his face and struck him with their fists. Others slapped him and said, 'Prophecy to us, Christ. Who hit you?'" (Matthew 26:67–68).

This time of triumph for Caiaphas and his cronies was a time of despair for Peter. He was trying to see what would happen to Jesus. But he had to keep moving around the courtyard of the high priest so that *he* wouldn't get arrested and killed, too.

At first, "Peter was sitting out in the courtyard" (Matthew 26:69). "A servant girl came to him [and said,] 'You also were with Jesus of Galilee . . .'" (Matthew 26:69). A number of people must have heard the girl's accusation. Because we are told that Peter "denied it before them all. 'I don't know what you're talking about,' he said" (Matthew 26:70).

Peter moved away from that group of inquisitive people and "went out to the gateway" (Matthew 26:71). However, "another girl saw him and said to the people there, 'This fellow was with Jesus of Nazareth.'" (Matthew 26:71). This time Peter was even more emphatic in his denial of the accusation. "He denied it again, with an oath: 'I don't know the man!'" (Matthew 26:72).

This was a lie. But in one sense, it is fascinating to realize that Peter really didn't "know the man." Even though he'd spent three years traveling with Jesus and learning from him, Peter still didn't really know Jesus.

Oh, Peter *thought* he knew Jesus very well. After all, he'd been the first disciple to say that Jesus was "the Christ, the Son of the living God" (Matthew 16:16).

But Peter assumed this meant that he would see Jesus "sitting at the right hand of the Mighty One and coming on the clouds of heaven" (Matthew 26:64). Peter envisioned Jesus fulfilling the prophecy in Daniel by receiving "authority, glory and sovereign power" so that "all peoples, nations and men of every language worshiped him" (Daniel 7:14).

Peter had never been able to accept the idea that Jesus would be the suffering servant prophesied in Isaiah. He couldn't bear to think of his beloved Jesus being "despised and rejected by men, a man of sorrows, and familiar with suffering" (Isaiah 53:3).

And so, Peter had refused to believe Jesus when he explained to his disciples:

> that he must go to Jerusalem and suffer many things at the hands of the elders, chief priests and teachers of the law, and that he must be killed and on the third day be raised to life.
>
> (Matthew 16:21)

Indeed, Peter had disagreed with Jesus so much about this depressing prediction that he "took [Jesus] aside and began to rebuke him, 'Never, Lord!' he said. 'This shall never happen to you!'" (Matthew 16:22). But now, the unthinkable was happening right in front of Peter's horrified eyes.

Peter simply had not yet been able to grasp that the reason Jesus would be "given authority, glory and sovereign power" so that "all peoples, nations and men of every language worshiped him" (Daniel 7:14) was because Jesus would be "pierced for our transgressions [and] crushed for our iniquities [so that] the punishment that brought us peace was upon him, and by his wounds we are healed" (Isaiah 53:5). And so, from this most fundamental, important perspective, Peter was right when he said, "I don't know the man!" (Matthew 26:72).

But when Peter denied he even knew Jesus, he meant it as a lie. And it was such a transparent lie that those around him quickly saw through it.

"After a little while, those standing there went up to Peter and said, 'Surely you are one of them, for your accent gives you away.'" (Matthew 26:73). To make matters even worse, "[o]ne of the high priest's servants, a relative of the man whose ear Peter had cut off" (John 18:26) was among those accusing Peter of being a disciple of Jesus. This servant of the high priest "challenged him, 'Didn't I see you with him in the olive grove?'" (John 18:26).

Peter's heart must have pounded. He panicked. "[H]e began to call down curses on himself and he swore to them, 'I don't know the man!'" (Matthew 26:74).

Apparently, all the noise and commotion attracted Jesus' attention. Because "[j]ust as he was speaking, the rooster crowed." And "[t]he Lord turned and looked straight at Peter" (Luke 22:60–61).

Imagine the look that Jesus must have given Peter.

Hurt must have filled Jesus' eyes. Even though Jesus had predicted Peter's denial, it still must have been a heavy blow to experience Peter's denial at this moment when Jesus was already in such distress.

And yet, that look from Jesus was just what Peter needed to bring him to his senses. "Then Peter remembered the word the Lord had spoken to him: 'Before the rooster crows today, you will disown me three times.'" (Luke 22:61).

I assume that Peter also remembered the cockiness with which he'd argued with Jesus. He had "insisted emphatically, 'Even if I have to die with you, I will never disown you.'" (Mark 14:31).

But events had proven that this was empty boasting. Peter hadn't even been able to stay awake to pray with Jesus in Gethsemane. He'd run away when Jesus was arrested. And in the courtyard of the high priest he'd repeatedly denied he even knew Jesus.

No wonder Peter "went outside and wept bitterly" (Luke 22:62).

I hope you never reach that point of despair where you have to weep bitterly. But, if you do, remember that even someone as great as Peter has been there before you.

And remember that Jesus is not looking at you with hurt in his eyes because he *hates* you. Jesus is looking at you with hurt in his eyes because he *loves* you.

After your bitter weeping is over, Jesus hopes you'll remember the rest of what he told Peter at the Last Supper—what Jesus tells all his disciples who fail him: ". . . Satan has asked to sift you as wheat. But I have prayed for you, . . . that your faith may not fail" (Luke 22:31–32).

After all, Jesus knows that "[w]e all, like sheep, have gone astray, each of us has turned to his own way" (Isaiah 53:6). But Jesus also knows that there is still hope for us. Even when we fail him miserably the way Peter failed him.

Jesus knew that Peter could find new hope after his bitter weeping was over. There was still hope for Peter. And there is always hope for us today. Even after we have failed Jesus miserably and have wept bitterly, we can still rejoice, finding the faith to say: "Give thanks to the LORD, for he is good. *His love endures forever*" (Psalm 118:1,29; Psalm 136)!

Such *hope* in the LORD's enduring *love* gives us the *faith* that brings us back to the Promised Land—the *faith* that makes us *love* Jesus who gives us *hope* because he sacrificed himself to save us (Colossians 1:3—6). His perfect sacrifice makes death "passover" God's people. His perfect sacrifice sets God's people free from their lives of sin. His perfect sacrifice brings us out of the Cursed Land of Sin's slavery into the Promised Land of the LORD's blessings (Exodus 20:1–2).

There is always hope—always strength to heal the Promised Land—because Jesus has been given authority, glory and sovereign power so that *all* peoples will be blessed by worshiping the LORD in spirit and in truth.

There is always hope—always the joy of the LORD that gives us strength to heal our Promised Land (Nehemiah 8:10)—because Jesus "took up our infirmities and carried our sorrows" (Isaiah 53:4). Jesus carried us and our sorrows to the Promised Land across the ocean of Sin that separated us from God!

Furthermore, by pouring out his life unto death, Jesus bore the sin of many (Isaiah 53:12). "[T]he punishment that brought us peace was upon him, and by his wounds we are healed" (Isaiah 53:5). By Jesus' wounds, our Promised Land is healed!

Therefore, "[g]ive thanks to the LORD, for he is good. *His love endures forever*" (Psalm 118:1,29; Psalm 136)!

Pilate Bows to the Political Pressure to Crucify Jesus

The Passover plot of Caiaphas and his cronies continued. Judas had played his part by betraying Jesus' whereabouts so Jesus could be arrested quietly away from the crowds. And Jesus had admitted that he was "the Christ, the Son of God" (Matthew 26:63–64), thereby clinching Caiaphas' case against him.

Things were going well. But speed was essential. Caiaphas needed a "rush to judgment" so that there would not be time for Jesus' supporters to rally support for him.

Therefore, "[e]arly in the morning, all the chief priests and the elders of the people came to the decision to put Jesus to death" (Matthew 27:1). They wasted no time implementing their judgment. "They bound him, led him away and handed him over to Pilate, the governor" (Matthew 27:2).[1]

Just as a judge does today when an alleged criminal is brought before him, "Pilate . . . asked, 'What charges are you bringing against this man?'" (John 18:29).

Caiaphas and his cronies presented a laundry list of charges that they hoped would convince Pilate to execute Jesus. "[T]hey began to accuse [Jesus], saying, 'We have found this man subverting our nation. He opposes payment of taxes to Caesar and claims to be Christ, a king.'" (Luke 23:2).

Pilate proceeded to investigate these charges. He "summoned Jesus and asked him, 'Are you the king of the Jews?' (John 18:33). 'What is it you have done?'" (John 18:35).

I wish we had a video of this confrontation between Pilate and Jesus. There are a number of ways that Pilate might have said these words.

Perhaps he said them in a professional, detached tone, the way a judge should. Perhaps he said them in a nasty, overbearing, angry tone, to intimidate the victim the way a Gestapo agent would.

I suspect Pilate said these words in a sarcastic, skeptical tone, the way a crafty politician would (especially when he was bleary-eyed and mad at being awakened so early in the morning to hear a case where the charges were ludicrous and were obviously brought in bad faith).

Pilate must have wondered how anybody could think that this pitiful, lonely figure could be "subverting" anybody's nation! By this time Jesus was already suffering from the ill-effects of abuse and lack of sleep. He'd been up all night. And, when Jesus claimed to be "the Christ, the Son of God," Caiaphas' cronies "spit in his face and struck him with their fists. Others slapped him and said, 'Prophesy to us, Christ. Who hit you?'" (Matthew 26:67–68).

Furthermore, Pilate may already have had enough information about Jesus and his teachings to know that much—if not all—of what Caiaphas and his cronies were saying were lies.

The Bible does not tell us what, if any, information the Roman authorities already had about Jesus before his trial. But it seems that Pilate and the other Romans must have noticed the excitement of the Jewish throng during Jesus' Triumphal Entry (Matthew 21:1–11). And the Roman "security forces" and informants must have reported the turmoil when Jesus drove the merchants and moneychangers out of the temple (Matthew 21:12–16).

The Bible hints that Pilate had such prior knowledge of the ulterior motives of Caiaphas and his cronies when it says that Pilate "knew it was out of envy that they had handed Jesus over to him" (Matthew 27:18).

Furthermore, Pilate may well have had specific knowledge that Caiaphas and his cronies were lying when they charged that Jesus "opposes payment of taxes to Caesar" (Luke 23:2).

Earlier that week, "the Pharisees went out and laid plans to trap [Jesus] in his words" (Matthew 22:15). They asked him, "Is it right to pay taxes to Caesar or not?" (Matthew 22:17). Presumably they included several people in their group who would report directly to the Romans what Jesus said. "But Jesus, knowing their evil intent" (Matthew 22:18), avoided their trap. He said, "You hypocrites, why are you trying to trap me?" (Matthew 22:18). And, after reminding them that their coins carried the portrait and inscription of Caesar, Jesus made his famous maxim: "Give to Caesar what is Caesar's, and to God what is God's" (Matthew 22:21).

It is reasonable to assume that an informant had already told the Romans about this statement by Jesus. In which case, Pilate knew that at least this part of the charges against Jesus was totally false.

Therefore, Pilate was probably inclined to believe Jesus' explanation that he was not the kind of king who the Romans needed to fear or execute. Jesus told Pilate, "My kingdom is not of this world. If it were, my servants would fight to prevent my arrest by the Jews. But now my kingdom is from another place" (John 18:36).

In a voice that I believe was tinged with amused sarcasm, Pilate quipped, "You are a king, then!" (John 18:37).

Jesus seized upon this mocking remark by Pilate to explain better who he was. "Jesus answered, 'You are right in saying I am a king. In fact, for this reason I was born, and for this I came into the world, to testify to the truth.'" (John 18:37).

Then Jesus went to the heart of Pilate's weakest character flaw as a politician—would he put the truth above his political ambitions? Jesus told him, "Everyone on the side of truth listens to me" (John 18:37).

Pilate evaded Jesus' assertion that "Everyone on the side of truth listens to me." In the timeworn tradition of politicians, Pilate refused to give a clear, unequivocal statement. Instead, he asked a question: "What is truth?" (John 18:38).

I believe that Pilate asked this question in a sneering, condescending tone of voice. As a cynical politician, I believe he thought that "the truth" counted for little, if anything, in the "real world." And Pilate's actions the rest of the day bear out my view that his actions were driven by fear rather than guided by the truth.

Many people intuitively think that Pilate asked the question "What is truth?" because he was sincerely uncertain what "the truth" was—either because of uncertainty regarding what the facts about Jesus were or because of philosophical doubts regarding whether truth is knowable at all. This interpretation of Pilate's question comes naturally to contemplative people such as theologians and philosophers—especially during the past century when so many doubts were expressed about whether there are absolute truths that are knowable with confidence by our finite minds.

But Pilate was not a theologian or a philosopher. He was a politician. And nothing in the story suggests that he had any doubts about what "the truth" was. Pilate *knew* that Jesus was innocent of the charges against him.

Pilate's problem was that—like many a politician before and after him—"the truth" was inconvenient and unpopular. And so, in the end, Pilate refused to act based on what he knew to be "the truth." Pilate acted instead based on what he knew to be "politically correct."

At first, Pilate tried to be "on the side of truth." After questioning Jesus, he went out to Jesus' accusers and said, "I find no basis for a charge against him" (John 18:38).

But Caiaphas and his cronies refused to accept this decision. "[T]hey insisted, 'He stirs up the people all over Judea by his teaching.'" (Luke 23:5).

At this point, Pilate should have ended the discussion, reiterated his decision that Jesus was innocent of the charges brought against him, and set Jesus free.

Instead, like many a politician before and after him, Pilate wavered. He knew the truth. But he also knew what the "public opinion polls" said. He wanted to avoid the political fallout of an unpopular decision.

A remark by Caiaphas and his cronies gave Pilate an idea how to avoid making a decision in this case. Caiaphas and his cronies said that Jesus started stirring up people "in Galilee and has come all the way here" (Luke 23:5). Pilate confirmed that Jesus was a Galilean. Then, since "Jesus was under Herod's jurisdiction, he sent him to Herod, who was also in Jerusalem at that time" (Luke 23:6–7).

Herod "was greatly pleased [to see Jesus] because for a long time he had been wanting to see him" (Luke 23:8). Not that Herod wanted to see Jesus for the right reasons. He didn't want Jesus to teach him how to love the Lord his God with all his heart and with all his soul and with all his mind and how to love his neighbor as himself. Instead, Herod wanted Jesus to entertain him with a miracle.

But Jesus refused to stoop to miraculous stunts to impress Herod or anyone else (Luke 23:8–9). Disappointed, Herod sought a different sort of entertainment from Jesus. "Herod and his soldiers ridiculed and mocked him" (Luke 23:11). This was the sort of amusement Herod liked.

"That day Herod and Pilate became friends" (Luke 23:12). But Herod did not solve Pilate's problem. Instead of taking responsibility for executing Jesus, Herod "[d]ress[ed] him in an elegant robe [and] sent him back to Pilate" (Luke 23:11).

Meanwhile, back in Pilate's palace, things were going from bad to worse.

His wife was nagging him. Even as "Pilate was sitting on the judge's seat" trying to decide what to do about Jesus, "his wife sent him this message: 'Don't have anything to do with that innocent man, for I have suffered a great deal today in a dream because of him.'" (Matthew 27:19). As every husband knows, when your wife wants something, you better do it. And nothing is more irritating (or ominous) than when your wife wants something so badly that she interrupts you during a bad day at work to nag you about it.

Moreover, a crowd was gathering. As a shrewd politician, Pilate tried to turn this problem into an opportunity. But his maneuvering backfired. He soon found himself under even more pressure to execute Jesus—even though it made his wife mad.

Apparently, it was normal for a crowd to gather on this day because "it was the governor's custom at the [Passover] Feast to release a prisoner chosen by the crowd" (Matthew 27:15). Pilate tried to steer the crowd toward choosing Jesus so he could save his life.

Pilate gave the crowd a choice between Barabbas and Jesus. Since Barabbas was "a notorious prisoner" (Matthew 27:16) who "had been thrown into prison for an insurrection in the city, and for murder" (Luke

23:19), Pilate may have thought that it was a "no-brainer." Surely the crowd would choose Jesus. Especially because Jesus had been so popular with the crowd during his Triumphal Entry and while he taught in the Temple.

But Pilate did not reckon with the fickleness of a crowd. They loved Jesus when he looked like a winner. They despised him when he looked like a loser.

Furthermore, this crowd may have been predisposed to choose Barabbas. After all, he'd been popular enough with some people in Jerusalem to stage an insurrection. Some of the people would demand the release of this popular terrorist being held by the army occupying their homeland.

Above all, Pilate underestimated the power and persuasiveness of Caiaphas and his cronies. "[T]he chief priests and the elders persuaded the crowd to ask for Barabbas and to have Jesus executed" (Matthew 27:20). When Pilate asked the crowd, "Which one do you want me to release to you: Barabbas, or Jesus who is called Christ?" (Matthew 27:17), he didn't get the answer he wanted. "With one voice they cried out, 'Away with this man! Release Barabbas to us!'" (Luke 23:18).

Now Pilate was caught between a rock and a hard place—fear of his wife and fear of the crowd. "Wanting to release Jesus, Pilate appealed to them again. But they kept shouting, 'Crucify him! Crucify him!'" (Luke 23:20–21).

Seeking desperately for a way out of this quagmire of fears, "Pilate answered, 'You take him and crucify him. As for me, I find no basis for a charge against him.'" (John 19:6).

This suggestion showed Pilate was a spineless politician. As long as he could avoid responsibility for crucifying Jesus, he was quite willing to stand aside and let someone else crucify Jesus. The truth and an innocent man's life counted for nothing as long as Pilate could find a politically correct way out of his quagmire of fears.

However, Caiaphas and his cronies did not accept this solution. They wanted Pilate to carry out the crucifixion. They "insisted, 'We have a law, and according to that law he must die, because he claimed to be the Son of God.'" (John 19:7).

"When Pilate heard this, he was even more afraid . . ." (John 19:8). In Roman mythology, the gods often mated with mortal women. Apparently this comment played upon Pilate's religious and superstitious fears. If Jesus was an offspring of a god mating with a woman, no wonder his wife had "suffered a great deal today in a dream because of him" (Matthew 27:19).

"From then on, Pilate tried to set Jesus free . . ." (John 19:12). But Caiaphas, his cronies and the crowd "kept shouting, 'If you let this man go, you are no friend of Caesar. Anyone who claims to be a king opposes Caesar.'" (John 19:12).

These shouts generated the ultimate fear in Pilate's life. If Caesar heard that he was not zealously putting down opposing kings, it would be the end of Pilate's career and, very possibly, the end of Pilate's life.[2]

Of course, such charges against Pilate would be lies and nonsense. But "What is truth?" against the power of a lie.

If we are not committed to serving on the side of truth, we will always be caught in a quagmire of fears fed by lies. If we do not hope in the LORD, our lives will ultimately be driven by fear instead of inspired by hope.

Caiaphas and his cronies had now found the greatest fear in the life of this career politician—the end of his career. Pilate lacked the backbone to sacrifice everything he had for the truth. Only Jesus had such courage and commitment that sad day in Jerusalem.

So "[w]hen Pilate heard this, he brought Jesus out and sat down on the judge's seat . . ." (John 19:13). In a voice that I imagine was now weary with stress and dismay, Pilate asked Caiaphas and his cronies: "Shall I crucify your king?" (John 19:15). "'We have no king but Caesar,' the chief priests answered" (John 19:15).

This statement by the chief priests is one of the saddest statements in the Bible.

When Ancient Israel first asked for a king, the Lord told Samuel "they have rejected me as their king" (1 Samuel 8:7). Even after Samuel warned the people about all the drawbacks of replacing God with a human king, the people insisted that they wanted a human king—a "Caesar." God's people said, "We want a king over us. Then we will be like all the other nations . . ." (1 Samuel 8:19–20).

Be careful what you ask for. You may get it.

The Ancient Israelites asked for a king. They became wicked like all the other nations. And, within a few centuries, Jerusalem and its temple were destroyed.

In Jesus' time, the chief priests rejected God as their king. They asked for Caesar instead. And the Romans destroyed Jerusalem, its temple and its high priests.

However, the destruction of Jerusalem, its temple and its high priests lay 40 years in the future as Pilate squirmed in his judgment chair. The crowd kept shouting: "Crucify him! Crucify him!" (Luke 23:21). "If you let this man go, you are no friend of Caesar. Anyone who claims to be a king opposes Caesar" (John 19:12).

At last, Pilate's fear for his career and fear for his life overcame his fear of his wife and his fear of superstition. But, being a politician, he made one last gesture to escape responsibility for a decision that he knew was contrary to the truth that Jesus was innocent.

"When Pilate saw that he was getting nowhere, but that instead an uproar was starting, he took water and washed his hands in front of the crowd. 'I am innocent of this man's blood,' he said. 'It is your responsibility!'" (Matthew 27:24).

This was a lie. It *was* his responsibility to determine Jesus' guilt or innocence. But "What is truth?" when a lie makes you look good?

"All the people answered, 'Let his blood be on us and on our children.'" (Matthew 27:25). The mob's contrived shouting did not absolve Pilate from his responsibility as governor to determine the truth about the charges against Jesus. The Roman government gave Pilate the responsibility to determine guilt or innocence. By condemning Jesus to death when he knew he was innocent, Pilate was guilty of Jesus' blood no matter how much he denied it and no matter how much he washed his hands in water.

As an excuse for their inexcusable persecution of Jews, Anti-Semites use this reply by the crowd to condemn other Jews who were not in the crowd, including Jews living today—2,000 years later. This is unfair and illogical. I'd hate to be held responsible for what my ancestors in England were saying and doing 2,000 years ago. Presumably they were Druids practicing human sacrifice!

Furthermore, the misapplication of the crowd's reply by Anti-Semites perversely distorts the fact that it is *good* to have the blood of Jesus on us and on our children! Not in the sense that we killed Jesus. But in the sense that Jesus knowingly became the sacrificial lamb who fulfilled the meaning of the Passover.

Remember that, in the original Passover when the Jews escaped from slavery in Egypt, death passed over the Jews because they covered their doorposts with blood from the passover lamb. So by saying that the blood of Jesus should "be on us and on our children" the crowd unwittingly declared the truth that Jesus was fulfilling the Passover. His blood would indeed be on them and on their children, offering them the gift of salvation that saves us from death and frees us from sin and its consequences.

This fulfillment of the Passover was coming true before the unknowing eyes of the crowd. Because the spineless Pilate "released Barabbas to them. But he had Jesus flogged, and handed him over to be crucified" (Matthew 27:26).

During our lives we each find ourselves in the position of Pilate many times. So learn from Pilate's mistakes.

When you're given responsibility to make a decision, always make it truthfully. Don't worry about the troubles and persecutions that "the crowd" may inflict on you. Don't allow yourself to be deflected from fulfilling your responsibilities truthfully even if the deceitfulness of wealth or the desire for other things (such as your career or escaping death) tempt you to shirk your responsibilities.

Be on the side of truth. Because, as Jesus told Pilate, "Everyone on the side of truth listens to [Jesus]" (John 18:37).

Jesus Forgives His Enemies and Trusts God

Caiaphas and his cronies had achieved their purpose. Jesus would be crucified. "So the [Roman] soldiers took charge of Jesus. Carrying his own cross, he went out to the place of the Skull (which in Aramaic is called Golgotha)" (John 19:16–17).

Jesus was already physically weak and tormented as he carried his cross. He'd been up all night. Caiaphas and his cronies had spit on him and slapped him (Matthew 26:67–68). Pilate "had Jesus flogged" (Matthew 27:26). His soldiers

> stripped [Jesus] and put a scarlet robe on him, and then twisted together a crown of thorns and set it on his head. They put a staff in his right hand and knelt in front of him and mocked him. "Hail, king of the Jews!" they said. They spit on him, and took the staff and struck him on the head again and again.
>
> (Matthew 27:28–30)

After such abuse and torture, Jesus lacked the strength to carry his cross far. "As they led him away, they seized Simon from Cyrene, who was on his way in from the country, and put the cross on him and made him carry it behind Jesus" (Luke 23:26).

Too late to make a difference, a crowd began to gather who did not want to see Jesus crucified. "A large number of people followed him, including women who mourned and wailed for him" (Luke 23:27).

The pitiful procession reached the place where Jesus would be crucified. This place of torture and execution was aptly called "the place of the Skull" known to us by its Aramaic name "Golgotha" (John 19:17).

"Here they crucified him, and with him two others—one on each side and Jesus in the middle" (John 19:18). Here, in this place of agony and shame, we see the incredible integrity of Jesus—a person who truly practiced what he preached.

In the Sermon on the Mount, Jesus taught: "Do not resist an evil person. If someone strikes you on the right cheek, turn to him the other also" (Matthew 5:39). And, in a similar vein, he taught: "Love your enemies and pray for those who persecute you" (Matthew 5:44).

It is easy to preach such platitudes from a pulpit. The hard part is to implement such inspiring truths when the Roman soldiers are stripping your clothes off you and are pounding nails through your hands and feet. Jesus passed this test. Because as he was being crucified, Jesus said, "Father, forgive them, for they do not know what they are doing" (Luke 23:34).

Unfortunately, those who most need such forgiveness for their sins seldom seek it. As Jesus observed during his Sermon on the Mount:

> [W]ide is the gate and broad is the road that leads to destruction, and many enter through it. But small is the gate and narrow the road that leads to life, and only a few find it.
>
> (Matthew 7:13–14)

Walking down that broad road that leads to destruction, many "who passed by hurled insults at him, shaking their heads and saying, 'So! You who are going to destroy the temple and build it in three days, come down from the cross and save yourself!'" (Mark 15:29–30).

Caiaphas and his cronies could not restrain their glee. "In the same way the chief priests and the teachers of the law mocked him among themselves. 'He saved others,' they said, 'but he can't save himself!'" (Mark 15:31).

In their gloating, they did not pause to reflect that the reason Jesus could not save himself was *because* that was the *only way* to save others. As perceived by the prophet centuries earlier, God's suffering servant had to follow "the LORD's will to crush him and cause him to suffer"

(Isaiah 53:10) because "the LORD has laid on him the iniquity of us all" (Isaiah 53:6). By voluntarily sacrificing his life on the cross, Jesus "took up our infirmities and carried our sorrows" (Isaiah 53:4) because "the punishment that brought us peace was upon him, and by his wounds we are healed" (Isaiah 53:5).

Evil people were not the only ones who could not understand why this dreadful punishment had befallen Jesus. His mother, Mary, stood near the cross. She watched her good, kind son suffering unjustly.

Jesus could not spare his mother this agony. Anymore than he could spare his own life. In order to save others, he could not save himself or his mother from this pain.

Instead, Jesus did all that a loving son could do to care for his mother's future well-being. "When Jesus saw his mother there, and the disciple [John] whom he loved standing nearby, he said to his mother, 'Dear woman, here is your son,' and to [John], 'Here is your mother.'" (John 19:26–27). Essentially, John was adopting Mary as his mother. He fulfilled this responsibility gladly. Because "[f]rom that time on, [John] took her into his home" (John 19:27).

Perhaps this simple act of love for his mother was what touched the heart of one of the criminals being crucified with Jesus.

At first, both criminals "heaped insults on him" (Mark 15:32). For example, "[o]ne of the criminals who hung there hurled insults at him: 'Aren't you the Christ? Save yourself and us!'" (Luke 23:39).

But after spending a while near Jesus, the other criminal had a change of heart. As the first criminal continued to hurl insults at Jesus, this "other criminal rebuked him. 'Don't you fear God,' he said, 'since you are under the same sentence? We are punished justly, for we are getting what our deeds deserve. But this man has done nothing wrong.'" (Luke 23:40–41).

This criminal who had a change of heart probably heard Jesus forgive those who were crucifying him. Now he sought such forgiveness for himself. He said, "Jesus, remember me when you come into your kingdom" (Luke 23:42).

Jesus did not lecture him about what he'd done wrong in the past. (And it must have been very bad if the man felt that he was "getting what [his] deeds deserve" and that he was being "punished justly" by suffering the agonies of crucifixion.) Nor did Jesus remind the criminal that earlier that very day he had joined the other criminal and the passers-by in heaping insults on Jesus.

Instead, Jesus simply forgave the criminal. And Jesus gave him hope. Because "Jesus answered him, 'I tell you the truth, today you will be with me in paradise.'" (Luke 23:43).

The forgiven criminal was going to need all the hope the Lord could give him. Darkness now "came over the whole land" (Mark 15:33) for about three hours. Apparently, little or nothing was said by Jesus during this time. The thirst and agony were just too great as the hours of torture crept by in nanoseconds filled with pain and shame.

But as the moment of his death approached, Jesus rallied his strength. He "cried out in a loud voice, '*Eloi, Eloi, lama sabachthani?*'—which means, 'My God, my God, why have you forsaken me?'" (Mark 15:34).

Jesus (who was with God and was God in the beginning (John 1:1)) now knew fully what it is like to be mortal. Jesus knew that dreadful feeling that, as things go wrong and as death approaches, God has forsaken us. Jesus knew that dread feeling that there is no more hope—not even hope in the LORD.

Had God really forsaken Jesus? Had Caiaphas and his cronies hopelessly outwitted the carpenter from Galilee? Was there no hope?

No! There is **_ALWAYS_** hope in the LORD!

Indeed, Jesus' brief, tortured words simultaneously re-affirmed his hope in the LORD while at the same time expressing his grief at the terrible events engulfing him. For the words "My God, my God, why have you forsaken me?" were not words that Jesus thought up on the spur of the moment. They were words that he memorized as a Jewish child because they were part of the 22nd Psalm.

In his thirst and physical weakness, Jesus could not repeat the whole psalm. Nevertheless, Jesus must have received comfort and hope by meditating on the words of this psalm as he hung in agony and shame on the cross.

The 22nd Psalm would have come to Jesus' mind that day at the foot of the cross as the soldiers stripped him naked. "[T]hey took his clothes, dividing them into four shares, one for each of them, with the undergarment remaining. This garment was seamless, woven in one piece from top to bottom" (John 19:23). This undergarment would have been worthless if they'd torn it into four equal parts. So the Roman soldiers said to one another, "Let's not tear it . . . . Let's decide by lot who will get it" (John 19:24). And that was what the soldiers did. As the Gospel of John noted, "[t]his happened that the scripture [in the 22d Psalm] might be fulfilled which said,

> "They divided my garments among
> > them
> > and cast lots for my clothing."

(John 19:24)

This Psalm (written centuries before Jesus was crucified) contains another passage that captures perfectly the horror of those hours that Jesus spent on the cross. So as Jesus heard the crowd's insults and as Jesus suffered, he knew this happened that the scripture in the 22d Psalm might be fulfilled which said:

> . . . I am a worm and not a man,
> > scorned by men and despised by the
> > > people.
> All who see me mock me;
> > they hurl insults, shaking their heads:
> "He trusts in the LORD;
> > let the LORD rescue him.
> Let him deliver him,
> > since he delights in him." . . . .

> I am poured out like water,
> > and all my bones are out of joint.
> My heart has turned to wax;
> > it has melted away within me.
> My strength is dried up like a
> > potsherd,
> > and my tongue sticks to the roof of
> > > my mouth;
> > you lay me in the dust of death.
> Dogs have surrounded me;
> > a band of evil men has encircled me,

they have pierced my hands and
> my feet.
I can count all my bones;
> people stare and gloat over me.

(Psalm 22:6–8,14–17)

As Jesus saw the anguish and despair on his mother's face, he re-membered this prayer for help in the 22nd Psalm:

. . . [Y]ou brought me out of the womb;
> you made me trust in you
> even at my mother's breast.
From birth I was cast upon you;
> from my mother's womb you have
> > been my God.
Do not be far from me,
> for trouble is near
> and there is no one to help.

(Psalm 22:9–11)

And Jesus found hope and courage as he remembered how the 22nd Psalm ended. Because, although this psalm begins on a note of tragic despair (with the question "My God, my God, why have you forsaken me?" (Psalm 22:1)), this psalm ends on this note of triumphant exulta-tion:

[The LORD] has not despised or disdained
> the suffering of the afflicted one;
he has not hidden his face from him
> but has listened to his cry for help . . . . .

The poor will eat and be satisfied;
> they who seek the LORD will praise
> > him—
> may your hearts live forever!
All the ends of the earth
> will remember and turn to the LORD,
and all the families of the nations
> will bow down before him,

for dominion belongs to the LORD
>   and he rules over the nations . . . . .

Posterity will serve him;
>   future generations will be told about
>   the Lord.
They will proclaim his righteousness
>   to a people yet unborn—
>   for he has done it.

(Psalm 22:24,26–28,30–31)

And so, confident that he had not been hopelessly outwitted by Caiaphas and his cronies, Jesus kept hoping in the LORD. Jesus knew that all his agony and shame happened so that the scripture in the 22d Psalm might be fulfilled which said that "[a]ll the ends of the earth will remember and turn to the LORD" (Psalm 22:27).

Comforted and encouraged by such thoughts, "Jesus called out with a loud voice, 'Father, into your hands I commit my spirit.' [And w]hen he had said this, he breathed his last" (Luke 23:46).

When we remember how Jesus sacrificed himself on the cross to save people from all the ends of the earth, to save people yet unborn, to save *each* of us, how can we keep from turning to the Lord to heal our Promised Land?

After our Promised Land is healed, we will be like Jesus. We will keep hoping in the LORD to bless us no matter how much agony and shame consume us. We will keep hoping in the LORD to establish the work of our hands no matter how much it may appear that evil people have outwitted us. We will be strong no matter how much pain we suffer. We will be courageous no matter how many insults we bear. We will experience the joy of the LORD that is our strength no matter how much it looks and feels as if God has forsaken us.

Because, after our Promised Land is healed, when we are feeling forsaken, feeling ashamed, suffering, or dying, we will worship the LORD in spirit and in truth, by saying: "Father, into your hands I commit my spirit."

PART SEVEN

*Jesus Resurrects Hope
by Defeating Death*

Caiaphas and Pilate Ensure No One Can Steal Jesus' Body

Jesus was dead. Hope died with him.

Jesus' devoted followers saw him breathe his last on the cross (Luke 23:46,49). And later, they saw a Roman soldier prove Jesus was dead by thrusting his spear into Jesus' side (John 19:33–35).

All that Jesus' followers could do now was bury him. And even the effort to give Jesus a decent burial was hopeless. There was too little time before the Sabbath. Nevertheless, all that could be done was done.

"As evening approached, there came a rich man from Arimathea, named Joseph, who had himself become a disciple of Jesus" (Matthew 27:57). Joseph was "a member of the Council, a good and upright man, who had not consented to their decision and action" (Luke 23:50–51) condemning Jesus to death. Joseph "was a disciple of Jesus, but secretly" because he feared other Jews (John 19:38).

Another member of the Council, Nicodemus, accompanied him. This was the same Nicodemus who had visited Jesus secretly at night and had the conversation during which Jesus told him, "You must be born again" (John 19:39; 3:1–3,7).

While Jesus was alive, Joseph and Nicodemus feared to make their love for him known. Now, when hope was gone, they courageously and publicly did the decent thing—they buried him.

"Going to Pilate, [Joseph] asked for Jesus' body, and Pilate ordered that it be given to him" (Matthew 27:58). "Nicodemus brought a mixture of myrrh and aloes, about seventy-five pounds. Taking Jesus' body, the two of them wrapped it, with the spices, in strips of linen. This was in accordance with Jewish burial customs" (John 19:39–40). They placed Jesus' body in Joseph's "own new tomb that he had cut out of the rock" (Matthew 27:60). This tomb was "in the garden" "[a]t the place where Jesus was crucified" (John 19:41).

Because evening was already approaching, they had little time to bury Jesus before the Sabbath began at sundown (Matthew 27:57; Luke 23:54). "[A]nd since the tomb was nearby, they laid Jesus there" (John 19:42). When they were done, Joseph "rolled a big stone in front of the entrance to the tomb and went away" (Matthew 27:60).

"The women who had come with Jesus from Galilee followed Joseph and saw the tomb and how his body was laid in it" (Luke 23:55). Among these women was Mary Magdalene. She sat "there opposite the tomb" (Matthew 27:61) and "saw where he was laid" (Mark 15:47).[1]

Evidently, the women were dissatisfied with the hasty manner in which Joseph and Nicodemus applied spices to Jesus' body. Just as my wife usually (always?) complains that I don't do housework well enough—and so she ends up doing it over again—these women 2,000 years ago apparently felt they had to improve on what Joseph and Nicodemus had done. Or, perhaps, these women simply loved Jesus so much that they felt compelled to do more for Jesus than Joseph and Nicodemus had had time to do.

Whatever their exact reasons, the women "went home and prepared spices and perfumes. But they rested on the Sabbath in obedience to the commandment" (Luke 23:56).

Joseph, Nicodemus and the women weren't the only ones worrying about whether Jesus was "properly" buried. Caiaphas and his cronies were also worried about how well Jesus was buried. However, instead of worrying about whether enough spices were applied to his body, they were worried about making sure that his body could not be stolen.

So "[t]he next day . . . the chief priests and the Pharisees went to Pilate" (Matthew 27:62). By this time, Pilate must have been tired of hearing Caiaphas and his cronies whine and complain.

No matter how much Pilate did for them, they always came back demanding more. Yesterday he'd executed an innocent man for them. Then they came back later and asked him to change the sign he'd placed over Jesus on the cross.

Pilate had had "a notice prepared and fastened to the cross. It read: JESUS OF NAZARETH, THE KING OF THE JEWS" (John 19:19). Pilate probably enjoyed this insult to the Jews by letting them ponder what the Romans could do to their "king."

Caiaphas and his cronies were not amused. They "protested to Pilate, 'Do not write "the King of the Jews," but that this man claimed to be king of the Jews.'" (John 19:21).

With no crowd to scare him, Pilate showed more backbone about saving his *sign* than about saving the *life* of an innocent man. And anyway, since Pilate was a cynical politician, he naturally cared more about the merits of his "press releases" than about the merits of his actions. Pilate stubbornly "answered, 'What I have written, I have written.'" (John 19:22).

Now Caiaphas and his cronies were back again with another request! But as Pilate listened to their reasoning, he could see the merit in *this* request.

"'Sir,' they said, 'we remember that while he was still alive that deceiver said, "After three days I will rise again." So give the order for the tomb to be made secure until the third day. Otherwise, his disciples may come and steal the body and tell the people that he has been raised from the dead. This last deception will be worse than the first.'" (Matthew 27:63–64).

Pilate understood the danger from deception. As a cynical politician, he knew the power of lies. And as for the power of truth, "What is truth?" against the power of lies?

Pilate was willing to make sure that no one believed that Jesus rose from the dead. That would never do!

Pilate wanted the Jews to realize that the power of the Roman Empire had crushed and crucified their King Jesus. That was why he insisted on keeping his exact language on the sign that hung over Jesus as he died. It would *never* do to have the rebellious Jews think that their king was somehow alive despite all that the Roman Empire could do to kill him!

Pilate acted decisively to ward off this peril. "'Take a guard,' Pilate answered. 'Go, make the tomb as secure as you know how.'" (Matthew 27:65).

There was no disagreement or bickering with Caiaphas and his cronies about the details of this order. "[T]hey went and made the tomb secure by putting a seal on the stone and posting the guard" (Matthew 27:66).

In reality, Caiaphas and his cronies need not have worried about anyone trying to steal Jesus' body. This is a perfect example of the proverb: "The wicked man flees though no one pursues" (Proverbs 28:1). There's no reason to believe that Jesus' disciples were trying to steal his body. Indeed, there's every reason to believe that they were *not* trying to steal his body.

It was only *after* Jesus' resurrection (when Jesus stood in their midst eating fish), that the disciples were at last able to comprehend that the Messiah, Jesus, *must* literally die and rise from the dead.

For example, soon after Peter first declared his belief that Jesus was "the Christ, the Son of the living God" (Matthew 16:16), "Jesus began to explain to his disciples that he must go to Jerusalem and suffer many things at the hands of the elders, chief priests and teachers of the law, and that he must be killed and on the third day be raised to life" (Matthew 16:21). But Peter immediately rejected the whole idea. He "took him aside and began to rebuke him. 'Never, Lord!' he said. 'This shall never happen to you!'" (Matthew 16:22).[2]

Jesus kept trying to convince the disciples, but without success.

A short time before his Triumphal Entry into Jerusalem, "Jesus took the Twelve aside and told them, 'We are going up to Jerusalem, and everything that is written by the prophets about the Son of Man will be fulfilled. He will be handed over to the Gentiles. They will mock him, insult him, spit on him, flog him and kill him. On the third day he will rise again.'" (Luke 18:31–33).

Despite this straightforward prediction by Jesus, "[t]he disciples did not understand any of this. Its meaning was hidden from them, and they did not know what he was talking about" (Luke 18:34).[3]

Even *after* they heard the first eyewitness accounts of Jesus' resurrection, they refused to believe it. On that first Easter morning, when the women hurried back from the tomb and told "the Eleven and . . . all the others" that Jesus was risen from the dead, "they did not believe the women, because their words seemed to them like nonsense" (Luke 24:9–11).

Furthermore, Jesus' disciples were hopelessly demoralized and disorganized after his arrest and crucifixion. One of their number, Judas, had betrayed Jesus and committed suicide (Matthew 26:14–16;27:1–5). Another of his key disciples, Peter, had denied he even knew Jesus and then "he broke down and wept" (Matthew 26:69–75; Mark 14:72).

Even on the evening of that first Easter, *after* they'd begun to hear the first amazing stories of Jesus' resurrection, "the disciples were together, with the doors locked for fear . . ." (John 20:19). Therefore, the disciples were far too worried about being arrested and crucified themselves to do something as bold and foolhardy as stealing Jesus' body from a sealed tomb that was guarded by Roman soldiers.

Furthermore, the disciples were as different as can be imagined from such fictional masters of covert operations as James Bond or the "Mission, Impossible" team. They were a collection of ordinary people such as fishermen (John 21:1–3). Not a bunch of CIA operatives.

Caiaphas and his cronies were worrying needlessly. There was no Passover plot except the one they hatched against Jesus.

But, since lies and deceptions were the favorite weapons of Caiaphas and his cronies,[4] it was natural that they assumed that Jesus' disciples would resort to the deception of stealing Jesus' body.

And so, God the Father hopelessly outwitted Caiaphas and his cronies. As the proverbs say: "An evil man is snared by his own sin" (Proverbs 29:6) and "What the wicked dreads will overtake him" (Proverbs 10:24). Truly, "the way of the wicked leads them astray" (Proverbs 12:26) because "the wicked are brought down by their own wickedness" (Proverbs 11:5).

Caiaphas and his cronies were so afraid that the disciples might try to steal Jesus' body, that they made *sure* it was impossible to steal the body! In their zeal to make it *impossible* for anyone to believe that Jesus rose from the dead, they unwittingly made it much *easier* to believe that

Jesus rose from the dead! Truly, "[t]he Lord works out everything for his own ends" (Proverbs 16:4).

Because, when the sealed tomb became empty and Jesus' body could not be found, it was *not reasonable* to believe that the demoralized, disorganized, fearful disciples stole the body right out from under the nose of the Roman guards. Thanks to Caiaphas and his cronies, it is *far more reasonable* to believe that Christ is risen! He is risen indeed![5]

God the Father Resurrects His Son, Jesus Christ

Caiaphas and his cronies were now about to learn the truth of another proverb: "There is no wisdom, no insight, no plan that can succeed against the LORD" (Proverbs 21:30).

In all their plotting against Jesus, Caiaphas and his cronies acted as if God was either unable or unwilling to intervene to help Jesus. Like a bully picking on my son, Andy, while I am watching nearby, Caiaphas and his cronies were now in for a rude awakening. They were about to experience a Father's love for his Son.

God the Father was indeed watching as Jesus hung on the cross. Nature itself showed the Father's grief as his Son "was pierced for our transgressions [and] was crushed for our iniquities" (Isaiah 53:5). Because "darkness came over all the land" (Matthew 27:45).

Darkness also clouded the special, intimate relationship that existed between the Father and his Son from before time began. As Jesus hung in agony and shame on the cross, he cried out, "My God, my God, why have you forsaken me?" (Matthew 27:46).

Only love for each of us prevented the Father from intervening in history at that moment to prove that he had not forsaken his Son. To save us from our sins, God the Father forsook Jesus for a short time—even though it grieved God the Father just as it would grieve me to stand aside and let bullies beat up Andy.

In that way, "the LORD . . . laid on [Jesus] the iniquity of us all" (Isaiah 53:6) and made "his life a guilt offering" (Isaiah 53:10) so that "the punishment that brought us peace was upon him, and by his wounds we are healed" (Isaiah 53:5). "For God so loved the world that he gave his one and only Son, that whoever believes in him shall not perish but have eternal life" (John 3:16).

Having faith that this feeling of separation—of being forsaken—was not permanent, Jesus affirmed his love and trust for his Father at the moment of his death by crying out with a loud voice, "Father, into your hands I commit my spirit" (Luke 23:46).

And, as Jesus died, the Father affirmed his grief at this voluntary sacrifice of his obedient Son. Because "[a]t that moment the curtain of the temple was torn in two from top to bottom" (Matthew 27:51).

There are several reasons why this tearing in two of the curtain in the temple from top to bottom (symbolically from heaven to earth) was a fitting way for God to intervene in history at this dark moment.

First, tearing one's clothes was a normal way to express grief in that culture. So the tearing of the curtain expressed the Father's grief at the death of his Son.[1]

Second, the curtain separated the Holy of Holies from the rest of the temple. The high priest entered the Holy of Holies only once each year to offer a sacrifice for the sins of the people. Therefore, it was fitting that at this moment (when Jesus once and for all made the perfect sacrifice for the sins of all people), the way should be opened symbolically for him to enter the Holy of Holies (Hebrews 7:24–28;9:11–15).[2]

And, third, Jesus was going to end the separation that had so long existed between God and people. The curtain symbolized that separation of God from ordinary people. Therefore, it was fitting that the curtain of separation was torn in two at the moment that Jesus—fully God and fully human—ended the separation of God from humans forever (Hebrews 9:15;10:15–17).[3]

The separation of God from humans ended forever that dark day because God the Father was not finished intervening in history to vindicate his Son. In fact, he had scarcely begun. And God will not stop intervening in history until everyone knows that Jesus Christ is Lord.

In a letter to the church at Philippi, the Apostle Paul expressed this truth by quoting words from one of the earliest hymns of the church.[4] Paul explained that:

> [because Jesus] humbled himself
> and became obedient to death—
>   even death on a cross!
> Therefore God exalted him to the highest place
>   and gave him the name that is above
>   every name,
> that at the name of Jesus every knee
>   should bow,
>   in heaven and on earth and under the earth,
> and every tongue confess that Jesus
>   Christ is Lord,
>   to the glory of God the Father.
>
> (Philippians 2:8–11)

God next intervened in history by showing how easily he could defeat the puny efforts of Pilate, Caiaphas and his cronies to "make the tomb as secure as [they knew] how . . . by putting a seal on the stone and posting the guard" (Matthew 27:65–66). "[A]t dawn on the first day of the week, . . . [t]here was a violent earthquake, for an angel of the Lord came down from heaven and, going to the tomb, rolled back the stone and sat on it. His appearance was like lightning, and his clothes were white as snow" (Matthew 28:1–3).

The reaction of the guards was what you would expect. "The guards were so afraid of him that they shook and became like dead men" (Matthew 28:4).

Then "some of the guards went into the city and reported to the chief priests everything that had happened" (Matthew 28:11). The reaction of Caiaphas and his cronies to the news that Jesus' body was missing was what you would expect. They tried to defeat the truth by a combination of lies and bribes. "When the chief priests had met with the elders and devised a plan, they gave the soldiers a large sum of money, telling them, 'You are to say, "His disciples came during the night and stole him away while we were asleep."'" (Matthew 28:12–13).

This was a pretty pitiful effort at a lie. How could the soldiers know what happened while they were asleep? Plus, the soldiers were reluctant to say they'd been asleep on guard duty—a breach of discipline that could cost them their lives.

But this pitiful lie regarding why the body of Jesus could not be found was the best lie that Caiaphas and his cronies could think up. So they told the soldiers that they would not be executed for sleeping on guard duty, assuring them that "[i]f this report gets to the governor, [Pilate,] we will satisfy him and keep you out of trouble" (Matthew 28:14). The implicit flip side of this promise was the unstated threat that, if the soldiers did not lie as requested, Caiaphas and his cronies would tell Pilate a lie so that he would execute the soldiers. (In much the same way as they threatened to tell Caesar a lie so that he would execute Pilate unless Pilate cooperated by crucifying Jesus.)

"So the soldiers took the money and did as they were instructed. And this story has been widely circulated . . . to this very day" (Matthew 28:15).

Caiaphas and his cronies must have gloated about their success at bribing people—using greed to get away with lies and violence. Their first bribe got Judas to betray Jesus, leading to the violent death of Jesus. Their second bribe got the soldiers to lie about Jesus' resurrection, leading to the violent persecution of Jesus' followers (Acts 5:40; 7:51–8:3; 12:1–4; 23:12–15; 25:1–12).

Caiaphas and his cronies were masters in the arts of greed, lies and violence. Nevertheless, these wicked people were doomed to failure because God is the master in the arts of faith, hope and love. And God's Truth was marching on!

The lies of Caiaphas and his cronies were weak even on the surface. No one can say what goes on while they are asleep. It was self-evident that the soldiers did not know whether the disciples had stolen the body.

So their pride in their lies and bribes came before their fall! As the proverbs say, "[t]he unfaithful are destroyed by their duplicity" (Proverbs 11:3) because "[a]n evil man is trapped by his sinful talk" (Proverbs 12:13).

Soon a much more serious flaw developed in their lie. They didn't merely have to explain why they couldn't find a dead body. Jesus was walking around talking to people!

Now it became even harder for Caiaphas and his cronies to come up with a plausible, consistent lie for *all* the evidence. Let's review their problem.

It was very hard for them to argue that Jesus had never died. Too many people saw him die.

Then there was the problem of the missing body. Even if Jesus somehow faked his death, how had he survived in the tomb and how had he gotten out?

And then, there was the problem of the many eyewitness accounts of people who were talking with Jesus, eating with him, and touching him. If all these people were lying or hallucinating, where was the dead body that could prove Jesus was still dead?

The full weight of the evidence proving the death and physical resurrection of Jesus Christ is lost if we only focus on each piece of evidence separately. The whole of the evidence is greater than the sum of its parts. Because even if you explain away one part of the evidence, how can you come up with a consistent, coherent explanation for *all* the rest of the evidence?

And the full weight of the evidence proving the death and physical resurrection of Jesus Christ is lost if we focus only on the *eyewitness* testimony in the New Testament without also considering the *written* testimony in the Old Testament. Because how can you come up with a consistent, coherent explanation for all the ways that the eyewitness evidence *also* aligns perfectly with numerous passages throughout the Old Testament that describe how God would save his people from Sin by sending a Savior, the Messiah. These passages accurately, reliably and perfectly describe the life, ministry, death and resurrection of Jesus even though *all these passages* in the Old Testament *were written hundreds of years before Jesus was born!*

For example, if you want to argue that Jesus was not dead when he was taken off the cross (only seriously injured), how do you explain that he was well enough a few days later to go walking along the road to Emmaus, a village seven miles from Jerusalem? (Luke 24:13–15,28–32). Because no one can doubt that Jesus was in terrible physical shape after being crucified. So even if you think he didn't die, you can scarcely think that he could have been healthy and walking long distances within a few days!

For another example, it's hard enough to think that the disorganized, demoralized disciples could pull off the "Mission, Impossible" of stealing the body from a sealed tomb guarded by Roman soldiers. But even if you think they stole the body, how do you explain so many eyewitness accounts of a resurrected Jesus?

Furthermore, many of these eyewitness accounts were by skeptical people who at first dismissed such tales as "nonsense" (Luke 24:11; John 20:24–29). Nevertheless, these eyewitnesses eventually became so convinced that Jesus rose from the dead by personally seeing, touching and talking with Jesus after his resurrection, that they willingly gave up everything to spread the good news of his resurrection—even to the point of suffering death themselves!

On top of this eyewitness testimony, there is also the written testimony of the Old Testament. As I've shown throughout my books about the Bible (*The Promised Land, Healing the Promised Land, Hoping in the LORD,* and *Lighting the World*), the written eyewitness accounts in the New Testament fulfill numerous passages throughout the Old Testament that describe how God would save his people from Sin by sending a Savior, the Messiah. Because these passages in the Old Testament were written *hundreds of years before Jesus was born*, the fact that their teachings and predictions match perfectly with the life, ministry, death and resurrection of Jesus is another extraordinarily strong reason for believing *all* that the Bible teaches us about the life, ministry, death and resurrection of Jesus Christ.

Therefore, in the face of lies and deceptions, God's Truth (as established by the testimony of eyewitnesses in the New Testament and by the testimony of Moses and the Prophets in the Old Testament) kept marching on. God succeeded in his "Mission, Impossible" of raising Jesus from the dead. Hope came alive again as the news spread that "Christ is risen! He is risen indeed!"

As Mary Cries, Jesus Comes and Calls Her by Name

Early on the first day of the week, while it was still dark, Mary Magdalene went to the tomb and saw that the stone had been removed from the entrance (John 20:1).

Mary was one of several women who went to the tomb very early that morning, just after sunrise, with spices to anoint Jesus' body (Mark 16:1–2; Luke 24:1). As "they were on their way to the tomb . . . they asked each other, 'Who will roll the stone away from the entrance of the tomb?'" (Mark 16:2–3). So it was quite a shock when Mary Magdalene saw that the entrance to the tomb was no longer blocked by the "big stone" (Matthew 27:60) that Joseph of Arimathea had rolled there.

I've always admired the loyalty and determination of these women. They went where they believed they could do the most good even though their task looked clearly hopeless. They didn't even have a way to get into the tomb. Yet they went.

So when I get discouraged and think that it's impossible to do something because a "big stone" blocks my way, I take courage from these women. Even if something looks impossible, start trying to do it. You never know how God will remove the "big stone" from your way. But he always does!

However, as so often in life, the good news that the "big stone" has been rolled away is misunderstood at first. The women jumped to the conclusion that someone had taken Jesus' body away so that now they didn't even have that much presence of Jesus to comfort them.

Mary Magdalene ran for help. "[S]he came running to Simon Peter and [John] and said, 'They have taken the Lord out of the tomb, and we don't know where they have put him!'" (John 20:2).

Peter and John ran to the tomb and went in. They saw "strips of linen lying there, as well as the burial cloth that had been around Jesus' head. The cloth was folded up by itself, separate from the linen" (John 20:6–7). But "[t]hey still did not understand from Scripture that Jesus had to rise from the dead" (John 20:9). So "the disciples went back to their homes" (John 20:10).

Typical males! Mary Magdalene desperately needed help and comfort. And they went back home!

It was more than Mary could stand. She "stood outside the tomb crying" (John 20:11).

"As she wept, she bent over to look into the tomb and saw two angels in white, seated where Jesus' body had been, one at the head and the other at the foot" (John 20:11–12). Few things soften my heart more than to see someone cry. And even angels must be touched by our tears. Because, like parents to a small child, the angels "asked her, 'Woman, why are you crying?'" (John 20:13).

Through sobs, Mary explained, "They have taken my Lord away . . . and I don't know where they have put him" (John 20:13).

"At this, she turned around and saw Jesus standing there, but she did not realize that it was Jesus" (John 20:14). It was not just the dark of dawn and the tears in her eyes that obscured her vision. It was the dark of her depression that kept her from perceiving that Jesus was there by her side.

All Mary could do was cry. So Jesus said, "Woman, . . . why are you crying? Who is it you are looking for?" (John 20:15).

Even now, Mary did not realize it was Jesus. "Thinking he was the gardener, she said, 'Sir, if you have carried him away, tell me where you have put him, and I will get him.'" (John 20:15).

Poor, distraught Mary. She was so desperate to find Jesus that she was offering to carry his corpse.

And then she found Jesus! Alive!

"Jesus said to her, 'Mary.'" (John 20:16).

"She turned toward him and cried out in Aramaic, 'Rabboni!' (which means Teacher)" (John 20:16).

When I enter into the emotions of this story, I always get a bit misty-eyed, thinking of Mary's joy when she recognized Jesus.

We aren't told how Mary was able to recognize Jesus. But it must have been something about the way Jesus said her name.

Jesus is "the good shepherd" (John 10:11) who "calls his own sheep by name and leads them out . . . . [H]is sheep follow him because they know his voice" (John 10:3–4). They follow his voice to "find pasture" (John 10:9)—a place where "they may have life, and have it to the full" (John 10:10). They follow Jesus' voice to the Promised Land.

Part of having life to the full is experiencing the joy of hearing Jesus say our name. To experience that revelation that God is not an abstract force far away. To experience that revelation that God is Jesus, our best friend who comes whenever we most need him—whenever we most need hope.

And the best part of having life to the full is experiencing the joy of having a life full of purpose. Because Jesus didn't merely end the tears in Mary's life. Jesus gave Mary something important to do.

As would be expected, Mary held Jesus close in that moment of joyous recognition. Then Jesus taught her that experiencing life to the full involves more than hearing him call your name and holding him close. There is work to be done.

Jesus is alive! Hope is alive! But other people in despair will not find Hope unless we tell them that Jesus is alive. Unless we tell them that there is Hope.

So "Jesus said, 'Do not hold on to me . . . . Go instead to my brothers and tell them . . .'" (John 20:17).

With new hope in her heart, Mary did as Jesus commanded her.

With new purpose in her life, she "went to the disciples with the news: 'I have seen the Lord!'" (John 20:18).

As a father, I do my best to be there with my children in their times of hopeless despair—when they stand alone at the empty tomb of their hopes and dreams, crying.

But since I cannot always be there when they most need me, I am glad to know that Jesus will always come to them—and to each of us—at such moments.

Listen. You will hear him call you by name.

That is how he brings hope back to your heart and purpose back to your life. That is how Jesus carries you across oceans of despair until you reach the Promised Land.

A Healthy Jesus Walks to Emmaus

Later that same first day of the week that Mary found the empty tomb and her risen Lord, two men left Jerusalem to go to Emmaus, a village about seven miles from Jerusalem (Luke 24:13). These two men left Jerusalem even though they had heard the first reports of Jesus' resurrection. It seems odd that in the midst of so much excitement, they would have left Jerusalem.

We don't know why they left. Maybe they had pressing business commitments elsewhere for the next day. Maybe they were afraid of being arrested and executed as Jesus had been.

Perhaps it's just as well that we don't know the specific reason why these two men left Jerusalem. This uncertainty helps us realize that there are many reasons—and many excuses—that we use to leave the very places where God is most at work.

Because, for whatever reason or reasons, these two men who had been following Jesus were walking away from the greatest event in history. They lacked the perception, interest or commitment to be personally involved in what God was doing in the world at that moment.

Instead—like a movie critic criticizing movies—they busied themselves with talking (and often criticizing) what God (the greatest movie director of all time) and other followers of Jesus were doing, believing and saying.[1]

Since they were talkers instead of doers, "[t]hey were talking with each other about everything that had happened" (Luke 24:14). And, as they talked, they walked further and further from where God was at work.

Fortunately for them, God intervened. He sent Jesus to walk and talk with them. He sent Jesus to turn their lives around so that they returned to the place where God was at work—the place where they needed to be.

"As they talked and discussed these things with each other, Jesus himself came up and walked along with them" (Luke 24:15).

It is comforting to realize that Jesus was willing to walk along with them even though they were heading in the wrong direction. Jesus is willing to be patient with us as we learn his ways better.

And it is wise to remember that, even though Jesus was right there with them, "they were kept from recognizing him" (Luke 24:16).[2] We are not told why Jesus kept these disciples from recognizing him while they walked together. But we often learn about God by going through experiences that seem to have nothing to do with God until, looking back at them—sometimes years later—we realize that God sent those experiences our way to make us wiser, better, more mature, more disciplined people.

In this case, I suspect that Jesus did not reveal himself to these disciples immediately because he had things to teach them that they'd learn better if they didn't recognize him immediately. In particular, it was necessary that these two disciples not immediately recognize Jesus from his physical appearance because he wanted to teach them that they should rely on the Scriptures to recognize Jesus and his ways.

As we've seen before, when Jesus teaches, he often starts with questions. That is why it is never wrong to question the things that people—even Christians—teach us. Often these questions come from God to help you know him and his ways better.

In this case, as Jesus walked along with them, he first "asked them, 'What are you discussing together as you walk along?'" (Luke 24:17). They did not answer quickly. "They stood still, their faces downcast" (Luke 24:17). Their hearts were in the right place, even though their feet were taking them the wrong way. They had deeply loved Jesus and his ways. Their downcast faces proved their sincere grief at the tragedy that befell him. All they needed was understanding and hope to get them walking in the right direction.

Similarly, if you keep your heart sincerely loving Jesus, he will find a way to get you walking in the right direction even if your downcast spirits temporarily lead you the wrong way.

At last, overcoming their grief enough to speak, "[o]ne of them, named Cleopas, asked him, 'Are you only a visitor to Jerusalem and do not know the things that have happened there in these days?'" (Luke 24:18). Of course, Jesus knew far better what was going on than these two men did. But before illuminating them about God and his ways, Jesus wanted these two men to explain what they believed. Jesus didn't want to talk over their heads. He wanted to understand what was going on in their hearts and minds before applying the "medicine" that would heal their downcast spirits. So Jesus asked the men another simple question: "What things?" (Luke 24:19).

Now their tongues loosened up. And their confusion and discouragement about life and God's ways came bursting forth:

"About Jesus of Nazareth," they replied. "He was a prophet, powerful in word and deed before God and all the people. The chief priests and our rulers handed him over to be sentenced to death, and they crucified him; but we had hoped that he was the one who was going to redeem Israel."

(Luke 24:19–21)

Perhaps at this point they paused in their story. They'd said quite a mouthful. They may have felt foolish telling a stranger that some women in their group were claiming that Jesus had risen from the dead.

There's no indication that Jesus said anything as they told him their distressing tale. Perhaps with a glance Jesus gave them the courage to tell him more about what perplexed and depressed them. So they continued:

"And what is more, it is the third day since all this took place. In addition, some of our women amazed us. They went to the tomb early this morning but didn't find his body. They came and told us

315

that they had seen a vision of angels, who said he was alive. Then some of our companions went to the tomb and found it just as the women had said, but him they did not see."

(Luke 24:21–24)

I imagine that as they talked with this stranger, they made it clear by their tone of voice that they didn't believe the women's foolish story that Jesus had risen from the dead.

But Jesus had heard *enough*. It was time to teach these men who was really being foolish. And it wasn't the determined, faithful women who loved him so much that they "foolishly" came to his tomb early that morning to anoint his body despite the apparently hopeless circumstances of the large stone, the Roman seal, and the Roman troops blocking their way. Jesus "said to them, 'How foolish you are, and how slow of heart to believe all that the prophets have spoken! Did not the Christ have to suffer these things and then enter his glory?'" (Luke 24:25–26).

To prove his point, Jesus did not rely on the credibility of the women who witnessed his resurrection. Nor did he reason from general philosophical principles. Jesus relied on the Scriptures to prove his point. "[B]eginning with Moses and all the Prophets, he explained to them what was said in all the Scriptures concerning himself" (Luke 24:27).

In the same way today, if you are walking the wrong way, discouraged and confused by the hopeless circumstances that swirl around you, look to the Scriptures for guidance. That is where you can find the answers to your confusion and the hope to walk the way you should walk. Because "[a]ll Scripture is God-breathed and is useful for teaching, rebuking, correcting and training in righteousness, so that the [person] of God may be thoroughly equipped for every good work" (2 Timothy 3:16–17)—thoroughly equipped to worship the Lord in spirit and in truth by blessing all peoples in the Promised Land.

And so, if you study the Scriptures sincerely and diligently, Jesus will walk with you, restoring hope to your heart and purpose to your life. Jesus will heal your Promised Land, enabling you to establish the work of your hands. However, he will seldom do so in as dramatic a fashion as he did that first Easter as he befriended the two men walking to Emmaus.

"As they approached the village . . ., Jesus acted as if he were going farther. But they urged him strongly, 'Stay with us, for it is nearly evening; the day is almost over.' So he went in to stay with them" (Luke 24:28–29).

Keep in mind that the men did not yet realize that their traveling companion was Jesus. Similarly, you may not at first realize that it is God himself who is helping you find hope and purpose from studying the Scriptures. But, as long as you feel strongly urged to keep studying the Scriptures, you can be confident that you are in the process by which God will make himself fully known to you. Eventually, you'll recognize that Jesus is the friendly traveling companion of your life.

The moment of recognition for these two men came as they shared a meal with their "new" friend. "When he was at the table with them, he took bread, gave thanks, broke it and began to give it to them. Then their eyes were opened and they recognized him . . ." (Luke 24:30–31). And, as soon as the men recognized Jesus, "he disappeared from their sight" (Luke 24:31).

We are not told how these two men recognized Jesus at that moment. Indeed, perhaps it is good that we are left to use our imaginations to search for ways that people can recognize Jesus. Because different people recognize Jesus for different reasons.

Some people may recognize Jesus from the close fellowship found by sharing a meal. Others may recognize Jesus as they begin to taste the good things he gives them—spiritual food such as hope in their heart and purpose in their life. Others may recognize Jesus when they see the nail holes in his hands as he gives them their spiritual food. When they realize that Jesus gave his life to save them, they recognize Jesus as their Savior.

Whatever specific act by Jesus opens your eyes so that you recognize that he has been walking with you and talking with you, I hope you feel as much excitement as these two men felt. Once they realized who they'd been with, "[t]hey asked each other, 'Were not our hearts burning within us while he talked with us on the road and opened the Scriptures to us?'" (Luke 24:32).

I hope that once you recognize Jesus, you will act on that revelation as quickly and decisively as these two men did. Jesus had taught the men what they needed to know. Now was the time for action. Not for sitting around the table eating. "They got up and returned at once to Jerusalem" (Luke 24:33).

Back in Jerusalem—the place where God wanted them to be—these two men found even more reason to have hope in their hearts and purpose in their lives. Because "[t]here they found the Eleven and those with them, assembled together and saying, 'It is true! The Lord has risen and has appeared to Simon.'" (Luke 24:33–34).

Furthermore, encouraged by the faith of other believers, these two men found a new purpose for their lives—giving hope to others by telling "what had happened on the way, and how Jesus was recognized by them when he broke the bread" (Luke 24:35).

Today, as on that first Easter, you can fill your heart with hope and your life with purpose by going to the place where God wants you to be—the place where God is at work. The Promised Land.

In the Promised Land, you will find best friends who believe that Jesus is alive. In the Promised Land, you will find best friends who feel their hearts burn within them as they open the Scriptures to learn more about Jesus and his ways. In the Promised Land, you will find best friends who worship Jesus Christ by joyfully proclaiming: "It is true! The Lord has risen."

In the Promised Land, you will find a new purpose for your life—blessing all peoples by giving them hope. How will you give all these peoples hope? By being best friends with them. And by telling these best friends the good news about Jesus.

You'll tell these best friends how Jesus walked with you through life before you even recognized him. You'll tell these best friends how your heart burned within you while you diligently and sincerely studied the Scriptures to learn about Jesus and his ways. You'll tell these best friends what Jesus did that opened your eyes so that you recognized him. You'll tell these best friends how to walk the way Jesus wants you to walk. You'll tell these best friends the way to reach the place where God wants you to be. You'll tell these best friends the way to reach the place where God is at work—the Promised Land. You'll tell these best friends how Jesus guided and carried you across oceans of hopeless confusion until you reached the Promised Land.

Jesus Tells the Disciples, "Peace Be with You!"

On the evening of that first Easter, "the disciples were together, with the doors locked for fear" (John 20:19). The disciples were afraid of Caiaphas and his cronies (John 20:19).[1] After crucifying Jesus, Caiaphas and his cronies could easily decide to "finish the job" by crucifying Jesus' closest followers.

Our fears today will differ from the fears of the disciples that first Easter evening. But each of us has rooms of our hearts that we lock because we are afraid of something. Perhaps we are afraid of other people laughing at us or insulting us. Perhaps we fear losing our jobs. Perhaps we fear sickness. Perhaps we fear death.

We can't overcome such fears merely by hearing about Jesus. To overcome such fears, we must personally meet the risen Lord Jesus Christ.

Because remember that the disciples already knew a great deal about Jesus. They'd heard him teach. They'd eaten meals with him. And, by the evening of that first Easter, they'd already heard that Jesus was risen from the dead. Yet still they feared.

Indeed, those first stories about the empty tomb and the risen Jesus may only have increased their fears. Was Jesus a ghost, haunting them? Were other people losing their minds, imagining that Jesus had risen from the dead? What was it all about?

So whether on that first Easter or today, there are always fears that beset our lives. Fears that keep us from hoping in the LORD. Fears that we can only conquer when we experience the truth of Jesus' promise: "I have come that they may have life, and have it to the full" (John 10:10)—that they may establish the work of their hands in the Promised Land by blessing all peoples.

And fortunately, Jesus always comes into the locked rooms of our heart.

He doesn't come the same way at every time and to every person. And he certainly doesn't come the exact way he came that first Easter evening when "Jesus came and stood among them and said, 'Peace be with you!'" (John 20:19). But one way or another Jesus always comes to us and says, "Peace be with you!"

We may have to wait much longer than we want. Those first disciples waited through the horror of Jesus' trial and crucifixion. Then they waited for days while Jesus lay in the tomb. But, in God's good time and in God's good way, Jesus comes and gives us new hope—regardless of how tightly our fears may have locked the rooms of our heart. That is how Jesus carries us across oceans of fears until we reach the Promised Land.

At that moment, we will experience the same hope in the LORD that followers of the risen Lord Jesus Christ have experienced ever since that first Easter evening—the hope that came at the moment that "[t]he disciples were overjoyed when they saw the Lord" (John 20:20).

Jesus Overcomes the Doubts of Doubting Thomas

Some of us have to wait longer than others until we see and hear Jesus clearly—until he enters the locked rooms of our hearts.

"Now Thomas (called Didymus), one of the Twelve, was not with the disciples when Jesus came" (John 20:24). And so Thomas became one of those people who have to wait longer than most to see and hear Jesus clearly. In fact, Thomas had to wait until he could *feel* the risen Jesus enter the locked rooms of his heart. And so he has become famous as "Doubting Thomas."

It wasn't enough for Doubting Thomas that "the other disciples told him, 'We have seen the Lord!'" (John 20:25). Doubting Thomas insisted, "Unless I see the nail marks in his hands and put my finger where the nails were, and put my hand into his side, I will not believe it" (John 20:25).

It wasn't enough for Doubting Thomas that Mary Magdalene and the other women had seen the empty tomb and spoken with the risen Jesus (Matthew 28:1–10).

It wasn't enough for Doubting Thomas that the two men walking to Emmaus had recognized Jesus and become convinced that, according to the Scriptures, "the Christ [had] to suffer these things and then enter his glory" (Luke 24:26).

It wasn't enough that many disciples saw Jesus in the locked room that first Easter evening and heard him say: "Peace be with you!" (John 20:19; Luke 24:36).

It wasn't even enough that the disciples had made sure that first Easter evening that Jesus was truly risen from the dead. Because, with Jesus' encouragement, they made sure that Jesus was not a ghost or a hallucination.

At first "[t]hey were startled and frightened, thinking they saw a ghost" (Luke 24:37). But Jesus reassured them. "He said to them, 'Why are you troubled, and why do doubts rise in your minds? Look at my hands and my feet. It is I myself! Touch me and see; a ghost does not have flesh and bones, as you see I have.'" (Luke 24:38–39).

After "he showed them his hands and feet . . . they still did not believe it because of joy and amazement" (Luke 24:40–41). So Jesus offered further physical proof that he was not a ghost or a hallucination. "[H]e asked them, 'Do you have anything here to eat?' They gave him a piece of broiled fish, and he took it and ate it in their presence" (Luke 24:41–43).

Having established the physical basis for believing he was alive, Jesus proceeded to establish the theological basis for believing he was alive and that he was the Messiah (called the "Christ" in Greek). "He said to them, 'This is what I told you while I was still with you: Everything must be fulfilled that is written about me in the Law of Moses, the Prophets and the Psalms.'" (Luke 24:44). The reference to "the Law of Moses, the Prophets and the Psalms" covers all of our Old Testament. And, as we have seen time and again, Jesus found passages from throughout the Old Testament that guided him in his ministry and foretold what would befall him.

Many of the passages from the Old Testament Scriptures that are referred to in our New Testament Scriptures presumably were cited by Jesus himself to these first disciples. Because "he opened their minds so they could understand the Scriptures. He told them, 'This is what is written: The Christ will suffer and rise from the dead on the third day, and repentance and forgiveness of sins will be preached in his name to all nations, beginning at Jerusalem.'" (Luke 24:45–47).

None of these eyewitness accounts was good enough for Doubting Thomas. Nor was he convinced merely by studying the Old Testament passages that the other disciples now realized were proof that Jesus was the Messiah.

Nevertheless, Doubting Thomas did *one* thing right. He continued meeting with those who had no such doubts. And, therefore, "[a] week later [when Jesus'] disciples were in the house again, . . . Thomas was with them.'" (John 20:26). So Doubting Thomas was present this time when Jesus came again to remove all doubts.

Just as on that first Easter evening one week before, "the doors were locked" (John 20:26). Nevertheless, the risen "Jesus came and stood among them and said, 'Peace be with you!'" (John 20:26). This was the same greeting he had used the week before (John 20:19). And this time Doubting Thomas was there to receive the peace that only the risen Lord Jesus Christ can give.

Jesus turned his attention directly to him and "said to Thomas, 'Put your finger here; see my hands. Reach out your hand and put it into my side. Stop doubting and believe.'" (John 20:27).

Now Doubting Thomas had the physical proof he needed. And he'd learned the theological significance of Jesus' death and resurrection from the Scriptures. His physical experiences and his intellectual knowledge complemented and illuminated each other. Thomas stopped doubting and believed. "Thomas said to [Jesus], 'My Lord and my God!'" (John 20:28).

When you have intellectual doubts about the truth regarding God, do not lose hope. Everyone feels doubts and confusion sometimes in the face of tragedies or skepticism. The important thing is *never* to give up your search for the truth despite your doubts. Because, if you persevere, Jesus will eventually satisfy your questioning.

Thomas' experiences as a doubter shed light on how to overcome such doubts.

First and foremost, do not stop gathering with other followers of Jesus! Even though you have doubts, stay near those who are patient enough to help you through your time of doubting.[1]

Second, do not limit yourself to one approach to perceiving truth. The doubts of Doubting Thomas come easily to those steeped in modern science. It is hard to find that intellectual balance between what physical evidence can prove and what the Scriptures teach. But never lose hope that, when properly understood, Science and the Scriptures will complement and illuminate each other.

There are several ways to think about this.

One way is to think of Science and the Scriptures as two different tools for discovering the truth about the universe. Just as both a microscope and a telescope are useful tools for discovering truth, both Science and the Scriptures are useful for discovering truth. But if we use the wrong tool to try to discover a particular aspect of the truth, we will become as befuddled as an astronomer trying to see a star with a microscope and as a biologist trying to study a virus with a telescope.

Another way is to think about Science and the Scriptures as two different wavelengths of electromagnetic radiation. Both are useful in discovering the truth about the universe, even though images taken in different wavelengths may look very different from each other. That is why we send satellites above the Earth's atmosphere to take pictures of the sky using different wavelengths (such as x-rays) than those wavelengths of light that penetrate the Earth's atmosphere.

A more down-to-Earth example of how different the same thing may look when we study it with different wavelengths of "light" is the difference between how your hand looks in a normal photograph compared to how it looks in an x-ray. Both photos are true and accurate. But one photo is more useful if you want to know how your hand looks to other people. And the other photo is more useful if you want to know whether you have a broken bone. The two photos complement and illuminate the truth about your hand just as Science and the Scriptures complement and illuminate the truth about the universe.

In God's good time and in God's good way, Jesus will reveal to you the right tools and the right photos to find him. Then you will be able to stop doubting. Then you will believe. And then you will say to Jesus, "My Lord and my God!"

I have two words of caution, however.

First, it may be a long time before Jesus reveals the right tools and photos to you. Thomas only had to wait one week. But other people have sincere doubts for years. Be patient while you work through your doubts. And always be patient with others who doubt, even if you have no such doubts.

Second, make sure your doubts are sincere. Some people insincerely use "doubts" merely as excuses for not following God's ways. In such cases of insincere questioning, you may never find the right tools and photos. Because no matter what you discover about God and his ways, you will always deny the truth (2 Timothy 3:7; Luke 9:57–62).

Then you become like the unfruitful soil in the Parable of the Sower. You will be unable to bear fruit for Jesus—not because of your doubts about the truth—but because of troubles, persecutions, worries, the deceitfulness of wealth, or the desire for other things.

And, finally, keep in mind that doubts can come at many times and about many things. Even if you are convinced that Jesus is your Lord and your God, doubts may arise over what God has called you to do with your life. Or doubts may arise about the morality of certain practices that you previously participated in such as astrology, gambling, abortion or war.

Do not despair in the face of doubts about what you should do and believe. No matter how many doors are locked in your heart and mind, Jesus always comes into them and says, "Peace be with you!" And then he provides the right mix of experiences from life and teachings from the Scriptures to end the doubts in your mind, bring hope to your heart, and give purpose to your life. That is how Jesus carries you across oceans of doubts until you reach the Promised Land.

Jesus Encourages Peter to Take Care of His Sheep

When God's people returned to the Promised Land from their exile in Babylon, they needed hope—hope that they could be restored to the place of fruitful service to God despite their past failings. And they found hope in these words from Isaiah:

> Even youths grow tired and weary,
>   and young men stumble and fall;
> but those who hope in the LORD
>   will renew their strength.
> They will soar on wings like eagles;
>   they will run and not grow weary,
>   they will walk and not be faint.
>
> (Isaiah 40:30–31)

As Peter tried to return to the Promised Land of following Jesus after an "exile" caused by Peter denying Jesus three times, he also needed such hope in the LORD—hope that he could be restored to the place of fruitful service to God despite his abysmal past failings.

Peter knew that he had started well in following Jesus. How could he ever forget that thrilling day when Jesus first called him to stop being a fisherman so that he could become a fisher of men?

It had happened several years earlier when Peter had "worked hard [fishing] all night and [hadn't] caught anything" (Luke 5:5). When Peter followed Jesus' command to try again in deeper water, Peter "caught such a large number of fish that [the] nets began to break" (Luke 5:6). Peter was so "astonished at the catch of fish" (Luke 5:9) that "he fell at Jesus' knees and said, 'Go away from me, Lord; I am a sinful man!'" (Luke 5:8). Nevertheless, "Jesus said to [Peter], 'Don't be afraid; from now on you will catch [people].' So [Peter] pulled [his] boat[] up on shore, left everything and followed him" (Luke 5:10–11).

For awhile all went well as Peter followed Jesus. In particular, Peter did well when he became the first disciple to tell Jesus: "You are the Christ, the Son of the living God" (Matthew 16:16). I'm sure Peter never forgot the thrill when Jesus replied:

"Blessed are you, Simon son of Jonah, for this was not revealed to you by man, but by my Father in heaven. And I tell you that you are Peter, and on this rock I will build my church, and the gates of Hades will not overcome it. I will give you the keys of the kingdom of heaven; whatever you bind on earth will be bound in heaven, and whatever you loose on earth will be loosed in heaven."

(Matthew 16:17–19)

Then the problems started. After receiving this blessing, Peter began to get an inflated ego, becoming a "legend in his own mind." Peter began thinking that he knew better than Jesus. Indeed, Peter was not shy about telling Jesus what to do.

The first example of Peter's ego problem occurred almost immediately after Jesus praised him for recognizing that Jesus was the Christ, the Son of the living God.

"From that time on Jesus began to explain to his disciples that he must go to Jerusalem and suffer many things at the hands of the elders, chief priests and teachers of the law, and that he must be killed and on the third day be raised to life" (Matthew 16:21).

Peter did not agree that this was what should befall the Christ, the Son of the living God. "Peter took [Jesus] aside and began to rebuke him, 'Never, Lord!' he said. 'This shall never happen to you!'" (Matthew 16:22).

Jesus did not mince words telling Peter that he was wrong. "Jesus turned and said to Peter, 'Get behind me, Satan! You are a stumbling block to me; you do not have in mind the things of God, but the things of men.'" (Matthew 16:23).

Despite this stern rebuke, Peter didn't learn his lesson. A mere six days later (Matthew 17:1) he again made the mistake of giving Jesus bad advice.

It happened during the event known as the Transfiguration. "Jesus took Peter, James and John with him and led them up a high mountain where . . . he was transfigured before them. His clothes became dazzling white, whiter than anyone in the world could bleach them. And there appeared before them Elijah and Moses, who were talking with Jesus" (Mark 9:2–4).

Peter "did not know what to say, they were so frightened" (Mark 9:6). But did this stop Peter from blurting out advice to Jesus? Of course not!

"Peter said to Jesus, 'Rabbi, it is good for us to be here. Let us put up three shelters—one for you, one for Moses and one for Elijah.'" (Mark 9:5).

The Bible does not explain what was wrong with this advice. I've heard several ideas that underscore Peter's error.

First of all, Peter was implying an equality between Jesus, Moses and Elijah. However, as the book of Hebrews explains at length, Jesus is far superior to any human, including humans as great as Moses and Elijah. Because Jesus Christ is the Messiah, the Son of the living God.

Second, Peter erred when he thought that following Jesus meant establishing fancy shrines. Peter still had to learn that following Jesus does not mean sitting down on a mountain top in dazzling clothes basking in glory. Following Jesus means taking up your cross and bearing it daily, no matter where such faithfulness leads you and no matter how much it costs you—even if it leads to your crucifixion.

Above all, Peter's error was his presumption that it was more important for Jesus to listen to Peter than for Peter to listen to Jesus. God the Father wasted no time setting Peter straight. "[A] cloud appeared and enveloped them, and a voice came from the cloud: 'This is my Son, whom I love. Listen to him!'" (Mark 9:7).

Nevertheless, Peter still did not learn his lesson. He failed Jesus again by his words and conduct on the night of the Last Supper—the night Jesus was betrayed by Judas and denied by Peter.

Right from the start of the Last Supper, Peter kept saying "the wrong thing." Jesus wanted to show the disciples that they should serve each other as symbolized by washing each other's feet (John 13:14–15). "[S]o he got up from the meal . . . and began to wash his disciples' feet" (John 13:4–5). When Jesus came to Peter, he objected. "'No,' said Peter, 'you shall never wash my feet.'" (John 13:8). Jesus insisted, saying, "Unless I wash you, you have no part with me" (John 13:8). Now the irrepressible Peter went overboard the other way, replying, "Then, Lord, . . . not just my feet but my hands and my head as well!" (John 13:9). So Jesus had to explain to Peter why he only needed to have his feet washed (John 13:10).

A bit later in the meal, Peter proved again that he could not seem to listen and learn from Jesus. Jesus warned him: "Simon, Simon, Satan has asked to sift you as wheat. But I have prayed for you, Simon, that your faith may not fail. And when you have turned back, strengthen your brothers" (Luke 22:31–32). Instead of listening to this warning, Peter argued with Jesus. He replied: "Lord, I am ready to go with you to prison and to death" (Luke 22:33).

Despite Peter's boasting, Jesus knew that despair and fear would grip Peter's heart later that night. Jesus warned him again: "I tell you, Peter, before the rooster crows today, you will deny three times that you know me" (Luke 22:34).

When they went to the olive grove in Gethsemane, Peter again failed to listen to Jesus and follow his advice. Jesus told Peter: "My soul is overwhelmed with sorrow to the point of death. Stay here and keep watch with me" (Matthew 26:38). Nevertheless, when Jesus checked on his disciples a while later, he "found them sleeping. 'Could you men not keep watch with me for one hour?' he asked Peter. 'Watch and pray so that you will not fall into temptation. The spirit is willing, but the body is weak.'" (Matthew 26:40–41).

Despite this rebuke, Peter *still* failed to listen to Jesus and follow his advice. Because when Jesus came back after praying, "he again found them sleeping" (Matthew 26:43).

The only way left for Peter to learn was the hard way. He was going to learn what happens when "Satan . . . sift[s] you as wheat" (Luke 22:31). He was going to learn what happens when you hear the words of Jesus and do not put them into practice, becoming "like a foolish man who built his house on sand" (Matthew 7:26). He was going to find out what it is like when "[t]he rain [comes] down, the streams [rise], and the winds [blow] and beat against that house, and it [falls] with a great crash" (Matthew 7:27).

Peter learned these bitter lessons in the courtyard of the high priest, as Jesus was being condemned. When Jesus most needed Peter's friendship, Peter denied three times that he even knew Jesus. As Peter shouted his denial,

> [t]he Lord turned and looked straight at Peter. Then Peter remembered the word the Lord had spoken to him: "Before the rooster crows today, you will disown me three times." And he went outside and wept bitterly.
>
> (Luke 22:60–62)

This picture of Peter weeping bitterly was the last we saw of Peter until Mary Magdalene ran to tell him that the tomb was empty on that first Easter morning. "Peter . . . got up and ran to the tomb. Bending over, he saw the strips of linen lying by themselves, and he went away, wondering to himself what had happened" (Luke 24:12).

By the evening of that first Easter, however, Peter knew the truth—Jesus was alive! Because when the two men who met Jesus on the road to Emmaus returned to Jerusalem that evening they heard: "It is true! The Lord has risen and has appeared to Simon [Peter]" (Luke 24:34).

We do not know any details of that first time that Peter met his risen Lord. But the Gospel of John provides a detailed account of a later meeting between Peter and Jesus.

This meeting took place near the Sea of Galilee while Peter was fishing. The circumstances were designed to remind Peter of that first time when Jesus called him to become a fisher of men. Once again Peter had fished all night without success. Once again Jesus urged him to try again. And once again Peter caught a huge number of fish (John 21:1–6).

Peter was overjoyed when he realized that Jesus had come again. In his enthusiasm to join Jesus, the always impulsive and irrepressible Peter "wrapped his outer garment around him (for he had taken it off) and jumped into the water" (John 21:7).

After the other disciples brought the boat into shore (John 21:8), Peter and the other disciples accepted Jesus' invitation: "Come and have breakfast" (John 21:12). (Jesus had already prepared "a fire of burning coals there with fish on it, and some bread" (John 21:9)).[1]

Then a shadow fell across the fellowship between Peter and Jesus. Peter had failed to listen to Jesus so often. Most of all, Peter had failed Jesus in that critical moment of testing when Peter denied Jesus three times.

Now, with other disciples there, Jesus knew that the time was right to clear the air between Peter and him. To let the other disciples know that Peter was fully forgiven. To let Peter and the rest of the disciples know that Jesus still had a purpose for Peter's life despite all his failures and failings. To heal Peter's Promised Land.

Peter had denied knowing Jesus three times. Now Peter told Jesus three times that he loved him (John 21:15–17).[2]

Peter had often acted as if he knew more than Jesus. Now Peter admitted: "Lord, you know all things; you know that I love you" (John 21:17).

Jesus put hope back into Peter's heart.

Yes, Peter had failed. He had fallen away from Jesus at a dark moment when Satan sifted him like wheat.

But now Jesus gave Peter hope that he would never deny Jesus again. Jesus predicted (correctly, according to tradition) that Peter would be crucified for following Jesus (John 21:18–19).[3] So, in the end, Peter would indeed keep the promise he made to Jesus at the Last Supper: "I will lay down my life for you" (John 13:37).

Furthermore, Jesus put purpose back into Peter's life. Despite the fact that Peter had failed Jesus in the past, Jesus still wanted Peter to be a fisher of men instead of a fisherman. Jesus still wanted Peter to "[f]eed my lambs," "[t]ake care of my sheep," and "[f]eed my sheep" (John 21:15–17).

So no matter how badly you've failed Jesus, never lose hope.

It doesn't matter exactly why and how you've failed Jesus. Perhaps you fell away because of troubles or persecutions. Or perhaps your fruitfulness was choked by worries, the deceitfulness of wealth, or the desire for other things.

Jesus still knows all things. Jesus still knows you love him.

Furthermore, Jesus still has a purpose for your life. There are many ways to care for his sheep—to bless all peoples in the Promised Land by becoming their "best friend."

You may be best at weeping with those who weep. You may be best at washing people's feet. You may be best at welcoming sinners. Or you may be best at taking children in your arms and blessing them.

Jesus still calls you—as he called Peter—with this command and with this challenge: "Follow me!" (John 21:19). And if you follow Jesus, he will carry you across oceans of denials and failures until you reach the Promised Land.

Therefore, follow Jesus as he calls you back home from the exile of your failures—as he heals your Promised Land. Follow Jesus as he brings hope to your heart—as he gives you the strength to establish the work of your hands in the Promised Land. Follow Jesus as he gives purpose to your life—as he gives you the joy and peace that come from lighting the world by blessing all peoples in the Promised Land.

Follow Jesus Christ because he rose from the dead, proving that in the Promised Land:

> [T]hose who hope in the LORD
>   will renew their strength.
> They will soar on wings like eagles;
>   they will run and not grow weary,
>   they will walk and not be faint.
>
> (Isaiah 40:31)

APPENDIX

Force Majeure: Does God Forgive Non-Christians?

In the text of "Jesus Blesses Peter," I state that "having the faith to follow Jesus Christ is the *only way* to cross the ocean of Sin that separates us from God—the *only way* to heal the Promised Land." I intentionally said "having the faith to follow Jesus Christ" instead of "following Christianity" to suggest the answer to a number of perplexing questions.

For example, Christians wonder how people such as Abraham who lived before Christ's death on the cross were forgiven for their sins so that they could enter heaven even though they never accepted Jesus Christ by faith as their personal Lord and Savior. Related debates surround the salvation of children, the salvation of people today who have never heard that Jesus died for their sins, and the salvation of people who never heard clearly that Jesus died for their sins because of the culture or religion in which they lived—such as Communism, Paganism, Judaism, Islam, Hinduism, or Buddhism.[1]

To help answer these perplexing questions, I believe that it is useful to use the legal concept of *force majeure* which is the Latin term for a force that is outside a person's control. In contracts, it is standard to include a *force majeure* clause that excuses non-performance of the contract's requirements if the non-performance is due to a reason that is outside the control of the non-performing person. For example, *force*

337

majeure clauses excuse non-performance that is due to reasons such as a hurricane, a blizzard, a strike, war, or terrorism. Despite such excuses for non-performance, however, a party is still required to make good faith efforts to perform to the extent feasible.

To explain how Abraham got into heaven without accepting Jesus Christ as his personal Lord and Savior, I believe that it is appropriate to use the concept of *force majeure*. Although Christians disagree about the answers to this question, I believe that the best answer is that (just like a judge in a contract law case) God does not penalize people who fail to perform properly due to reasons outside their control. Therefore, God did not penalize Abraham for his failure to accept Jesus Christ as his personal Lord and Savior (Abraham's failure to perform his side of the applicable "contract, covenant, dispensation") because Abraham's failure to perform was outside his control (Jesus hadn't yet died on the cross for Abraham's sins). Furthermore, as required by contract law, Abraham made good faith efforts to perform to the extent feasible. In other words, Abraham was a repentant sinner who sincerely sought God in good faith to the best of his abilities and opportunities. Therefore, God (who loves to forgive repentant sinners) treated Abraham *as if* Abraham had the faith to follow Jesus Christ.

In summary, *force majeure* excuses Abraham because he lived at the wrong time to follow Jesus. *Force majeure* excuses a young child because he or she died too young to follow Jesus. *Force majeure* excuses a repentant sinner from another culture or religion who never heard of Jesus because—like Abraham—they can't be expected to follow someone who they never heard of. And (although this seems less certain to me) it appears logical that *force majeure* excuses someone from another culture or religion if (and only if) God (who sees the hearts and motives of people perfectly) determines that the repentant sinner never heard the message about Jesus clearly enough to understand it. *Force majeure* enables such repentant sinners who sincerely seek God in good faith to the best of their abilities and opportunities to reach the Promised Land because God (who is perfectly just *and* perfectly merciful) excuses their failure to say "Jesus is Lord" for the same reason that a human judge excuses a failure to perform a contract: Because the failure is caused by a reason that is outside the control of the "breaching" party. Therefore,

God (who is perfectly just *and* perfectly merciful) treats such repentant sinners who sincerely sought God in good faith to the best of their abilities and opportunities *as if* they had the faith to follow Jesus Christ (*as if* they had the faith to accept Jesus Christ as their personal Lord and Savior), so that they can cross the ocean of Sin and reach the Promised Land. (*See* Matthew 25:31–46; Luke 16:22–26; Romans 2:13–16).

Let's illustrate this by an example from what happens to an employee who does not come to work. The general rule is that an employee who does not come to work is fired. But now let's consider what happens if there's a blizzard—an event of *force majeure*.

If the blizzard is so bad that the government closes the roads so that it is illegal to drive to work, no fair-minded employer is going to fire their employee for not coming to work. This illustrates the situation of repentant sinners such as Abraham, a baby, and someone who never heard about Jesus. Although they sincerely wanted to "come to work" (to say that "Jesus is Lord"), it was absolutely impossible to do so for reasons outside their control and, therefore, God does not "fire them" (condemn them to an eternity of punishment).

A fair-minded employer's reaction is harder to predict, however, if the blizzard is not bad enough to make the government close the roads. Depending on all the facts and circumstances (for example, how deep the snow is, how low the visibility is, how well the road is plowed, how far the employee had to come, and how hard the employee tried to overcome these obstacles), the employer may or may not decide to fire the employee. This is the situation of children who are old enough to begin understanding about Jesus and of people who hear some things about Jesus but are from a different culture and/or religion and, therefore, either: (i) do not hear very much about Jesus; and/or (ii) what they hear is not heard clearly. Depending on all the facts and circumstances, God may excuse the failure of these people to say "Jesus is Lord" or God may say, "Depart from me, you who are cursed, into the eternal fire prepared for the devil and his angels" (Matthew 25:41).

Unfortunately, when considering these crucial issues of eternal blessing or punishment, many people make the mistake that I made on the first draft of my "third year paper" at Harvard Law School. My faculty adviser, Professor Richard Baxter, was the United States representative on the World Court at The Hague. He noted that I committed the mistake of almost all people when first tackling international legal issues. I started my analysis at the difficult to understand, gray areas of international law and ended up with a pile of mush. Instead, he told me that in international law (as in any difficult issue to analyze), I should start from what is definitely known, set those propositions up as firm starting points, and then reason as best I could to the gray, uncertain areas. By reasoning this way, we give people meaningful guidance rather than a "pile of mush."

When Dr. Gary Walsh was the Senior Pastor at Pearce Memorial Church, he made a similar observation regarding the development of our positions on abortion. He told us to start with the clear cases in which abortion is morally wrong (for example, people get an abortion because it's inconvenient to have a baby at that time or because they don't want their sin to be discovered) rather than starting with the morally difficult cases in which abortion is considered because of rape, incest, or the threat to the mother's life.

In the case of whether people receive eternal blessings or eternal punishment, what are these clear doctrines taught in the Bible from which our reasoning must start? First, there are both eternal blessings *and* eternal punishment (Matthew 25:31–46; Mark 9:42–48; Luke 16:19–31; John 8:24). Second, *everyone* (even those who follow Jesus) would receive eternal punishment except that Jesus died to be the sacrifice for our sins (John 3:16; 11:49–52; Ephesians 2:1–13; Hebrews 9:22; 10:4,14; Revelation 5:1–14). And third, to be saved from eternal punishment we must "[b]elieve in the Lord Jesus" (Acts 16:30–31). The only "wiggle room" in these three essential truths is whether God excuses a repentant sinner's failure to "believe in the Lord Jesus" *explicitly* due to reasons beyond their control (*force majeure*) because God realizes that the repentant sinner believes in the Lord Jesus *implicitly* (Matthew 25:31–40; John 9:41; Romans 2:14–16).

The sacrifices for sin in Ancient Israel are consistent with my hypothesis that God waives the usual requirement for the forgiveness of sins if the failure to satisfy the requirement (in this case the requirement to follow Jesus Christ by having the faith to accept Jesus as their personal Lord and Savior) is due to *force majeure*, a reason outside the control of a repentant sinner who sincerely sought God in good faith to the best of their abilities and opportunities. The general rule in the Old Testament *and* the New Testament is that "without the shedding of blood there is no forgiveness" (Hebrews 9:22). In the New Testament, the shed blood is the blood of Jesus Christ (Hebrews 10:14). In the Old Testament, the shed blood was the blood of sacrificial animals (which Christians now realize was a foreshadowing of the "perfect sacrifice"— the Lamb of God, Jesus Christ) (Hebrews 10:1–4).

In the Old Testament, therefore, the usual sacrifice for sin was the blood from an expensive animal such as a lamb (Leviticus 4:1–6:30). Nevertheless, there was an exception for people who were too poor to buy an expensive animal for a sacrifice. For those repentant sinners who were unable to obtain the required sacrifice due to a reason outside their control (in this case, their poverty) a different sacrifice—two birds— could be substituted for the lamb (Leviticus 5:7–10). Furthermore, in the case of a very poor person, the repentant sinner could sacrifice two quarts of fine flour—*even though this different kind of sacrifice did not shed any blood* (Leviticus 5:11–13).

It seems reasonable to me, therefore, that in the New Testament God is willing to forgive a repentant sinner if, due to reasons outside their control (*force majeure*), they were unable to acknowledge the proper sacrifice for their sins (the Lamb of God, Jesus Christ) even though they sincerely sought God in good faith to the best of their abilities and opportunities. At the end of *The Chronicles of Narnia*, C.S. Lewis made this point that God looks at the "substance" of our faith instead of at the "form" of our faith by having Aslan forgive (and welcome into heaven) a worshiper of the false god, Taslan, because this repentant sinner had, in effect, been worshiping Aslan under the wrong name.

Endnotes

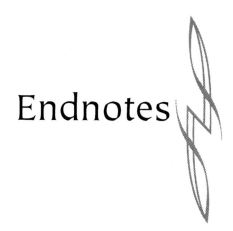

PART ONE: God Gives Us Jesus To Give Us Hope

Joseph Marries Mary

[1]See the note to Matthew 1:20 in *The NIV Study Bible*, Kenneth Barker, general editor, (Grand Rapids, Michigan, Zondervan, 1995) (hereinafter referred to as "*The NIV Study Bible*").

[2]Although Nazareth was called a city, I'm sure it was a "small town" by today's standards.

[3]See the notes to Matthew 1:16 and to Luke 3:23–38 in *The NIV Study Bible*.

[4]Matthew 1:21,25 and the footnote to verse 21 in my 1984 edition of the New International Version of the Bible (Grand Rapids, Michigan: Zondervan, 1984) (hereinafter referred to as "*The 1984 NIV*") and *The NIV Study Bible*.

[5]I remember Dr. Donald Joy making this point as part of a sermon he gave at Pearce Memorial Church about what a great father Joseph was.

Jesus Is Born

[1]Matthew 1:23, citing Isaiah 7:14; Matthew 2:5–6, citing Micah 5:2; Matthew 2:15, citing Hosea 11:1; Matthew 2:17–18, citing Jeremiah 31:15; and Matthew 2:23, apparently not citing a specific passage or prophet, but referring in general to those prophetic passages predicting that the messiah would be despised and rejected just like people from Nazareth were despised (as shown by Nathanael expressing his contempt for Nazareth when he said after learning that Jesus was from Nazareth, "Nazareth! Can anything good come from there?" John 1:46). Another possibility is suggested in The New Scofield Reference Bible (copyright 1967 by Oxford University Press) (hereinafter referred to as "*The 1967 New Scofield*" given to me by my parents when I was baptized. In that Bible, the footnote to Matthew 2:23 says that the phrase "'He shall be called a Nazarene' probably refers to Isa. 11:1, where the Messiah is spoken of as 'a rod [*netzer*] out of the stem of Jesse.'"

[2]See the note to Matthew 2:1 in *The NIV Study Bible.*

[3]See the Introduction to Romans in *The NIV Study Bible.*

[4]This phenomenon is known as "Murphy's Law."

[5]Pastor Charles Ellis used to stress this point when he told the nativity story. He was my pastor when I was a boy at Westside Baptist Church in Greece, New York and when I was a teenager at Clarkson Community Church.

[6]When he was the Senior Pastor at Pearce Memorial Church, Dr. Gary Walsh stressed that the point of the story of the Good Samaritan was that we should actively be looking for people in need so that we can be a good neighbor to as many people as possible. In contrast, the "expert in the law" incorrectly was trying to define the concept of "a neighbor" to apply to as small a group as possible so that he wouldn't have to help people who he didn't want to help. Dr. Walsh subsequently became president of the Evangelical Fellowship of Canada.

[7]I'd never thought about this until I heard a sermon by Jerry Young, the pastor of the Baptist church in Bristol, Connecticut that I

attended when I was a law clerk during the year after I graduated from law school.

The Shepherds Find Jesus

[1]See the footnote to Luke 2:11 in *The NIV Study Bible*.

The Magi Follow the Star

[1]See the explanation of who the various Herods were in a geneaological table titled "House of Herod" found near chapter 2 of Matthew in *The NIV Study Bible*.
[2]See the note to Matthew 2:1 in *The NIV Study Bible*.
[3]My daughter Sarah and I shared this experience when we strolled on Kaanapali Beach on Maui at sunrise less than a month before I first drafted this passage.

Hoping in the Lord

[1]Pastor Tom Kilburn was the Youth Pastor at Pearce Memorial Church. (Subsequently, he became the Chaplain at Roberts Wesleyan College, the Christian College adjacent to Pearce Memorial Church.) He was replacing Senior Pastor Art Brown in the pulpit that Sunday. Needless to say, we paid close attention to his vivid descriptions about how planes crash because we were nervous about flying to Hawaii.

PART TWO: God Calls Jesus To Set Us Free from Sin

Mary and Joseph Lose Jesus in Jerusalem

[1]A similar difference in priorities can be seen in the story of Mary and Martha. Martha was distracted by her housework. But Mary put learning from Jesus at the top of her priority list (Luke 10:38–42).
[2]I remember Professor Warren Woolsey making these points when I took his course in Biblical Literature during my Freshman Year at Houghton College.

Much of the course centered on the "life of Christ" because Professor Woolsey taught an immensely popular class called "The Life Of Christ." I'm sure that many of the ideas in these letters spring from seeds he planted in that one semester survey of the Bible, even though I am no longer able to remember most of them well enough to give him the credit in footnotes.

Unfortunately, I was never able to get into his course on the life of Christ. I tried and tried. But it was always oversubscribed.

Jesus Is Tempted

[1]I am going to discuss the temptations in the order they are given in Luke 4:1–13.

As you may know, the temptations are listed in a different order in Matthew 4:1–11. In both accounts, the temptation to make bread from stones is listed first. However, the accounts reverse the order of the last two temptations.

In Luke, Jesus is first tempted to worship the devil and then tempted to jump from the Temple. In Matthew, Jesus is first tempted to jump from the Temple and then tempted to worship the devil.

Obviously, one or both of the accounts is listing the temptations in a thematic order instead of in a chronological order.

Furthermore, the temptations probably did not come in well-separated, distinct moments.

If temptations came to Jesus like they come to me, they came all jumbled up together. Tempting thoughts flashed back and forth from one to another and vanished for a while only to reappear again later.

When it comes to temptation, the whole is greater than the sum of its parts—the temptations reinforce each other instead of detracting from each other.

[2]I remember a senior partner at Nixon Hargrave, making a similar point early in my legal career when he made numerous revisions in a legal document I had drafted. Sensing my discouragement, he said something like, "Your draft was really pretty good. The

reason I'm spending so much time teaching you how to make it even better is because you're so good that you can really benefit from my advice. I don't bother telling these things to the people who aren't as good as you."

[3]Dr. Arthur Brown, the Senior Pastor of Pearce Memorial Church, raised this question when we studied this passage in our small group that met Sunday evenings. Subsequently, Dr. Brown became Executive Director of Free Methodist World Missions.

[4]Mike Linkins raised this point when we studied this passage in our small group that met Sunday evenings.

[5]Wendy Barrett made this point when we studied this passage in our small group that met Sunday evenings.

[6]For example, at the end of Joshua's life, he called the people to throw away their "foreign gods" and serve only the LORD (Joshua 24:14–24). Throughout the book of Judges, there was a continual struggle to free the worship of the LORD from the entanglements of the religions of the other inhabitants of the Promised Land. King Solomon himself—who had built the temple in Jerusalem for the LORD—strayed away from the LORD because his many foreign wives "led him astray. As Solomon grew old, his wives turned his heart after other gods, and his heart was not fully devoted to the LORD his God, as the heart of David his father had been" (1 Kings 11:3–4).

King Ahab made the mistake of letting his foreign wife, Jezebel, strengthen the worship of Baal in the northern kingdom of Israel (1 Kings 16:30–33; 21:25).

And King Ahaz built an altar in Jerusalem modeled after an Assyrian altar that he saw while visiting his new "friend" and "ally" Tiglath-Pileser king of Assyria (2 Kings 16:7–14).

In a classic example about how we want to worship both the Lord and other gods, depending on what is most convenient, King Ahaz ordered that the daily sacrifices be offered on the Assyrian altar, but when he needed guidance, he used the traditional altar of the LORD (2 Kings 16:15–18).

King Ahaz was like so many people today. They sacrifice the best years of their life to "gods" of their own choosing. They ignore the Living God until they're in trouble. Then they expect God to give them the guidance and help they need to get out of the mess that their sins have led them into.

[7]Exodus 17:1–7 and the footnote to verse 7 in the New International Version.

[8]See Numbers 20:1–13 and the footnote to verse 13 in *The NIV Study Bible*.

[9]I discuss these issues regarding the accuracy, reliability and application of the Bible at length in the appendices to *The Promised Land*.

[10]It was Rod Bassett's class at Pearce Memorial Church about a year before I first drafted this letter. Dr. Rod Bassett is a psychology professor at Roberts Wesleyan College.

[11]I always stayed at the Loew's Summit directly across the street from the Waldorf-Astoria.

PART THREE: Jesus Shows He Is the Messiah

Jesus Turns Water into Wine

[1]As you may know, it is difficult to be sure of the exact chronological order of certain events in Jesus' life.

This is an especially difficult problem when comparing the events in the Gospel of John with the events in the other gospels. The other gospels are based on fairly similar source material and cover many of the same events. But John covers many events that the other gospels do not mention such as this miracle of Jesus changing water to wine at the wedding in Cana.

Rather than enter into scholarly debates about chronology in my writings, I am going to use the chronology for Jesus' life given at the back of *The 1984 NIV* under the heading "The Ministry of Jesus," unless noted to the contrary. Even if this chronology is inaccurate, the inaccuracies will not be material to my purposes in writing these letters.

[2]Since Mary asks Jesus to help with the wine instead of Joseph, there is a reasonable inference that Joseph has died. This inference is strengthened by the fact that Joseph is never mentioned in the

Bible after the story about the boy Jesus in the Temple. However, we do not know for certain when Joseph died.

[3]Jesus did not object to providing more wine. Obviously, Jesus did not believe in total abstinence from wine. However, in that culture with its lack of refrigeration and soft drinks, there was little else to drink! So even I would have had to serve and consume alcoholic beverages. Therefore, Jesus' example on this point does not change my mind that it is wisest to abstain from alcoholic beverages.

[4]This insight into the story comes from a sermon preached by Pastor Paul Toms at Park Street Church in Boston when I was in law school.

Jesus Tells Nicodemus He Must Be Born Again

[1]One of the reasons my denomination was called "Free Methodists" was because we refused to go along with such a practice that was quite common 150 years ago—charging people for pews. The other two reasons that our denomination was called "free" was that we believed in freeing the slaves before the Civil War and because we believed in freedom to worship God in a variety of ways (ways that were generally more emotional and musical than many grim-faced saints felt appropriate 150 years ago).

[2]Presumably, this is the same as the "Sanhedrin" mentioned elsewhere in the Gospels.

[3]John 3:3 and the note to this verse in *The NIV Study Bible*.

Jesus Preaches in His Hometown of Nazareth

[1]In the chronology of Jesus' life, it's not certain when Jesus made this visit to Nazareth. I think it could be either before or after his conversations with Nicodemus and the Samaritan woman. However, the chronology of Jesus' life in *The 1984 NIV* puts this story in Luke after the stories about Nicodemus and the Samaritan woman in John so I will discuss it in that order.

[2]This phrase is used in the famous summary of Jesus' life titled "A Solitary Life."

[3]This account and a parallel account in Mark 6:1–6 appear in a different place in the narrative of those gospels than in Luke. The authors of the gospels most likely grouped the events so as to best convey their thoughts without adhering strictly to the actual chronology of events. Even if the accounts relate to a different visit to Nazareth by Jesus, the reasoning of his detractors would have been similar to the reasoning of those who tried to throw him off the cliff in Luke's account.

Despite His Family's Wishes, Jesus Continues His Work

[1]See the discussion of this point in the chapter titled, "Mary and Joseph Lose Jesus In Jerusalem."

[2]As you may recall, Abraham Lincoln applied this illustration by Jesus in the Lincoln-Douglas debates to explain why slavery must be abolished. He insisted that the United States could not remain half slave and half free—but that there would either be freedom for all or freedom for none. Otherwise, America would be a house divided against itself and would surely fall.

[3]This idea that concepts that apply traditionally in one area of life (such as family life) should be applied in other areas of life (such as business relationships) is similar to some thoughts that Professor Roberto Unger taught in his course about Jurisprudence (the philosophy of Law) that I took at Harvard Law School.

Jesus Tells the Parable of the Sower

[1]Many people have struggled to analyze and understand Jesus' statement in Matthew 12:31–32 that "every sin and blasphemy will be forgiven men, but the blasphemy against the Spirit will not be forgiven. Anyone who speaks a word against the Son of Man will be forgiven, but anyone who speaks against the Holy Spirit will not be forgiven, either in this age or in the age to

come." Here is my contribution to understanding this difficult text.

I wonder if Jesus is making a point akin to an idea that I discuss in the Appendix to this book titled: "*Force Majeure*: Does God Forgive Non-Christians?" In that Appendix, I reason that God is willing to forgive certain people (Abraham is the most indisputable example) who for reasons outside their control (*force majeure*) cannot say the necessary confession of their faith "Jesus is Lord," but who nevertheless follow God by loving him with all of their heart, soul and mind, and by loving their neighbors as themselves. Therefore, God forgives them for not using the right words about Jesus on the basis that they are truly followers of Jesus in the more important sense of doing what Jesus commands by producing the fruit of the Holy Spirit in their lives. (Matthew 21:28–32). Paul makes a similar point by noting that non-Jews are sometimes justified by their consciences (Romans 2:14–15).

Similarly here, this passage is followed immediately by Jesus' statement that a tree is recognized by its fruit. And Jesus denounces his detractors because "how can you who are evil say anything good?" (Matthew 12:33–37). Therefore, good faith misunderstandings about Jesus are forgiven by God, but God does not forgive those who love evil rather than good (the fruit of the Holy Spirit: love, joy, peace, patience, kindness, goodness, faithfulness, gentleness and self-control (Galatians 5:22–23)).

[2] The Senior Pastor at Pearce Memorial Church, Dr. Gary Walsh, stressed this point in a sermon about the Parable of the Sower. Subsequently, Dr. Walsh became the president of the Evangelical Fellowship of Canada.

PART FOUR: Jesus Tells His Disciples He Is the Messiah

Jesus Feeds Five Thousand People

[1] Mark 6:46 tells us that Jesus went up on the mountainside to pray.

Jesus Blesses Peter

[1]I was uncertain how to "splice together" the passages in John after the Feeding of the Five Thousand with the accounts in Matthew, Mark and Luke that cover roughly the same period of time. Finally, I decided to go first with the account of John because it sheds so much light on the significance of Feeding the Five Thousand by comparing it to Moses feeding the people manna and by Jesus explaining to people that he is the true bread of life from heaven. Then I decided to transition directly into Peter's declaration that Jesus was the Christ in Matthew after a similar declaration in John because the accounts in Matthew, Mark and Luke end with Jesus confirming the truth of Peter's declaration and Jesus warning his disciples not to tell anyone. This gives a closure to the conversation that is not present in the account in John.

Furthermore, although I do not know if the declaration by Peter as recorded in John occurred in the same conversation as Peter's declaration recorded in Matthew, Mark and Luke, there is a natural flow to such a conversation the way I've spliced the accounts together. After Peter burst out that the Twelve won't also desert Jesus because they have no place else to go and because Jesus was "the Holy One of God," Jesus responded to Peter's dramatic declaration by "cross-examining" the Twelve about who Jesus was. When Peter confirmed in unequivocal words his belief that Jesus was the Christ (which is Greek for the Hebrew word "Messiah"), Jesus responded by confirming the truth of what Peter said, praising Peter for saying it, and warning everyone not to tell anyone else.

[2]The session was taught by Ron Lambert of EMME Associates, Inc. to Upstate Farms Cooperative, Inc. employees at the Batavia Party House on June 19 & 20, 1997.

[3]Other examples of Jesus claiming authority are Luke 6:1–5 (making the astounding claim that he "is Lord of the Sabbath"), Luke 7:1–10 (the centurion recognizing that Jesus had sufficient authority to heal his servant from a distance), and John 2:13–

22 (Jesus claiming authority to drive the money changers and merchants from "my Father's house"—the temple in Jerusalem).

[4]This reference to Jesus as "the Holy One of God" seems to mean that Peter believed that Jesus was the Messiah. It echoes Isaiah's frequent references to "the Holy One of Israel." Furthermore, at roughly this same time, Peter declared unambiguously that Jesus was the "Messiah" (as the term is translated from Hebrew) or the "Christ" (as the term is translated from Greek). (See, for example, the footnote to John 7:26 in *The NIV Study Bible*. And see the definitions of "Christ" and "Messiah" in the Dictionary-Concordance in *The 1984 NIV*).

This unambiguous declaration by Peter is recorded in the Gospels of Matthew, Mark and Luke. Since the story we have just been discussing appears in John, but not in Matthew, Mark or Luke, we cannot be certain how the stories relate chronologically. But it is entirely possible that the stories in Matthew, Mark and Luke represent a continuation of the conversation recorded in John. See endnote 1 to this chapter.

[5]The setting for this conversation was "[o]nce when Jesus was praying in private and his disciples were with him." We again see a key way that Jesus combated the fears, insecurities and depression that would have overwhelmed most people in his situation—he prayed in private frequently.

[6]My view is that the most likely purpose of these words praising Peter is to emphasize Peter's authority to permit Gentiles, as well as Jews, to become members of the Church. Peter's role in this key transformation of the early church is set forth in the story of the conversion of the Roman centurion, Cornelius, in Acts 10 and 11.

If this was indeed the purpose of Jesus' praise for Peter recorded at Matthew 16:17–19, that would help explain why these words of Jesus are only recorded in the Gospel of Matthew. Since the Gospel of Matthew tends to focus on issues that are of interest to Jews, the author probably wanted to stress that Peter had the authority to allow Gentiles, as well as Jews, to become members of the Church.

Such a grant of authority to Peter from Jesus would, therefore, not extend to any successors of Peter. And, indeed, there is nothing in the words of Jesus that extends any grant of authority to Peter to any future line of people such as the popes.

Furthermore, even Peter himself was not considered to be an infallible, all-powerful leader of the Church. For example, a council was called in Jerusalem to consider whether Peter had acted properly in preaching to the Roman centurion Cornelius, baptizing Cornelius, and thereby allowing Gentiles to become Christians without first converting to Judaism. Acts 11:1–18. And at a church council in Jerusalem recorded in Acts 15:1–34, although Peter was an important leader, James was actually presiding over the council. Acts 15:19–21. Furthermore, the wording of a letter from that council in Jerusalem "[t]o the Gentile believers in Antioch, Syria and Cilicia" came from all of "[t]he apostles and elders, your brothers." Acts 15:23. This letter (that the early church seemed to treat as authoritative as described in Acts 15:24,30–31) did not, therefore, state or imply that Peter had any special status as a ruler of the early church. Nor did Paul hesitate to criticize Peter for hypocrisy when Peter started treating Gentile Christians differently from Jewish Christians. Indeed, Paul wrote to the churches in Galatia: "When Peter came to Antioch, I opposed him to his face, because he was clearly in the wrong." Galatians 2:11.

[7]See the footnote to 1 Timothy 3:1 in *The NIV Study Bible*.

[8]I am discussing authority within the Church in this passage, but I believe that a similar principle applies in any relationship where someone exercises authority over someone else.

For example, under ordinary circumstances, we follow the principle of submission to governmental authority set forth in 1 Peter 2:13–14: "Submit yourselves for the Lord's sake to every authority instituted among men: whether to the king, as the supreme authority, or to governors, who are sent by him to punish those who do wrong and to commend those who do right."

But under extraordinary circumstances, the governing authorities have departed so far from the conduct and moral principles that legitimize their exercise of authority, that rebellion or disobedience is not only permissible, but mandatory to fulfill our responsibility to treat all people as our neighbors by doing to them what we would have them do to us.

Sometimes the entire government must be overthrown, as justified by the Declaration of Independence during the Revolutionary War (interestingly, I first drafted this footnote on the Fourth of July, 1997) or as attempted by Germans such as Dietrich Bonhoeffer who tried to overthrow Hitler and the Nazis.

Other times, it is only one aspect of governmental authority which must be ignored or resisted, as when people helped slaves run away to freedom before the Civil War despite state and Federal laws to the contrary, as when people helped Jews escape the Nazis, and as when Martin Luther King, Jr. led civil disobedience to end legally enforced discrimination and segregation.

Similar principles apply to marriages.

Under ordinary circumstances, husbands and wives should "[s]ubmit to one another out of reverence for Christ." Ephesians 5:21.

But under extraordinary circumstances where the other spouse refuses to remain faithful as required by the wedding vows or where one spouse abuses the other spouse, the offending spouse has departed so far from the conduct and legitimizing principles of marriage that the marriage is already ended "in substance" and, therefore, the victimized spouse is justified in ending the marriage "in form" by obtaining a divorce.

PART FIVE: Jesus Trains His Disciples How To Be Great

Jesus Tells the Rich, Young Ruler How To Follow Him

[1] I remember that Professor Abe Chayes, my professor at Harvard Law School for the second semester of Civil Procedure and for

a course in International Legal Process, was notorious for never answering any question except by asking you another question. Such a Socratic approach to learning (named after another great and good teacher—Socrates) is essential to becoming an educated person who does not memorize answers but who learns how to analyze and solve problems on his or her own.

[2]I use the capitalized term "Sin" differently from the terms "sin" or "sins."

When used with the lower case "s" the term sin or sins refers to particular instances of thinking or doing the wrong thing. Even those who have surrendered their lives to Christ can commit lower case sins (1 John 1:8–10).

When capitalized, the term "Sin" refers to that general state of rebellion against God that is the initial attitude of every human. It is this general state of rebellion that means that each human will walk away from God until he or she reaches hell (1 John 1:6;2:11;3:6), unless he or she changes the direction of his or her life by surrendering his or her life to Christ so that he or she begins walking with God until he or she reaches heaven (1 John 1:7,9;2:6).

One of my favorite ways to illuminate this difference between capitalized Sin and lower case "sins" comes from late in the Civil War. Abraham Lincoln authorized one last attempt to negotiate a peaceful settlement with the Confederate States. On his side, Abraham Lincoln would give in on details of what the Confederate States wanted. But Abraham Lincoln insisted that the Confederate States end their rebellion and submit to the United States government. On their side, the Confederate States would give in on any details of what the United States wanted. But the Confederate States insisted that they must be allowed to retain their own separate, sovereign government independent from the authority of the United States.

Therefore, the ultimate issue between the United States and the Confederate States was not individual details (sins). The ultimate issue between the United States and the Confederate States was rebellion ("Sin"). Unfortunately, the Confederate States refused to end their rebellion and therefore the United States used military force to crush them and punish them (sent them to hell).

This final effort at finding a peaceful end to the rebellion of the Confederate States is described (albeit in less theological terms) in *The Army of the Potomac: A Stillness at Appomattox* by Bruce Catton (Garden City, New York: Doubleday, 1953), 331–334.

The Good Samaritan

[1] These points were made by Dr. Gary Walsh in a sermon at Pearce Memorial Church when he was the Senior Pastor. Subsequently, Dr. Walsh became president of the Evangelical Fellowship of Canada.

PART SIX: Jesus Sacrifices Himself To Save Others

Jesus Raises Lazarus from the Dead

[1] The depth and sincerity of the grief of Mary, Martha, and Jesus are details that help prove that Lazarus was really dead—that this was not a faked death and a fake raising from the dead. Mary and Martha knew that Lazarus had been gravely ill and had died. And Jesus was deeply moved to the point of weeping because he was not play acting—he knew that Lazarus had suffered the agonies of death and that the grief of Mary and Martha was genuine.

[2] This is one of those details that helps prove that Lazarus was really dead—that this was not a faked death and a fake raising from the dead. Martha was very much aware that Lazarus had been deathly ill and she was certain that he was dead when he was placed in the tomb. That was why she made this spontaneous outburst that opening the tomb would release a bad odor.

Caiaphas Tells the Sanhedrin That Jesus Must Die

[1] This quote is taken from the definition of "Sanhedrin" in the Dictionary-Concordance of *The* 1984 *NIV*.

[2] See the note to John 11:48 in the New International Version.

[3] Indeed, I remember when the Israelis re-occupied the "Wailing Wall" (all that remains of the temple grounds where Jesus taught) and the rest of ancient Jerusalem during the Six Day War in 1967 for the first time in almost 2,000 years. Mostly, I remember the immense joy of the Israeli troops who reached the site of the ancient Jewish temple and then paused in the midst of the battle to pray at the Wailing Wall.

Jesus Tells Judas Iscariot To Leave Mary Alone

[1] The chronology of Jesus' life in *The* 1984 *NIV* says that this anointing of Jesus took place on Tuesday of the Last Week with the Triumphal Entry taking place two days before on Sunday.

As you may know, scholars have spent considerable effort trying to reconcile the chronology of events that take place during Holy Week.

After much thought, I decided to describe the dinner where Jesus was anointed as taking place before the Triumphal Entry. I reached this decision because, after the Gospel of John describes Mary anointing Jesus, the Gospel says: "The next day the great crowd that had come for the Feast heard that Jesus was on his way to Jerusalem. They took palm branches and went out to meet him . . . ." John 12:12. This passage seems to me to fix Jesus' anointing as occurring on the day before the Triumphal Entry.

On the other hand, the accounts in Matthew and Luke give an account of Jesus' anointing immediately after a reference to the Passover being only two days away. In my chronology, those two gospels "flashback" to the story of Jesus' anointing a few days earlier to give background for why Judas went to the chief priests to betray Jesus two days before the Passover.

A similar "flashback" occurs when some of the gospels describe the death of John the Baptist. They give the news of his death at the correct chronological point in the story (just as the gospels give the correct chronological point in the story for Judas going to betray Jesus). But for purposes of organizing their narrative they give the events leading to John the Baptist's death at that point instead of earlier in the flow of their narrative. See Matthew 14:1–12 and Mark 6:14–29.

For example, I was going to organize my narrative the same way that it appears in Matthew and Mark (by not mentioning the dinner where Jesus was anointed until two days before the Passover) until I decided to discuss the story of Jesus raising Lazarus from the dead (a story that only appears in the Gospel of John). Once I took the time to explain who Mary, Martha and Lazarus were and (like the Gospel of John) chose to emphasize that raising Lazarus from the dead helped trigger the decision to arrest Jesus and execute him, it was better for me to organize my materials in the same way the Gospel of John did by putting the story of the dinner where Jesus was anointed on the day before the Triumphal Entry.

None of this uncertainty about the exact day of the week that something happened during Holy Week changes the substance of the account.

Furthermore, I want to emphasize that the uncertainty about the exact chronology does not mean the Bible has mistakes in it. It merely means that the four accurate accounts in the four gospels leave some ambiguities about the chronology that scholars must do their best to unravel 2,000 years later.

As an attorney, it does not surprise me that there are such ambiguities and uncertainties. I always find such ambiguities and uncertainties when piecing together truthful accounts by several different people. Indeed, I become suspicious that people are lying to me and have rehearsed their testimony if no such ambiguities and uncertainties exist among their accounts.

[2]Luke 10:38–42 tells us that, during an earlier visit by Jesus, Martha complained that Mary was so intent on listening to Jesus that Martha was left to do all the housework.

³The Bible does not say that anyone was worried whether wiping Jesus' feet with her hair might be too intimate, sensual an act for Mary to engage in with Jesus. Perhaps in the context it was clear that Mary was acting like a slave rather than like a seductress. Or perhaps the disciples thought it was "safer" to criticize Mary for not caring enough about the poor than to criticize her for showing too much love toward Jesus.

Judas Betrays Jesus for Thirty Silver Coins

¹Jesus himself was predicting such a disaster. After Jesus praised the widow for giving her tiny copper coins, "[s]ome of his disciples were remarking about how the temple was adorned with beautiful stones and with gifts dedicated to God. But Jesus said, 'As for what you see here, the time will come when not one stone will be left on another; every one of them will be thrown down.'" (Luke 21:5–6).

²I believe her eyes glowed with joy "for God loves a cheerful giver" (2 Corinthians 9:7) and "[i]t is more blessed to give than to receive." (Acts 20:35).

The Last Supper

¹Obviously, I do not know for certain how to splice together the differing accounts of the four gospels regarding Jesus commenting on Judas' betrayal. But a plausible way to understand how they fit together is that a few of the comments were made quietly, so no one could hear them except who Jesus wanted to hear them. That would explain how Jesus could explicitly tell Judas he was the traitor and could identify Judas as the traitor at the request of Peter and John by handing Judas a piece of bread, yet the disciples still had no idea who the traitor was or why Jesus told Judas to do quickly what he was going to do.

Such difficulty in hearing what is going on elsewhere at the table is common at any large gathering. For example, think how impossible it is to follow every conversation and whispered comment during Thanksgiving dinner (and, in our family, we usually have less than thirteen adults come to our house for Thanksgiving dinner).

The important thing to keep in mind is that, even though the accounts differ, that does not mean that any of the accounts err in any way. It merely means that in each narrative the author highlighted different aspects of the meal to make the dramatic points that were most important to the teachings the author was trying to convey.

Similarly, I am organizing the material in a way that best conveys the dramatic points that are most important to the teachings I am trying to convey—highlighting the dramatic confrontations between Jesus, Judas and Peter, and making us realize how easy it is for us to share the failings of a Judas or a Peter.

[2]This thought (as well as some of the other ideas in this chapter) came from comments made by Rod Bassett and members of his Sunday School Class when we discussed this passage in the Sunday School Class that Rod taught at Pearce Memorial Church during the 1996–1997 school year.

[3]See endnote 1 of this chapter for the reasons I infer that this conversation between Judas and Jesus took place quietly so that the others at the table did not hear it (or at least so that the others did not understand what Judas and Jesus were talking about).

[4]Peter may or may not have spoken this question quietly. Frankly, I have trouble imagining Peter ever speaking quietly. And since Peter "motioned" to John, I suspect that they were reclining fairly far apart at the table.

The literal words from the Gospel of John that are believed to describe John are "the disciple whom Jesus loved" (John 13:23). It is believed by many scholars that this is a euphemism for the disciple John who did not want to refer to himself in the first person or by name, but who wanted instead to emphasize that Jesus loved him. To make it easier to understand the narrative, I decided to replace the words "whom Jesus loved" with the name "John."

[5]See endnote 1 of this chapter for the reasons I infer that this conversation between John and Jesus took place quietly so that the others at the table did not hear it (or at least did not understand what John and Jesus were talking about). This inference is strengthened with regard to this conversation because we are told that John leaned back against Jesus to ask his question, suggesting that the men were very close together and were talking quietly to each other.

[6]See endnote 1 of this chapter for the reasons I infer that this conversation between Jesus and John took place quietly so that the others at the table did not hear it (or at least did not understand what Jesus and John were talking about). This inference is strengthened with regard to this conversation because we are told that John leaned back against Jesus to ask his question, suggesting that the men were very close together and were talking quietly to each other.

[7]Obviously, I do not know for certain how to splice together the differing accounts of the four gospels about Jesus telling Peter that Peter would deny him three times that very night. I decided to have Jesus tell Peter this three times with minor variations each time.

One reason I did this was to have symmetry with Peter denying Jesus three times and Jesus asking Peter three times whether he loves Jesus (John 21:15–17).

It also seemed likely that Jesus would have to repeat himself several times before Peter would stop arguing with Jesus about how wrong Jesus was. Peter never could seem to resist arguing with Jesus. Nor could Peter ever seem to sit quietly while listening to Jesus. Furthermore, the comment in Mark 14:31 that Peter "insisted emphatically" that he would die with Jesus rather than disown him supports the idea that Jesus had to argue with Peter about this several times.

Furthermore, splicing the comments together this way gives a coherent account of the conversation as recorded in the four gospels. It is reasonable to conclude that the issue first came up when Peter was protesting that he wanted to follow Jesus anywhere, even if it meant dying with Jesus. Then, when Jesus explained that the Scriptures taught that everyone would fall away, Peter boasted that, even if everyone else fell away, he would remain loyal. Then, when Jesus contradicted this boast by telling Peter that Satan desired to sift him like wheat, Peter again protested that not even prison or death would cause him to deny Jesus. And, despite these overconfident, boastful assertions by Peter, Jesus continued to insist that Peter would deny him three times that very night.

[8]See the note to Matthew 16:18 in *The NIV Study Bible*.

The Garden of Gethsemene

[1]By making these statements, I do not mean to limit the sovereignty of God. With his creativity and power, God might well have been able to devise other ways to achieve the key purposes served by the incarnation, crucifixion and resurrection: a demonstration of God's love and amazing grace that vindicates God's holiness, justice and mercy. However, by the time that Jesus was in the Garden of Gethsemene, there was no alternative to going through with the crucifixion that had been foretold by the Old Testament, considering all of the historical facts and circumstances that had been caused or permitted by God.

My emphasis on the importance of the crucifixion follows Paul's example when preaching in Corinth. Like Paul, I want my books to teach people to learn about "Jesus Christ and him crucified" (1 Corinthians 2:2). Because even though Christ (the Messiah) being crucified is a stumbling block to some and foolishness to others, his crucifixion reveals the "power of God and the wisdom of God" (1 Corinthians 1:22–25).

The importance of the incarnation, the crucifixion and the resurrection is explained in those portions of *Visions of America, Visions of the Church* that discuss the Truth of Christmas and the Truth of Easter.

[2]I worked in Building 502, a large stockroom, during the summers after my Freshman, Sophomore and Junior years.

[3]See the footnote to Matthew 26:50 in *The NIV Study Bible*.

Jesus Allows Himself To Be Arrested Without a Fight

[1]See, for example, Matthew 16:21; Mark 8:31–32,10:32–34; and Luke 9:22,18:31–34.

[2]In the book of Acts, Philip came across an Ethiopian eunuch who was reading that passage from Isaiah. "The eunuch asked Philip, 'Tell me, please, who is the prophet talking about, himself or someone else?' Then Philip began with that very passage of Scripture and told him the good news about Jesus" (Acts 8:34–35).

3This claim by Jesus caused Pilate to ask his famous question, "What is truth?" (John 18:38).

Jesus Tells the High Priest That He Is the Messiah

[1]See the footnote to Matthew 26:63 in *The NIV Study Bible*.

[2]Just a few days earlier in the temple Jesus had used this prophetic passage from the psalms to hint that he was the Messiah. His opponents became so afraid of the implications that they didn't dare to ask him anymore questions (Matthew 22:41–46).

Pilate Bows to the Political Pressure to Crucify Jesus

[1]I have read a number of discussions speculating why the Sanhedrin felt it was necessary to have Pilate execute Jesus instead of just doing it themselves.

At first, Pilate told the Jewish leaders, "'Take [Jesus] yourselves and judge him by your own law.' 'But we have no right to execute anyone' the Jews objected" (John 18:31).

Some scholars dispute this claim after reviewing the historical record about the powers of the Sanhedrin. Furthermore, the first recorded Christian martyr, Stephen, was stoned to death for blasphemy after an appearance at the Sanhedrin (Acts 6:8–8:1)—the same charge that Caiaphas and his cronies used for condemning Jesus. But it's hard enough to be certain about the powers and jurisdictions of modern courts, much less to discern such legal technicalities across a chasm of 2,000 years.

I suspect that the difference between Jesus' case and Stephen's case may be that Jesus was a far more prominent figure than Stephen was.

The Sanhedrin didn't dare have a mob stone Jesus to death. They needed to go through the motions of a sham trial.

Furthermore, from a public relations standpoint, it was far better if the Romans took responsibility for executing Jesus. Not only would this take some of the political backlash away from Caiaphas and his cronies when people who liked Jesus heard that he was dead. It also served a useful political purpose with the Romans by letting Caiaphas and his cronies pose as loyal servants of Rome who could be trusted by Roman leaders and who should be supported by Roman largesse and legions. (Of course, Pilate would know this was a lie, but "What is truth?") Note that, if Caiaphas and his cronies were lying or exaggerating about their lack of power to execute Jesus, then Pilate wasn't the only one who didn't want to take full responsibility for his actions that day.

[2]See the note to John 19:12 in *The NIV Study Bible*.

PART SEVEN: Jesus Resurrects Hope by Defeating Death

Caiaphas and Pilate Ensure No One Can Steal Jesus' Body

[1]Notice how there can be no doubt that Jesus was actually dead. In addition to the proof afforded by the Roman soldier who thrust his spear in Jesus' side to make sure that the blood did not flow in the manner it would if he were still alive, there were multiple witnesses to the fact that Jesus was buried (not administered emergency medical treatment) and that his body was inside the tomb when the rock was rolled across the entrance. There was also little time for any medical treatment or theft of the body because Jesus was buried so quickly and so near the site of his crucifixion.

[2]Mark 8:31–33 makes the same point.

[3]See also John 16:16–33. Since the Eleven transmitted and supervised these early traditions regarding themselves, the natural tendency would have been for them to try to make themselves look good. Therefore, great credibility attaches to statements such as these that the Eleven did not understand what Jesus was talking about.

[4]Remember that Caiaphas and his cronies had lots of experience deceiving people.

They'd sent spies to try to trick Jesus into saying something like "Don't pay taxes to Caesar" so that they could turn Jesus in to the Romans as a traitor (Luke 20:20–26).

When Jesus shrewdly avoided their traps, they went ahead and told lies to Pilate to justify their accusations (Luke 23:1–2).

Pilate easily saw through their deception and declared that Jesus was innocent (Luke 23:4). But Caiaphas and his cronies weren't going to let the truth about Jesus stop their plans. So they resorted to another lie. They threatened to tell Rome that Pilate was not putting down a rebellion by King Jesus. This blackmail worked. Pilate did their bidding (John 19:12–16).

[5]These are the words of the traditional Easter morning greeting of the Orthodox Church: "Christ is risen! He is risen indeed!"

God the Father Resurrects His Son, Jesus Christ

[1]I have not heard this idea before. But it is a logical inference from realizing that the tearing of the curtain took place at the moment of death—the very same moment when someone in that culture would tear their clothes.

[2]I heard Pastor Charles Ellis discuss this thought many times. He was a masterful storyteller with the soul of a poet. So as I was growing up, I heard many marvelous sermons from Pastor Ellis that made the story of Jesus' death and resurrection become vivid and meaningful. I'm sure that forgotten details from these sermons subconsciously undergird many of the thoughts in my books.

[3]I heard Pastor Ellis discuss this related thought many times.

[4]See the note to Philippians 2:6–11 in *The NIV Study Bible*.

A Healthy Jesus Walks to Emmaus

[1]This way of describing their attitude arises from a discussion question in the margin of my 10th Anniversary edition of the Serendipity Bible (Grand Rapids, Michigan: Zondervan, 1988, 1996) for Luke 6:37–49: "Would you rather be a movie director or a movie critic? Why?" In the Fall of 1998, we discussed this question in our caring and sharing group that met every other Sunday evening.

[2]It may not have been very hard to keep these two men from recognizing Jesus because they weren't expecting to see him. Indeed, on the day I finished revising these writings about Jesus' resurrection (Saturday, March 27, 1999), I experienced the difficulty of recognizing someone when I wasn't expecting to see them.

After completing all of the revisions, Suzanne, Sarah, Andy and I went to the Easter musical, *The Choice*, that Pearce Memorial Church was presenting at the Roberts Cultural Life Center.

As we walked through the parking lot to enter the building, I heard a woman call "Tim Harner!" I turned toward a smiling, attractive woman approaching with her young son. I said hello, but I couldn't recognize who she was. It didn't help that the sun was at her back.

Finally, seeing my confusion, she said, "It's Linda! Linda Risewick!" *Then* I recognized her.

She'd been out of work a month and a half since having a baby. But I still should have recognized her.

We both worked at Upstate's corporate office in LeRoy that only had about 50 employees. Furthermore, we sometimes worked together because she paid the milk checks to our dairy farmers and legal questions sometimes arose that she asked me about.

The problem was that I had no idea she was coming to the musical. And LeRoy (where she lives) is about 20 miles away. So when I started trying to figure out who she was, I drew a blank. Similarly, when Mary Magdalene didn't recognize Jesus standing near her (even when he started talking to her) and these two men didn't recognize Jesus as he was talking to them, it was very difficult for them to recognize Jesus because they were absolutely sure that he was dead and that the person they were talking to could *not* be Jesus. A similar problem of recognition arose when Peter and the disciples first saw Jesus in the story where Peter tells Jesus three times that he loves him (John 21:4).

If you keep in mind the difficulty of recognizing someone when you don't expect to see them, you will not fall into an error such as thinking that the people who "saw" Jesus were hallucinating, engaging in wishful thinking, merely "seeing" Jesus with the "eyes of faith," or mythologically thinking about Jesus when they saw someone who reminded them of him.

On the contrary, their initial failure to recognize Jesus is a natural, human touch to the stories of Jesus' physical appearances after his resurrection that reinforces their authenticity, accuracy and reliability.

Jesus Tells the Disciples, "Peace Be With You!"

[1] I prefer using the phrase "Caiaphas and his cronies" to specify the small group of people who actually plotted to kill Jesus, instead of using the term "the Jews" which Anti-Semites wrongly take out of context to condemn all the Jews then and throughout the 2,000 years since Jesus was crucified.

Jesus Overcomes the Doubts of Doubting Thomas

[1] To be sure, Jesus became "impatient" with the two men walking to Emmaus when he said to them, "How foolish you are, and how slow of heart to believe all that the prophets have spoken!" (Luke 24:25). However, I believe this remark was prompted by the two men acting as if the women who met the risen Jesus were foolish people who talked "nonsense" (Luke 24:11). If you have sincere doubts, seek answers to your questionings diligently and respectfully. Never scoff at believers in Jesus Christ for being foolish people who talk nonsense.

Jesus Encourages Peter To Take Care of His Sheep

[1]Obviously, many fascinating insights can be drawn by pondering the symbolism of "burning coals," "fish" and "bread." As always, the poetic eye and soul of John fathomed deep meanings from the otherwise mundane details of what he observed.

But I prefer to keep this chapter focused on the interaction between Peter and Jesus, and on the way that Jesus restored hope and purpose to Peter's life. I also want to emphasize that this is a literal, historical account of an actual meeting between Peter and Jesus, rather than implying that this story is a myth composed to symbolize a number of teachings about Peter and Jesus.

[2]I know that a number of commentators draw a variety of inferences from the difference between the Greek words for "love" that appear in this passage (see the note to John 21:15–17 in *The NIV Study Bible*).

However, I decided not to get into that level of detail because: (1) I want to emphasize the parallel between three denials of knowing Jesus and three affirmations of loving Jesus; and (2) since I'm not a Greek scholar, I'm really not the best person to discuss the nuances of which Greek word for "love" is being used.

[3]See the note to John 21:19 in *The NIV Study Bible*.

APPENDIX

Force Majeure: Does God Forgive Non-Christians?

[1]These issues are explored with theological and philosophical rigor in Burson and Walls, 209–214, 226–234.

How to Order the General Counsel Series

As a "war of civilizations" threatens Humanity, read the following books of the General Counsel Series to discover the civilization that is good, that is very good—the Promised Land:

The Promised Land (Vol. 1) draws upon high points of the Bible—from Genesis through Ruth—to teach us how to find the Promised Land, how to establish the work of our hands, and how to be strong and courageous.

Healing the Promised Land (Vol. 2) draws upon high points of the Bible—from the rise of the Monarchy in Ancient Israel to the renewal of Jerusalem after the Babylonian Exile—to teach us how to heal our personal Promised Lands and how to heal God's Promised Land.

Hoping in the LORD (Vol. 3) draws upon high points of the Bible—from Matthew to John—to teach us how Jesus carries us to the Promised Land.

Lighting the World (Vol. 4) draws upon high points of the Bible—from Acts through Revelation—to teach us how to light the world, not by might, nor by power, but by God's Spirit so that we reach the Promised Land.

Visions of America, Visions of the Church (Vol. 5) draws upon high points of American and Church history to teach us how Humanity can find peace and joy in the Promised Land.

Each volume of the General Counsel Series is available by calling 1-877-421-READ(7323) or by visiting www.pleasantword.com, www.amazon.com, or www.barnesandnoble.com